GPO'S DEPOSITORY LIBRARY PROGRAM:

A Descriptive Analysis

PETER HERNON
University of Arizona

CHARLES R. McCLURE
University of Oklahoma

GARY R. PURCELL
University of Tennessee

ABLEX PUBLISHING CORPORATION
NORWOOD, NEW JERSEY

Library of Congress Cataloging in Publication Data

Hernon, Peter.
  GPO's depository library program

  Bibliography: p.
  Includes index.
  1. Libraries, Depository—United States.   2. Libraries—Special collections—
Government publications.   3. United States—Government publications.   4. United
States, Government Printing Office.   I. McClure, Charles R.   II. Purcell, Gary R.
III. Title.
Z675.D4H43 1985   021.8   85–6038
ISBN 0–89391–313–8

ABLEX Publishing Corporation
355 Chestnut Street
Norwood, New Jersey 07648

Contents

List of Figures

List of Maps

List of Charts

Preface

Depository programs by which governments distribute publications free to designated libraries are maintained within the United States by federal, state, and local governments; in such countries as Australia and Canada; and in the United Nations and other international organizations. Those countries which do not have depository arrangements may follow a principle of legal deposit, which represents a historical commitment to preserve national culture. Such a concept has been applied with greater or less effectiveness to government publications.

While it is not our purpose to discuss the variety of depository programs or argue for the establishment of such programs, the book does analyze the depository program operated by the U.S. Government Printing Office (GPO). The book provides a state-of-the-art assessment of the depository program; in particular, it examines the historical development of the program, the current composition of member libraries, as well as the published literature on the program. After providing a descriptive assessment of the program and the published literature, we will assess the process by which the GPO and the Joint Committee on Printing (JCP), the congressional oversight committee, collect and analyze data on the depository program. The book will also examine the possible uses that can be made of the data for decision making and planning, and offer recommendations for specific strategies by which the program can become more effective and better meet the information needs of the public.

Briefly stated, the book is written to accomplish specific objectives:

- to review the historical development of the program (see Chapter 1)
- to review and analyze the existing literature and research related to the program, noting areas requiring additional research (see Chapter 2)
- to provide a state-of-the-art description and assessment of the depository program (see Chapters 3 and 4)
- to provide a profile of member libraries (see Chapters 3 and 4)

- to examine those libraries having relinquished depository status and see if they offer insights relevant for current depositories (see Chapter 5)
- to offer specific strategies and recommendations by which the depository program can increase its overall effectiveness and better meet the information needs of the public (see Chapters 6 and 7)
- to suggest how basic GPO data-gathering forms, and the actual data collected, may be useful for planning—the setting of goals and objectives for the depository program as a whole and individual libraries; developing programs and activities to accomplish those objectives; and evaluating these programs and activities against the objectives (see Chapters 6 and 7)

The final chapter outlines a recommended course of action appropriate for the GPO, if the depository program is to realize its potential. The planning process recommended in the final two chapters is central to that course of action; every effort should be made to implement this planning process, extending to resource inputs and service outcomes, as well as the formulation and implementation of performance measures.

At present, many depository librarians regard the state plans, initiated by the GPO and the Depository Library Council to the Public Printer, as effective models for planning. This simplistic view of planning has been challenged elsewhere (Hernon and McClure, 1984), in part because measurable objectives have not been set, because key terms are ill-defined, and because no formal evaluation component has been articulated or detailed. Complicating the planning process even more are the facts that many depository libraries have not formulated collection development policies (Hernon and Purcell, 1982), that the depository program does not have clear and measurable objectives (Hernon and McClure, 1984), and that the data collection process has a number of fundamental weaknesses. If official questionnaires call for a sampling of reference services, the sampling frame may be insufficient. Questions asked may be ambiguous, key terms may go undefined, and the categories for responding to a question may not be mutually exclusive or provide equal intervals. Further, data analysis may be limited to mere percentages and may not make comparisons to the type of factors reported in Chapters 3 and 4. These weaknesses affect the planning process for the GPO depository program and, perhaps, other depository programs as well.

One barrier to preparing for the future and the development of an interlocking network is that depository programs, such as the one operated by the GPO, are deeply rooted in tradition. They have seldom been subjected to the rigors of scientific evaluation and rarely have official questionnaires, designed to elicit basic factual data, been linked to objectives, matched to formal hypotheses, or submitted to rigorous statistical analysis. In fact, few investigations have gathered the type of descriptive data essential for the formulation of appropriate goals, objectives, and performance measures. It is our hope that the baseline data reported here can provide a basis from which these weaknesses can be corrected. In an attempt to obtain data about the depository program, the GPO and the JCP may be asking important questions, but the problem is that their data collection instruments and analysis do not permit ongoing comparisons and rigorous analysis.

In another work (Hernon and McClure, 1984), alternative structures for the GPO depository program have been identified. However, before the implementation of one of these, or the making of other than patchwork improvements, it is essential that baseline data be collected and widely reported. This is critical given the quantity of publications distributed to depository libraries, the cost of production and distribution, the financial commitment made by depository libraries, as well as the effort made by the private sector in the preparation of bibliographic aids and microform sets, and by all concerned with the identification of source material and improved bibliographic control.

To repeat, it is our intent to provide a detailed, descriptive analysis of the GPO depository program so that participants in, and overseers of, the program will have a more complete understanding of the program. The baseline data will be useful for those wanting to make comparisons between the GPO and other depository programs and for those wanting to update, or to make comparisons to, the baseline data. Further, depository programs other than the one administered by the GPO may want to apply the discussion of the planning process to their only situations. They may want to review program goals, objectives, and evaluation mechanisms, as well as establish performance measures.

In short, this book should have value to libraries participating in the GPO depository program, the GPO itself, the JCP, the library profession at large, government officials operating other depository programs, and libraries participating in these programs. Researchers might use the data reported on depository libraries to draw samples to represent subgroups in the population. They might, for example, develop sampling procedures by which they can limit their study to academic, baccalaureate institutions, or they might select some libraries integrating their entire documents collection into the general collection and make comparisons to libraries handling their documents in other ways. Depository staff, and their administrators, would be able to see how their library fits into the GPO depository program at large as well as determine critical issues affecting their continued participation. These issues might relate to the ways in which they are evaluated by the GPO. Decision makers in the GPO and on the JCP should also benefit from the characterizations of libraries participating in the depository program and from the specific recommendations for improving the program, data collection, and data analysis.

To the end of updating our database and increasing the types of data analysis which can be performed with it (as well as recognizing the needs of subsequent researchers to use a database similar to the one which we developed), we are willing to discuss arrangements by which the database may be used. Only through the formal establishment, maintenance, and use of such a database can the performance and effectiveness of the depository program be improved.

Peter Hernon
Charles R. McClure
Gary R. Purcell

December 1984

Acknowledgments

We are indebted to many people who made this book possible. Our sincere appreciation is expressed to staff members from those current and defunct depositories responding to our query for descriptive information. Kristine Hillier of the Graduate Library School, University of Arizona, looked in various print sources and recorded descriptive data on each depository library. She also transposed this information to data coding sheets.

Martha Trivett of the Graduate School of Library and Information Science, University of Tennessee, assisted in the inputting of these data into the School's microcomputer and in the preparation of the mail questionnaire for depository library distribution.

Computer analysis was performed at the University of Tennessee. We are grateful to this institution for its support of this analysis.

We also wish to thank the publisher, Walter J. Johnson, and his staff, for their consistently cooperative attitude and their financial support for the collection of the data serving as the foundation of the book.

Finally, we owe a special debt to our families (Elinor, Alison, and Linsay Hernon; Vicky and Wendy McClure; and Carolyn, Kay, Margaret, Kristen, Beth, Ronald, and Benjamin Purcell) for their support, patience, and sacrifice during the completion of this book.

Chapter *1*

Historical Background

At present, the depository program of the Government Printing Office (GPO) consists of approximately 1,400 libraries classified as either regional or partial depositories, or as receiving depository status by congressional designation, federal law,[1] or special legislation.[2] In fiscal year 1982, the budget of the GPO totaled $809,176,000, including the expenses financed by the sale of publications and reimbursements from government agencies; the Superintendent of Documents, a division within the GPO, received $86,889,000 of this total, while the depository library program was allotted $21,559,000 (Letter, Taylor, 1982).[3] Further, it has been estimated that printing and distribution costs for publications sent to depository libraries average $11,000 per depository (*Federal Government Printing and Publishing*, 1979). Undoubtedly, the dollar amount is increasing each year because of rising publishing costs and inflation. One final set of statistics is relevant; the GPO estimates that the monetary value of a depository collection for one year, with the cost based on an estimated commercial value of the publications, is $100,000 for a regional and $35,000 for a partial depository selecting 35% of the available item numbers (*Administrative Notes*, 1983).

Table 1-1, which depicts the number of publications distributed to depository libraries, shows that in a six-year period over 350,000 titles were distributed; these titles accounted for more than 137 million copies! During the same period, 41.7% of all the titles distributed were in a microfiche, rather than paper, format. This percentage, however, is misleading;

---

[1] This category encompasses the following: two libraries designated by the mayor of the District of Columbia, one library designated by the governor of American Samoa, one library named by the governor of Guam, two libraries specified by the governor of the Virgin Islands, highest state appellate court libraries, state libraries, land grant colleges, federal executive departments located in the District of Columbia, independent and other agencies of the federal government, accredited law school libraries, and academy libraries of the U.S. Air Force, Army, Coast Guard, Merchant Marine, and Navy.

[2] This category encompasses the public library of the District of Columbia, the Boston Athenaeum, and the American Antiquarian Society.

[3] See also *Annual Report of the U.S. Government Printing Office, Fiscal Year 1981* (1982), p. 30.

Table 1-1. Number of Publications Distributed to Depository Libraries
by Fiscal Year*

| | Hardcopy | | Microfiche | | Total** | |
Year	Titles	Copies	Titles	Copies	Titles	Copies
1978	32,142	12,928,901	4,045	1,544,755	36,187	14,473,656
1979	69,878	19,580,302	16,553	7,473,049	86,431	27,053,351
1980	34,234	9,395,283	24,438	10,651,385	58,672	20,046,668
1981	37,385	11,923,321	27,993	12,820,265	65,378	24,743,586
1982	15,849	7,023,392	27,974	13,686,010	43,823	20,709,402
1983	18,292	8,553,839	43,850	21,748,730	62,142	30,302,569
Total	207,780	69,405,038	144,853	67,924,194	352,633	137,329,232

* The following data are derived from *Administrative Notes* (Washington, D.C.: GPO), 4, no. 16 (October 1983): 3.
** In some instances, the same work may be available in a dual format. Therefore, the totals represent an inflated estimation of the number of unique titles produced and distributed.

in the years 1982 and 1983, microfiche became the preferred format for depository distribution. Clearly, the GPO is trying to improve bibliographic control over what the federal government publishes annually, but in the most cost-beneficial manner (Hernon and McClure, 1984).

Regional depositories must take everything available for depository distribution, while partial depositories can select those item numbers of value to their clientele. The libraries, then, receive the publications free of charge, but incur costs related to organization, storage, and servicing, as well as the purchase of additional reference sources for improving access to these publications.

As shown in Table 1-2, between 1895 and 1983, the number of depository libraries has increased by 953, or 327.4 percent! The Depository Library Act of 1962, to be discussed later in this chapter, has accounted for the dramatic increase in membership. The library community is quite obviously committed to the program and the belief that government publications have value to their constituent groups.

Given the dimensions of the depository library program (e.g., the number of member libraries and titles distributed annually, and the cost of the program to both the federal government and participating libraries), as well as the existence of the program for well over a century, one might expect, therefore, that the program has formal goals and objectives, that an effective inspection program is in place, and that basic data relevant to planning and decision making are regularly collected. Further, it might be assumed that a detailed profile of current and past depositories is maintained. This book challenges such assumptions.

This chapter sets the background for subsequent chapters through the tracing of the historical development of the GPO's depository library pro-

Table 1-2. The Number of Depository Libraries for Selected Years*

Year	Number of Libraries	Year	Number of Libraries
1983	1,373**	1928	477
1982	1,365	1924	446
1981	1,346	1923	421
1979	1,311	1920	476
1978	1,227	1918	482
1976	1,189	1917	484
1975	1,167	1916	484
1973	1,110	1915	482
1972	1,074	1912	464
1971	1,045	1907	474
1962	594	1904	500
1947	558	1898	510
1933	499	1897	478
1932	504	1896	445
1931	498	1895	419
1930	500	1859	12
1929	492		

* The following figures were reported in the *Annual Report of the Public Printer* (Washington, D.C.: GPO) or *Government Depository Libraries* (Washington, D.C.: GPO) for those years. It should be noted that the number of depository libraries is not given in each *Annual Report* through the years.
** This figure represents the total at the time that the survey reported in subsequent chapters was conducted.

gram. The discussion identifies relevant statutory law and documentation governing the depository program. In so doing, the chapter places the program in historical perspective and shows its evolutionary nature.

Much of the relevant federal legislation has been library inspired. Further, the depository program is one of cooperation between the federal government and specific libraries, with both groups gaining from the special relationship. Libraries are not forced to participate but do so by choice.[4]

Development of the Program

In 1789, the new government turned to newspapers to publish laws, orders, and resolutions of Congress. As a result, some Washington newspapermen became publishers for Congress and were permitted to record congressional debates. The House of Representatives produced a limited edition of its journal for the first session, while the Senate, whose proceedings were secret, did not immediately issue a journal. An appropriation for public printing was not made until 1794. For the five years previous, printing

[4] See Schwarzkopf (1982), pp. 7–33.

was paid from a contingent fund available to Congress and the executive branch, without being specified by law.

Those newspapers which became official organs for a political party and which represented the interests of the party in power received special printing orders from the executive departments. The State Department, and its Secretary, became the custodian of the acts of Congress and selected those newspapers which would publish authentic copies of laws and regulations. By 1795, copies of federal statutes were also distributed to the states, through their governors, in part so that rural areas inadequately served by newspapers could be informed of official policies and activities.

Any official publishing necessitated special legislation which would permit the printing of a sufficient number of copies of the journals of each house of Congress for distribution to state executives and state and territorial legislatures. Provision was made, at times, for the distribution of these journals, as well as acts, documents, and reports to incorporated universities, colleges, and historical societies.

On December 27, 1813, a resolution was adopted incorporating the provisions which had theretofore been covered by the special legislation and making them applicable to "every future Congress." The number of copies printed was limited to 200, in addition to the usual number. The librarian of the Library of Congress was authorized to distribute these publications, and government printing became a more profitable enterprise for printing firms. With this resolution, Congress became committed to the formal and regular distribution of its publications. On December 1, 1814, the American Antiquarian Society, Worcester, Massachusetts, became the first non-governmental body to receive government distributed publications; it therefore became the first depository library (Nakata, 1979, p. 9).

Still, the Secretary of State continued to distribute publications, although his office had no specific authority to do so. By joint resolutions of 1840 and 1844, the number of copies of journals and documents printed was increased to 250 and then to 300.

Dissatisfaction with newspaper patronage, charges of misuse and corruption in printing contracts, concern about the cost of official printing, and criticism of presidential news organs led to various attempts to reform printing and distribution methods. At the 1853 Librarian's Conference, a resolution was adopted and this precipitated Congress' first move toward revision of the 1813 distribution system. As a result of various efforts, legislation of the late 1850s placed the depository library program on a firm basis[5] and also created the GPO.

---

[5] For a discussion of this time period see Miller (1980).

By resolutions of 1857 and 1858, distribution authority was transferred from the Library of Congress and the State Department to the Secretary of the Interior. The Secretary was charged with distribution to

> such colleges, public libraries, atheneums, literary and scientific institutions, and boards of trade or public associations as may be designated to him by the Representative in Congress from each Congressional district, and by the Delegate from each Territory in the United States.

Depository designation was assigned by members of Congress, with those states having greater population density eligible for larger representation in the depository program. The framework for the present-day depository library program was set (*Government Depository Libraries*, 1982, p. 4); "the principle of congressional designation as the basis for the depository library system was . . . established, with an apparent intent to provide distribution on an equal basis throughout the country" (Schwarzkopf, 1982, p. 10).

An act of 1859 provided for depository designation by members of the Senate and for the permanent retention of depository publications by libraries. The Secretary of the Interior was charged with "receiving, arranging, safe-keeping, and distribution" of public documents "of every nature," printed or purchased for the use of the government, "except such as are for the special use of Congress or the Executive Departments." The Secretary was also empowered to remove, and retain, publications stored in the Congressional Library or deposited with the Secretary of State.

By an act of March 1861, the Secretary of the Interior could decide which libraries received publications when there were insufficient copies for distribution to all depository libraries. Further, depository libraries were to receive publications, unless the Secretary viewed them as no longer suitable to be recipients of these publications. Here is the first suggestion of an inspection authority or a supervisory capacity to the depository program (Ibid.).

In 1869, the Superintendent of Public Documents was created, as an office within the Department of the Interior, and charged with the custody of government publications and their distribution. Still, Congress and executive departments often maintained their own distribution practices and policies. These policies became so indiscriminate that the first Superintendent of Documents noted that many organizations, including depository libraries, received unwanted and duplicate publications. In his view, the receipt of unsolicited publications was counterproductive; these publications were "regarded with contempt" and publications of the federal government lacked credibility with the public (*100 GPO Years, 1861–1961*, 1961, pp. 79, 90).

Anne Boyd and Rae E. Rips, in their guide to government publications, agreed with the view of the first Superintendent of Documents and added the following criticism:

> The methods of distribution were haphazard and highly unsatisfactory; largely in the hands of Congressmen who were allotted large numbers for distribution and who used the privilege for political purposes. Scholars, librarians and those who actually needed the publications were dependent upon the favor of their local Representative or Senator for securing them. (1949, p. 29)

The demand for reform in printing and distribution practices resulted in the general printing act of January 1895. The provisions of the Act paralleled the recommendations emanating from the library community for decades.

The 1895 Act consolidated existing laws governing the printing, binding, and distribution of government publications. It transferred the Office of the Superintendent of Public Documents from the Department of the Interior to the GPO, which had been created in 1860 and had begun operations in 1861. The office was renamed the Superintendent of Documents, and charged with directing bibliographic control efforts, distributing public documents, selling documents to the public, and maintaining the depository library program. To accomplish its charge, the office began to gather an extensive collection of government publications; in 1972, these publications were transferred to the National Archives and Records Service.[6]

The Act also specified that the number of legislative journals distributed would be limited to three per state, but granted authority for the distribution of the *Congressional Record*. For the first time, executive department publications—except those of a confidential, internal, or administrative nature—were eligible for depository distribution; in the past, however, many of these publications had been republished as congressional documents, by order of Congress, and distributed to libraries as part of the *Serial Set*.

Since government printing, publishing, and distribution had become a function of both the legislative and executive branches, the Act attempted to centralize government printing under the GPO. Another provision stipulated that a catalog of government publications be prepared by the Superintendent of Documents on the first day of each month, to identify the documents "printed" during the preceding month. The purpose was to keep the public and libraries informed of the publications issued by the

---

[6] For a discussion of the transfer of this collection to the National Archives and the subsequent history of this collection, see Schwarzkopf (1984), pp. 27–47.

government. The Superintendent of Documents interpreted the word "printed" very broadly so that it could extend to material reproduced by any duplicating process.

The 1895 Act also expanded the types of libraries which could become depositories. State libraries, executive department libraries, and libraries of military academies all became eligible to serve in the program. Depository status, therefore, could be gained either from designation by a member of Congress or by legal designation.

Section 70 of the Act provided for the Superintendent of Documents to "investigate the condition of all" depository libraries and to remove any which were not maintained as a public libraries or which allowed the number of books other than government publications to fall below 1,000; college libraries, however, were exempted from this minimal number. Irregularly, thereafter, the *Annual Report of the Public Printer* summarized the results of a survey of depository libraries and their handling of depository publications. The first such survey was conducted in 1895. According to F. A. Crandall, then the Superintendent of Documents, no more than 50 of the 419 depository libraries had "the public documents in their possession so well and intelligibly catalogued that they can readily find whatever they wish to find in them" (*Annual Report of the Public Printer*, 1895, p. 75).

As this example illustrates, the 1895 Act did not attack all the problems of the time, many of which related to individual libraries, their collection and service policies and practices. Libraries were receiving vast quantities of publications, but treated many of these as second-class resources requiring minimal attention. The problems relating to the depository library program went beyond the fact that libraries could not make selection decisions but had to retain whatever was sent. The intent was to ensure that each congressional district would receive a similar quantity of publications. With the increasing volume of publications distributed and the need for their permanent retention, many libraries let publications accumulate and stored them in separate areas of the library. Thus, storage decisions often predominated over use, utility, and other factors. In some cases, libraries could not even find shelf space to store publications (*Annual Report of the Public Printer*, 1936, p. 64).

The waste in printing, paper, and distribution, as well as in library handling and storage, was recognized but not attacked for years. Partial remedies considered but not implemented included a reduction in the number of depositories, and in the flow of publications distributed gratis (*100 GPO Years*, 1961, p. 90), and revision of existing statutes to enable libraries to select the publications which they wanted to receive.

Under an act of 1905, depository distribution of reports on private bills (covering the relief of private parties, pensions, removal of political disabilities, and the survey of rivers and harbors) and simple and concurrent resolutions was discontinued. An act of 1907 provided that libraries of land grant colleges could become depository libraries; this stipulation expanded the type of libraries which could receive depository status under a "law" designation. In 1913, legislation was enacted so that a member of Congress, at the beginning of a session, could no longer withdraw and reassign depository status at will. Depository designations had seldom been changed; however, this particular act guarded against the possibility of that happening and stated that a library retained depository status unless it ceased to exist or voluntarily relinquished its privilege. The Superintendent of Documents could terminate status of those libraries failing to comply with existing laws.

From 1913 until 1923, depository libraries returned to the GPO some 1,226,558 publications for which they lacked storage space or which were of no interest to their clientele (*Annual Report of the Public Printer*, 1923, p. 13). Since depository libraries had to accept and retain whatever was distributed, they often tried to return unwanted publications to the Superintendent of Documents. The government not only had to pay for the printing of these unwanted publications but also frequently absorbed the transportation costs to and from the libraries. According to the *Annual Report of the Public Printer*, there were instances in which

> volumes with pretty bindings or attractive titles are taken out from the shipments and placed upon the shelves, and the remainder are dumped in attics or cellars to await an opportunity to return them to this office; and this sort of thing will continue so long as the Government insists upon forcing upon libraries quantities of books for which they have no need. (1907, p. 353)

It was also estimated that, contrary to federal law, depository libraries discarded many publications, rather than returning them to the Superintendent of Documents (*Annual Report of the Public Printer*, 1923, p. 13).

The high cost, in comparison to the low benefit, of these publications, as well as the "gross waste" (Ibid.), led to a new policy. The appropriations act for fiscal year 1923 advanced the concept of selective depositories; depository libraries could select those categories of publications suitable to their clientele.

When the appropriations act went into effect, 51 libraries did not submit selection profiles and, therefore, were dropped from membership in the depository program. In addition,

> only 51 other libraries out of 421 depositories requested that the Superintendent of Documents continue to send them all the publications issued by this office. Sixty-nine libraries asked for more than two-thirds of the publications. On the other hand, 152 libraries requested to be released from nearly half of the publications, and 149 others wanted less than half of the Govern-

ment list. Thus 301 out of 421 depository libraries, or nearly three-fourths, are now taking half or less than half of the number of Government publications that have been unloaded on them for many years. (*Annual Report of the Public Printer*, 1923, p. 13)

An immediate consequence of the act was that the cost of publications distributed to depository libraries decreased from $119,999.12 in 1921 to $73,753.45 in 1923, for a savings of over $46,000 (Ibid). Another benefit was that libraries could plan collection growth—minimize the receipt and retention of unwanted publications and anticipate the amount of shelf space needed to handle the collection. This was important because for just one year, 1929, a complete depository collection would have required 150 feet of shelf space (*Annual Report of the Public Printer*, 1929, p. 38).[7]

During the 1930s, both the Superintendent of Documents and the library community recognized the need to gather basic data on depository libraries: their methods of classification and shelving depository publications, their means for making documents accessible to the public, the practices followed in the disposition of obsolete and useless publications, volume and title counts, hours of service, number of users served, and capacity for collection expansion. The Superintendent of Documents also wanted the opinions of depository librarians and members of the Public Documents Committee, American Library Association, about the number, types, and composition of libraries to participate in the depository program. Additional opinion was wanted about the procedure for the designation of depository libraries and funding for depository inspection.[8]

---

[7] In comparison, it required almost 50 feet of shelf space to accommodate the publications distributed in 1907 (*Annual Report of the Public Printer*, 1907, p. 355).

[8] It might be useful to quote extensively from the *Annual Report of the Public Printer* (1931) to show the types of questions for which the Superintendent of Documents wanted comment "before any further legislation relating to depository libraries is enacted by Congress":

1. Should the number of libraries be increased?
2. Should provisions be made for the same classes of special depositories as now provided by law . . .?
3. Shall the Superintendent of Documents act independently in designation of libraries or should the responsibility for the selection and designation be placed upon Members of Congress, as now, or upon the State library commission or some other authorized body of the State?
4. Should the law specify the character of library eligible for designation, such as public, school, college, university, etc., or arrange for [the] class of libraries to be determined by regulations?
5. Should the law include specific requirements for designation or should this be handled by regulations?
6. If class of library determined on as eligible for a depository does not include all that are now on the list, should the law provide for their being continued as a depository?
7. Should the law prescribe how the libraries are to be apportioned among the various States and Territories?
8. Should the distribution be on a population or a geographical basis?
9. Should Congress be asked to provide funds for the investigation of libraries by an agency of the Government, or should such investigation to determine their fitness or whether their publications are available for free, public use be left to some State organization? (pp. 40–41)

The purpose for gathering the assorted factual information and opinion was to provide a detailed state-of-the-art assessment of the depository program for use in identifying and documenting existing problem areas,[9] and for proposing further legislation relating to the depository program. The survey was expected to show "the class of library eligible to become a depository, and where it should be located" (*Annual Report of the Public Printer*, 1938, p. 112).[10] For the rest of the decade, the basic issues, in regard to the survey, related to how the data would be collected, by whom, and who would pay for the data collection.

At this time, the GPO had limited staff and travel funds to inspect the current condition of depository libraries, as stipulated in section 70 of the 1895 printing act. Moreover, it did not want to request an additional budgetary allocation from Congress for an inspection program or for gathering detailed factual information and opinion on the depository program. As a consequence, the GPO considered a mail questionnaire to depository libraries as the best means to collect data and to let the libraries "express an opinion of the real value of the depository privilege and submit comments on the present service together with suggestions for improvements" (*Annual Report of the Public Printer*, 1932, p. 92). This particular survey was not initiated because it was realized that a volunteer solicitation of general views would not provide adequate insights into the program as a whole.

In spite of the need for basic documentation on the depository program, the GPO was unwilling to even fund a general, detailed survey on current practices and conditions. Instead, it turned to the Public Documents Committee, American Library Association, for assistance in both drafting a questionnaire and obtaining the necessary funding for data collection and analysis. If the American Library Association would not underwrite the cost of the survey, the Committee was encouraged to seek

---

[9] The GPO was already aware of certain problems with the depository library program, e.g., limited space for collection expansion in a number of libraries; the need to control waste in the distribution of publications; an inability to get copies of all printed and processed material eligible for distribution; maldistribution in the placement of depository libraries around the nation or a state; and the need to improve distribution mechanisms (*Annual Report of the Public Printer*, 1947, p. 213).

[10] The law governing the depository program needed to be placed "on a more sound and equitable basis." According to the *Annual Report of the Public Printer*,

> Although population figures, metropolitan areas, size of book collections, and much of the other necessary statistical data can be accumulated readily to show that the present law has defeated its purpose, a comprehensive field survey of all depositories is necessary in order that no present designated depository will be deprived of its privilege if it can show conclusively that it has adequately housed the Federal public documents and that their constant demand and use in that institution is of sufficient magnitude to justify its continuance as a depository notwithstanding the fact that the statistical data may be against it.
>
> The survey will supply the information that is required to determine the class of library eligible to become a depository, and where it should be located. (1938, pp. 111–112)

outside funding. Still, the GPO wanted to be able to critique a draft of the questionnaire to ensure that the types of questions for which it needed answers were included.[11] However, the Committee was unable to obtain financial support from either the American Library Association or an outside funding source prior to the outbreak of World War II.

An act of 1938 reversed the 1905 act and expanded the categories of congressional publications authorized for depository distribution to include reports on private bills and simple and concurrent resolutions. It also broadened distribution to include the journal of each house of Congress and all publications, except those of an administrative and confidential nature ordered by a congressional committee; distribution of the House and Senate journals was no longer limited to three sets per state. In 1941, congressional hearings became available for depository distribution.

After the end of World War II, attention reverted to the need for basic information on the depository library program and the possible introduction of new legislation in Congress. It might be hypothesized that the GPO was trying to cope with the increased volume of source material resulting from the war effort and to supply libraries with source material in the most cost-beneficial manner. Further, there was increased dissatisfaction with the depository program as then constituted. The Superintendent of Documents believed that a number of libraries regarded participation in the program "merely as an opportunity to obtain free publications." "Criticisms" even reached members of Congress that some "depositories are not being maintained as public libraries" and that "documents are stored in basements or are lost or destroyed instead of being made available for general public reference." Given the annual cost to the government of providing depository libraries with free copies, the GPO and Congress wanted to see that funds were not wasted (*Annual Report of the Public Printer*, 1947, p. 213).

Although the GPO lacked the necessary travel funds to carry out "any comprehensive program of regular and thorough inspection of the condition of depository libraries" (Ibid.), it now recognized the need, as well as its *responsibility*, to do so. However, the GPO did not believe that all libraries had to be inspected in person. The preference was to do the evaluation at the lowest cost. As a result, in its budget for fiscal year 1949, the GPO requested funding for a regular survey of depository libraries. With the approval of the budget, the *Biennial Survey* was initiated in 1950.

This survey is important for two reasons: first, the GPO had become committed to a formal and regular investigation of depository libraries. Although the GPO recognized that responses to a questionnaire were not totally satisfactory (*Annual Report of the Public Printer*, 1937, p. 65), the

---

[11] For a discussion of the proposed survey and the climate of the times, see Wilcox (1938), pp. 26–66.

belief was that a survey was better than nothing and that it might lead to a comprehensive investigation (*Annual Report of the Public Printer*, 1947, p. 213). The *Biennial Survey*, as can be seen, reflected the extent to which the GPO was willing to go, at that time, to collect data on depository libraries and to monitor their handling of depository publications. And, second, with the survey, the GPO recognized the importance of the government in funding a means of gathering information on depository libraries and monitoring their performance as members of the depository program. Clearly, the GPO viewed surveys as a legitimate and acceptable means for monitoring the performance of those libraries participating in its depository program.

No major changes in the legislation governing the depository program emerged until 1962 and the Depository Library Act of that year. The legislation leading to this act generated substantial support from the library community, for a variety of reasons. Some of these included

- "a real desire for more worthwhile publications with which to better serve the public"
- "getting something for nothing"
- inflexibility of the present method of depository distribution
- the need to expand the number of depositories
- the prestige of holding depository status (U.S. Congress, 1962, p. 173)

The American Library Association, and many leaders in the library profession, were active proponents for revision of the law and expanding the number of depository libraries. There was some concern expressed in the hearings about the cost of the program, especially if many libraries joined the program. However, as Senator Frank J. Lausche, of Ohio, pointed out,

> If the depository library system were not available, the Government would be required to expend additional millions of dollars each year to provide comparable facilities to make its documents available to the American people. Hence, the educational as well as the monetary value of the libraries' services to the country should not and cannot be minimized. (Ibid., p. 26)

Although it was recognized that libraries will seek depository status for reasons of self-interest or the desire to better serve their own constituents, the legislation was recognized as beneficial to both the government and the library community. Nonetheless, a number of compromises were necessary as the provisions of the legislation took shape.

The 1962 act, which consolidated existing statutes, increased the potential number of depository libraries. Now, members of the House could name two depositories per congressional district, and each senator could designate two per state. The number of federal (executive branch and independent agencies) depositories was also increased. Table 1-2 illustrates the rapid expansion in the number of depository libraries since the enactment of this legislation.

The act formalized pilot programs already in effect in both Wisconsin and New York (depository libraries in both states could transfer control of publications held at least twenty-five years to the State Library in New York or the State Historical Society of Wisconsin, with the permission of the Superintendent of Documents) and created the system of regional libraries. These libraries, limited to two per state, were charged with the maintenance of comprehensive collections held permanently (some ephemeral and superseded publications did not have to be retained), the provision of interlibrary loan and reference service, and assistance to other depositories in the disposition of unwanted publications.

The overwhelming majority of libraries became selective depositories, meaning that they could limit their holdings to high-interest publications and, with the permission of a regional library, discard those not needed after a five-year retention period. Federal government depositories were exempted from the authority of regional libraries and could dispose of unwanted publications after first offering them to the Library of Congress and the National Archives.

All government publications, including those labeled as non-GPO publications, ones printed at field printing plants by federal agencies and not printed at the GPO, became eligible for depository distribution. The only exceptions to this generalization related to publications intended only for official use, required for strictly administrative or operational purposes, classified for reasons of national security, and having no public interest or educational value.[12] However, neither then nor subsequently were these exceptions defined in detail, with corresponding guidelines developed.

The wording of the 1895 act was modified so that depository collections should be "maintained so as to be accessible to the public" but the library need not be maintained as a public library. Further, there was an increase from 1,000 to 10,000 as the number of non-government publications which a library had to hold to qualify, minimally, as a depository.

---

[12] The Superintendent of Documents opposed a provision proposed for the 1962 act, whereby regional depositories needing to conserve space could receive microform copies of older material. The year 1976 marked a reversal in the position of the Superintendent of Documents; at that time, the GPO became a producer and distributor of microfiche. From that time onward, the number of microfiche publications has increased dramatically each year until microfiche has become the preferred format for depository distribution. Microfiche offers the GPO the most cost-beneficial format for the production and distribution of large numbers of titles each year.

Depository libraries were also required to report "every two years on their condition"; the reporting took the form of the *Biennial Survey*. The Superintendent of Documents was empowered to "make first hand investigation of conditions for which need is indicated" and include the results of these investigations in his annual report. Any library having fewer than the required 10,000 books, not "properly maintaining" its depository holdings, or ceasing to be "maintained so as to be accessible to the public," could be removed from the roster of depositories if it did not correct the "unsatisfactory conditions within six months." These provisions still reflected a narrow vision of the inspection authority of the Superintendent of Documents; inspection was limited to those libraries "for which need is indicated." The need for inspection was based on responses, or the lack thereof, to the *Biennial Survey*.

The Superintendent of Documents was, by the provisions of the 1962 act, required to "issue a classified list of Government publications in suitable form, containing annotations of contents and listed by item identification numbers" to assist depository libraries in making their selections.

In subsequent years, the 1962 act has been modified only in two instances. First, an act of 1972 authorized special designation for the highest appellate court of each state; these libraries were exempt from the requirement of public access. Second, in 1978, accredited law schools could become depositories under the "law," rather than congressional, designation. The purpose was to expand the number of depository libraries; law schools holding their status under a congressional designation could transfer their status to a law designation, thereby freeing a congressional designation in the district for another library.

The Depository Library Council to the Public Printer was established in 1972 to advise the Public Printer and the Superintendent of Documents on matters relating to the depository program. Its members are appointed by the Public Printer based on recommendations made by professional associations, Council members, and librarians at large. In 1975, this Council prevailed on the Superintendent of Documents to give a liberal interpretation to Title 44 and the inspection of depository libraries.[13] A formal inspection program was created and three inspectors were charged to inspect each depository library at least every three years. In addition, there would be "a full investigation of any concern that is purported to be a violation of statutory law." In other words, depending on the nature of the infraction reported to the GPO, JCP, or a member of Congress, there

---

[13] This title of the *United States Code* codifies existing statutory law on "public printing and documents." The depository library program administered by the GPO is covered in Chapter 19 of Title 44.

might be a separate investigation of a depository library and its handling of the depository collection.[14]

The next year the Council adopted the "Minimum Standards for the Depository Library System," which established very general areas of responsibility for the Superintendent of Documents and libraries participating in the depository library program.

In July 1976, the GPO requested approval from the JCP to start microform distribution to depository libraries. In March 1977, Senator Howard W. Cannon, chairperson of the JCP, wrote a letter to the Public Printer granting authorization for the GPO micropublishing program and for conversion to microfiche.[15] Table 1-1 shows the significance of the decision to let the GPO become a micropublisher.

Also in 1977, the Council adopted, with the support of the Superintendent of Documents, the *Guidelines for the Depository Library System*, which delineated the purpose of the depository program, its objectives, and the duties and obligations of member libraries. The *Guidelines* and the "Minimum Standards" provide the framework under which depository libraries are inspected; these documents therefore take on the effect of administrative law and specify the requirements with which depository libraries must comply.

The *Guidelines* introduced several refinements in the depository program. First, it established a procedure which libraries seeking depository status should follow. Second, libraries seeking depository status were required to possess a minimum of 15,000 titles other than government publications. This provision raised by 5,000 the number recommended in the 1962 act, and specified a title count, whereas previous statutes had not sufficiently differed between volume and title counts.[16] And third, each depository was encouraged to maintain a "basic collection" of twenty-three reference titles and to select a minimum of 25% of the available item

---

[14] According to Michael F. DiMario, a recent Superintendent of Documents, in the past "some infractions of general GPO policy were inadvertent due to lack of information or experience on the part of librarians or administrators, but that once all responsibilities were clarified, situations resolved themselves internally at the institution where the problem arose" (Letter, DiMario, 1983).

[15] For a historical overview of the GPO micropublishing program, see Chapter 8, Hernon and McClure (1984).

[16] The emphasis on title counts is interesting because, as will be discussed later, many depository libraries have more reliable information about volume counts. It would seem that many libraries do not keep title counts or else only report, in the literature cited in Chapter 3, the higher figure, be it a title or volume count. Since the GPO is only seeking information about small collections of non-government publications (trying to determine that the number exceeds 15,000), information on title counts is irrelevant for many individual libraries. However, it is relevant for some of the library types discussed in Chapters 3 and 4.

numbers. Yet, both determinations were based on the collective opinion of Council members, and staff of the GPO and the JCP, rather than on research findings. The research, although in a preliminary phase, seems to call into question the wisdom of making all these titles common to all depository library types, and of establishing 25% as the recommended minimum (Hernon and McClure, 1984).

If a depository library prefers to select a lesser percentage, it can do so; as shown in Chapters 3 and 4, a significant proportion of depository libraries make fewer selections. The GPO recognizes that since many depository libraries have limited resources, they should be encouraged to assess their own needs and to determine the usefulness of the collection to their constituents. As shown by the trend data reported in Chapter 3, the percentage of libraries taking fewer than the recommended percentage is not decreasing with each *Biennial Survey.* As a consequence, the recommended percentage does not comprise a realistic goal for a large number of participating libraries. Recommendations for title inclusions should be offered within the context of specific subject areas and take into account the diverse types of libraries comprising membership in the depository program (Hernon and Purcell, 1982), while recommended percentages for minimal selections should be based on library types and their particular mission, goals, and objectives.

For additional information about the minimum number of item numbers which a depository library should receive, one of the authors of this book requested a formal clarification from the Superintendent of Documents. Apparently, a library is free to select whatever percentage it so desires. However, if by chance a library decided not to select *any* items from the *Classified List,* it would be contacted "to determine if the originally expressed need for U.S. government publications had ceased or if there were any problems that GPO could help the library deal with." In short, the depository library system does not recognize inactivity; a library either selects item numbers or it "ceases to exist" as a depository (Letter, DiMario, 1983).

In the late 1970s, legislation for a National Publications Act was introduced in Congress. Among some of its provisions was an expanded definition of government publication and an increase in the formats of materials available for depository distribution to include machine-readable files and audiovisual materials. The legislation also proposed the restructuring of the depository library program. The exact nature of the structure was vague and subject to interpretation, apparently because the framers did not have a specific plan or organization in mind, and because they wanted a general bill so that they could legislate later by regulation. The proposed legislation, which also recommended the abolition of regional depositories, further assumed that a comprehensive index to government publishing was both desirable and possible. For a variety of reasons, the legislation died in committee (Schwarzkopf, 1982, pp. 28–29). Since then, there has been no major attempt to revise Title 44 of the *United States Code* and the depository library program.

In the summer of 1983, the Supreme Court issued a landmark decision, the *Immigration and Naturalization Service* v. *Jagdish Rai Chadha* (103 S. Ct. 2764, 1983), which struck down the one-house legislative veto as a violation of the separation of powers clause of the U.S. Constitution. As a direct result of the decision that a congressional committee could not promulgate rules binding on another branch of government, the broad powers of the JCP over executive-branch printing and dissemination of federal publications have been curtailed. According to Zagami (1985), General Counsel to the JCP, the decision should not seriously interrupt the "flow of documents published by the federal government, including the executive branch" to depository libraries. In his opinion, the efforts of the Reagan administration and the Office of Management and Budget to place publishing limitations on federal agencies will have potentially greater impact on the number of titles produced and distributed through the depository program. The administration is, indeed, "weakening publishing programs and the ability to provide the public with information about government services, programs, functions, and activities" (Hernon and McClure, 1984, p. 31). Still, as shown in Table 1-1, the number of titles distributed in both paper copy and microfiche is large and more than many depository libraries can already absorb (Hernon and Purcell, 1982; also see Chapters 3 and 4 of this book).

In the *Congressional Record* for November 11, 1983 (pp. H9709–H9713), the Joint Committee on Printing proposed new regulations covering a broad range of topics related to government printing and information dissemination. These regulations, especially in their application to the depository program, do not deal with the "complicated problem of public access" (McClure, 1984d). These regulations may well have some short-term benefits but they demonstrate the inability of Congress to revise Title 44 and the dated statutes regulating government printing and information dissemination. As subsequent chapters will show, Title 44 is badly in need of revision, coherent national information policies should be developed, and meaningful evaluation of the effectiveness of the depository library program must be implemented.

In conclusion, with the 1923 appropriations act, libraries could become selective depositories able to decide which publication categories they wanted to receive. The intention was to ensure that libraries had the publications "of real interest to their respective readers" and that there was an end to "the gross waste of publications that are of little or no use to many depositories." (*Annual Report of the Public Printer*, 1929, p. 38). In a sense, this legislation encouraged libraries to practice collection development (guiding the collection to meet predetermined goals and objectives, and the selection and retention, by selective depositories of high interest publications). Ironically, many selective depositories, today, do not practice collection development. They neither engage in formal needs assessments nor have written collection development policy statements advancing goals and objectives, and containing an evaluation component. Even the quality and utility of written statements vary substantially (Hernon and Purcell, 1982). The implications of these findings will be discussed in subsequent chapters.

As will be shown in Chapters 3 and 4, many libraries are highly selective in the item numbers taken. Obviously, many of the more than 5,500 item numbers have limited appeal. If machine-readable files, audiovisual resources, etc., become eligible for depository distribution, their appeal will be limited (Ibid.). With this in mind, as well as the types of issues presented in Chapters 6 and 7, program goals and objectives and program evaluation must be highlighted before concluding this chapter.

Program Goals and Objectives

Section 1911, Title 44, of the *United States Code* labels the basic purpose of the depository library program as "to provide reference collections of official publications in the 435 congressional districts of the 50 states and in the outlying territories of the United States, where they will be accessible free of charge to the public." However, this section was intended as "one of the conditions that libraries must satisfy to retain their depository status, and not as a statement of the basic purpose of the program" (Schwarzkopf, 1982, p. 8).

According to *Government Depository Libraries* (1983), the depository library program is based upon certain "principles" predicated on the right of the public to know about government programs, policies, procedures, and publishing activities. This document further notes that

> 1) With certain specified exceptions, all government publications shall be made available to depository libraries; 2) depository libraries shall be located in each State and Congressional district in order to make government publications widely available; and 3) these government publications shall be available for the free use of the general public. (p. 1)

The *Guidelines* themselves do not differentiate between goals and objectives. The three objectives actually comprise one goal—to make "U.S. government publications easily accessible to the general public and to insure their continued availability in the future." The other two statements support this long-term aspiration. The *Guidelines* then skip to specific points around which objectives could be developed. These points emphasize *resources* (inputs into the program) rather than *outputs* (services and the quality and staff performance). Objectives (short-term, specific, and measurable statements which attempt to allow the organization to strive to achieve its goals) are absent.

The *Guidelines*, as can be seen, advance a goal statement relating to public accessibility and a condition which libraries must meet—the availability of these publications for the future. However, the concept of "easily accessible" is not defined, and those highest appellate court libraries serving as depositories are exempted from the goal. Supporting information about the goal statement ignores this exemption; instead, one can locate it in Title 44, *United States Code.*

Schwarzkopf, who has studied the relevant federal statutes and their corresponding legislative histories, has found it most difficult to discern a better written goal statement for the depository library program. The best or most complete statement, he believes, is located in Senate report 87-1587 (H.R. 8141, the Depository Library Act of 1962) and states

> The depository library system is a long-established cooperative program between the federal government and designated major libraries throughout the United States under which certain classes of government publications are supplied free of cost to those libraries for the purpose of making such publications more readily accessible to the American public. (p. 31)

This statement shows that both the government and the library community benefit from this relationship. However, critical weaknesses to this goal are that depository libraries are located in both U.S. territories and the United States proper and that the highest appellate court libraries now comprise an exemption. The concept of making "publications more readily accessible to the...public" is vague and open to interpretation. This would create problems for anyone trying to take this goal and develop measurable objectives acceptable to the federal government, depository libraries, and the public.

As the three goal statements in this section show, the intended purpose is to provide public access to publications emanating from the government. Surprisingly, however, one statement of purpose is intended to cover all areas of responsibility related to the government and participating libraries. Additional goals merit formulation and should extend to service, resource management (collections, staff, and facilities), and administration (e.g., planning and cooperation).[17]

---

[17] For examples of goal statements and objectives see Palmour, Bellassai, and De Wath (1980).

Program Evaluation

As will be shown in subsequent chapters, evaluation of the depository program through an inspection program or other mechanisms is impossible without the formulation of meaningful goals and objectives. Complicating the implementation of the *Guidelines* as administrative law is the fact that key terms (e.g., depository libraries will provide "sufficient staff" and "space") are never defined. Depository libraries are also instructed to provide reference service, but the quality of that service is not addressed. Quality becomes a critical issue in light of the findings of a study which showed that seventeen academic depository libraries scrutinized by unobtrusive testing could answer correctly an average of only 37% of the requests for factual information and bibliographic citations (McClure and Hernon, 1983).

The *Guidelines* further assume that what is "good" for one depository is "good" for all the other libraries in the program. Yet the program consists of academic, public, state, federal, appellate court, and other special libraries—each of which has different missions and goals. Instead of defining public access and setting the objectives by which the extent and type of such access can be measured, both the *Guidelines* and the "Minimum Standards" do not provide an adequate basis for determining and improving current practices and dealing with program weaknesses.

The *Instructions to Depository Libraries* (1977) provide general information on the depository program in an attempt to assist depository libraries in meeting their duties and obligations. Again, the language is often vague and open to interpretation. For example, in accepting designation as a depository library, the director of that library signs a formal agreement which states, in part, that ". . . reasonable care will be exercised in selecting publications to be furnished to this library so as to prevent waste of government funds appropriated for distribution of depository publications." In signing the agreement, the library agrees to ". . . abide by the law governing depository libraries, and such regulations and instructions as have been or may be issued by the Superintendent of Documents in administering the law." One stipulation is that the libraries complete the *Biennial Survey* "fully" and return it "promptly." However, using the 1981 survey as an example, 5% of the current depositories did not return the completed questionnaire. Apparently, from the data presented in Chapter 5, noncompliance with the law has not resulted in the withdrawal of depository status. It is probably, however, an issue raised at the time of the next inspection.

The *Instructions* do present some supplementary information not found elsewhere. For example, section 1 states that libraries failing to unpack and process depository shipments "as they are received" could lose their depository status. As is evident, information about the depository program and the responsibilities of the government and participating libraries are scattered among a variety of sources: the *United States Code*, the *Guidelines*, the "Minimum Standards," the *Instructions*, the form used during the library inspection, as well as policy interpretations and regulations emanating from the GPO and the JCP.

The weaknesses addressed thus far have a direct relationship to the data collected from surveys such as the *Biennial Survey* and the quality of the information gathered from the *GPO U.S. Depository Library Inspection Visit Form* (n.d.). This form and the inspection program have been critiqued elsewhere:[18] suffice to say, they attempt to implement the *Guidelines* but contain questions which are vague, subject to interpretation, and difficult to quantify from the categories provided. Further, since an element of subjectivity enters the scoring, the validity of the instrument and the evaluation process is questionable.

A central theme of this book is that much remains before the government, library community, and the public can determine whether the depository program is both effective and efficient. The purpose of this book is to provide a factual description of the depository program and to offer concrete recommendations for developing an effective evaluation mechanism for the depository library program.

---

[18] For a discussion of the inspection program and the data gathering form see McClure and Hernon (1983), and Hernon and McClure (1984).

Chapter 2

Review of the Research Literature on the Depository Program

This chapter reviews the significant research pertinent to the operation of the Government Printing Office (GPO) depository library program, and to the utilization of government publications received by depository libraries through that program. It is the intent of this chapter to discuss the value of research, to offer observations about existing research concerned with the depository program, and to identify selected research works and their contribution to documents librarianship. The chapter will also advocate the expansion of research related to theory and practice as well as issue a challenge to the field.

Value of Research

In the documents field, new source material is disseminated regularly; agencies reorganize, effect policy changes, plan new programs and directions, improve dissemination capabilities, seek greater cost-benefit with their publishing programs, and make assorted decisions that have an impact on libraries, scholarship, and the information needs of various groups. Libraries, their staff members, and the private sector are also not static with their programs, activities, and expectations. Monitoring developments in all these areas is a difficult task, one involving the identification of outcomes, the steps leading to them, the factors contributing to them, viable alternatives, and the factual basis upon which decisions are made. Accumulating this knowledge enables libraries to best serve the public good by planning for inter-institutional cooperation and appropriate referral, as well as the collection, storage, and dissemination of information that will be needed and used by their clientele.

An awareness of the role and value of research and the relationship between research findings and the decision-making process is crucial for all who are involved in the GPO depository library program if it is to attain its potential for meeting the information needs of the public. Research is integrally related to the development of a theoretical base upon which further research and other works of scholarship can build to broaden the knowledge base availability for the decision-making process. An awareness of the role of research and the relationship between research and theory and practice will enable documents librarians and those responsible for the depository program to adapt to new environments and new situations, while at the same time constantly subjecting existing values, beliefs, and practices to a process of review and evaluation. The absence of both research and a theoretical base results in a static state of affairs, where changes in the depository library program only occur at the procedural level and not at a level which materially improves the understanding and meeting of the goals and objectives of the program, and the ability of the program to respond to external demands placed on it. The depository program needs reliable and valid research data so that decision making does not rest on intuition and supposition. However, in much of the writing on the program, the authors state what they want or hope the field to be, without considering the realities that exist. For example, some people advocate the distribution of more government publications (print, nonprint, and electronic) through the depository program without adequately considering the inability of many depository libraries to cope with the amount of source material already distributed.

Much of the discussion of increased dissemination of government information in a microformat centers on issues related to cost savings to government agencies, access to more information available on deposit, reduced library processing time, and space savings for depository collections. User needs, use patterns, and format preferences are not fully taken into consideration. The assumption is that users want increased access to information and that format is not a significant factor. Such an assumption ignores the research into information-seeking strategies and the "overload" of information that scholars and other client groups experience. These groups are asked to digest additional information and to spend even more time in information gathering. It is much easier for them to rationalize the ephemeral nature for much of this publishing, to assume that the more important publications will eventually appear in their subject literature, or to turn to alternative sources of information, especially looseleaf services which capsulize the essential information (Hernon, 1984). Increased microform production and distribution may encourage the development of new looseleaf services. The result may be further use of general reference collections and not the use of original documents.

Given this state of affairs, definite questions need to be raised:

- why do all government publications need to enter the depository program?
- should more attention be given to identifying and improving access to those documents likely to generate the most demand?
- is the depository program cost-beneficial, cost-effective, and used to its potential?
- does the program comprise an effective and efficient means for the prompt and reliable delivery of documents to users?
- how can depository libraries gain access to technology of the future so that they can make new information readily available?
- how many depository libraries are actually necessary?

We all have opinions on these questions. There is, however, an insufficient base of data to answer them objectively and dispassionately. In the process of investigating these and similar questions, we may find it necessary to explore ways outside the depository program to enhance public access to government publications. At any rate, the assumptions underlying the depository program must be reevaluated in light of today's information environment.

Observations about Research Pertinent to the GPO Depository Library Program

Research has a direct relationship to problem solving, and can be characterized as encompassing certain prescribed activities:

- identification of a problem
- conducting a literature search to place the problem in its proper context
- formulation of a logical or theoretical framework, with goals, objectives, and hypotheses
- adoption of research designs and methodologies appropriate to the examination of the problem
- collection and analysis of data
- formulation of conclusions derived from the data
- development of recommendations for further study

Unfortunately, most of the writing concerned with government publications, and with the depository program in particular, do not exhibit all seven activities. Instead, they may merely report the results of a survey questionnaire, without the establishment of a clear problem statement and formal objectives and hypotheses.

In this section, observations about research concerned with the depository library program will be viewed in the context of these basic questions:

- what are the general characteristics of the research
- who is conducting the research
- what methods of research are being used

Two additional questions of importance will be answered in the next section, which highlights the findings of selected research literature. These questions are

- what topics are addressed in the research literature?
- what are the research findings that are of value in the decision-making process?

To answer the latter question, a brief summary of the major findings of the studies must be presented.

General Observations

An examination of the research pertinent to the depository library program shows that most of the substantive work has been published within the past decade. Earlier writings concerned with the depository program, in most cases, did not exhibit the characteristics of research, as defined above. The level of sophistication of the studies has increased during the past few years, with the result that more higher-quality research in this field has been produced since the late 1970s than at any prior time. However, the number of high-quality research studies is still very limited. Furthermore, most of the work is of a "one-shot" nature in that it is neither based on nor compatible with previous research. Authors have generally conducted a survey which has not been subsequently updated, or the updating is done irregularly. Therefore, longitudinal studies cannot show trend data over time. Research on the depository program frequently does not build and elaborate on the findings of previous works. Knowledge, therefore, is fragmented and not accumulated. Decision makers are forced to rely on outdated, superficial, and questionable data.

Who Is Conducting the Research

The conducting of research pertinent to the depository library program is within the sphere of interest of several groups. Persons engaged in practice, working either in depository libraries or for the GPO or other government agencies, have a vested interest in adding to the base of knowledge available for decision making. Library educators involved in teaching government publications courses constitute another group that should have an interest in conducting research in this area. A third group consists of library science students, either at the master's or doctoral level. A fourth group is comprised of research organizations, inside or outside of government, that might conduct or fund studies on a contractual basis. Organizations outside of government would include independent consulting firms fulfilling a contract. An example of an agency inside government that has recently completed a study of the depository library program is the General Accounting Office (1984).

The four groups *should* have an interest in conducting research pertinent to the depository library program. An examination of current research writings indicates that very few individuals from any of these groups are actually engaged in conducting significant research. Most of the research and writing originate from a small number of faculty members in library education, with some additional writing coming from a few persons employed in depository libraries. The GPO and other government agencies such as the Joint Committee on Printing have, from time to time, authorized surveys to be conducted, but these surveys frequently do not meet the definition of research previously advanced.

It might be expected that master's and doctoral students engaged in thesis or dissertation research would be a productive source of research in this area. However, such is not the case. A review of graduate research in government publications reports the number and subject of dissertations and theses concerned with government publications (Richardson, 1983). This report shows that from 1928 through mid-1982, 169 graduate dissertations or theses were completed which dealt with federal government publications. However, few of these studies have related specifically to the depository library program. The impact of this body of research has been limited for several reasons. First, the quality of graduate research is uneven and the topics treated vary significantly in their value to practicing librarians. It is not uncommon for these studies to treat one library or small geographical area. Second, physical accessibility to theses and dissertations may be difficult because of the interlibrary loan policies of individual institutions. The key question then becomes, "Is the research important enough to justify the effort to obtain it?" Clearly, as long as the general answer remains "no," thesis and dissertation research will remain outside of the mainstream of availability of documents research.

The conclusion to be drawn is that the population of active investigators concerned with the depository library program is exceedingly small, and consequently the number of research articles and monographs is very limited. If the few individuals who have been active investigators were to cease their activity, the thrust of the research effort would come to a standstill. If there is to be an increase in the body of research knowledge by those involved in government documents practice and education, more interaction is required among the spheres depicted in Figure 2-1. The purpose is to increase the number of researchers and studies, and to stimulate further existing researchers so that they have a continued interest in adding to the knowledge base of documents librarianship.

What Methods of Research Are Being Used

Based upon an analysis of 37 research studies completed between 1970 and 1977 in the documents field, Richardson found that 65% were concerned with U.S. government publications, 8% with state government, 3% with local government, 5% with the U.N. and international organizations, and 19% with other countries. Further,

> Nearly half (48 percent) of the research employed a form of survey methodology. Arranged in descending order of frequency, the remaining methods are: historical analysis 28 percent, citation and content analysis 14 percent, and experimental design 10 percent. Apparently no theoretical or operations research has been done. (Richardson, 1977, p. 363)

Figure 2-1. Role of Research in Documents Field

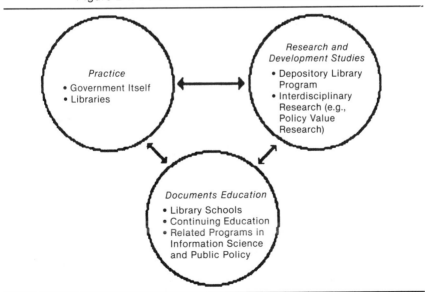

The survey still comprises the major means of data collection used to study library practices, librarian attitudes and information-gathering techniques, user perceptions, and use patterns. Most surveys are conducted through mail questionnaires, but in-person and telephone interviews have been used to a limited extent. Studies are seldom replicated so that it is difficult to monitor how, if at all, situations have changed over time. Where there is repetition among the questions asked by different surveys, the data are usually not compatible because the questions are worded differently, cover different populations, reflect different time periods, or are not compatible in other ways. This is a result of a "go-it-alone" philosophy that seems to be all too common in documents research. It represents a lost opportunity for the benefits that could be derived from longitudinal studies comparing data over time. In addition to the problems noted above, most surveys concerned with the depository library program do not provide reliability and validity measures. The result is that the reader cannot assume the reliability of their findings, hence the information has limited value for decision making.

The second most commonly used method for study of the depository library program is still historical. This method has value because a knowledge of the historical development of the depository program provides a context for understanding current issues. Methods such as citation and content analysis, comparisons of treatment and control groups using an experimental design, unobtrusive testing, and obtrusive testing have been used infrequently to study the depository program. The next section of the chapter identifies specific writings to illustrate the areas in which research related to the depository program has been carried out.

Identification of Selected Research

Figure 2-2 offers a visual depiction of the topics which will be treated here. To see how these diverse topics fit together, readers are encouraged to consult Hernon and McClure (1984). Using the concept of "public access" to government information as their theme, they suggest areas where change is required if public access is to be improved, identify a strategy for bringing about change, and provide a research agenda to further the process of change. The value of their work is that for the first time the central issue with which the depository library program should be concerned (public access to government information) is addressed in a comprehensive fashion. Further, they provide a conceptual basis from which further theoretical and practical research can occur.

Figure 2-2. Research Topics on the Depository Library Program

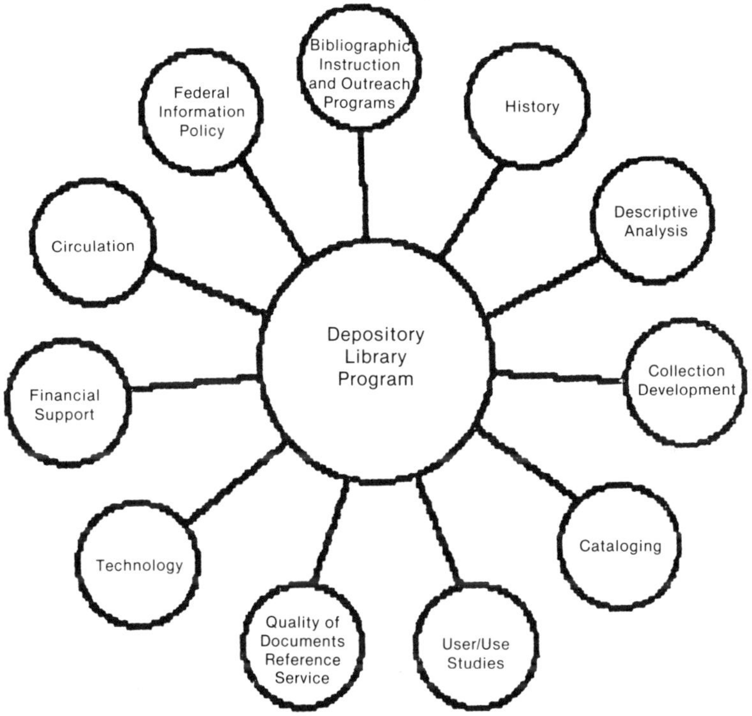

History

Several writers have provided an historical account of some aspects of the depository library program. Chapter 1 of this book is the most complete general overview of the history of the program to date. A more detailed account, but one limited to the years 1813 to 1895, was the product of a doctoral dissertation (Miller, 1980). Summary accounts of the development of the depository library program are found in two articles which trace the history of the program from early times through its present operation (Schwarzkopf, 1978, 1982). Another article by the same author provides a condensed history of regional depositories (Schwarzkopf, 1975). Another historical article provides a valuable perspective on the long-standing controversy on the question of whether a separate or a distributed collection serves the use of the depository collection better (Waldo, 1977). Finally, a review of documents reference service in academic libraries up to the year 1962 shows that, when viewed historically, this is a relatively new type of service for libraries to offer (Hernon, 1978).

It is not possible to characterize fully the contribution of each of the historical works cited above. However, taken in the aggregate, these writings provide an enlarged understanding of how the depository library program developed. They also indicate those forces that have helped to shape it and the responses of documents librarians to the development of the program. Many of the present-day issues and problems involved with the program have persisted for years. These studies collectively provide a challenge for other historical investigators to identify other topical areas for historical research and to synthesize their findings into the larger picture.

Descriptive Analysis

A number of studies have provided descriptive information about depository libraries and the depository program. Almost without exception, these descriptive studies have exemplified the "one-shot" survey syndrome described earlier in this chapter. The authors of this book have endeavored to avoid that by building on the *Biennial Survey* and on an earlier survey of the libraries participating in the program (Whitbeck, Hernon, and Richardson, 1978). The 1978 article had as its purpose to identify and report on "key variables, or characteristics, related to U.S. federal document depositories and to explore possibly significant relationships between these variables" (Ibid., p. 266). Because the research reported in Chapters 3, 4, and 5 builds on this study, it is possible to derive some trend data on the depository program for some of the variables. One example of this is the treatment in Chapter 5 of depositories that have surrendered depository status.

Illustrative of descriptive studies that are isolated efforts unconnected to previous work and that seemingly do not lead toward subsequent research is the report of a survey undertaken by the General Accounting Office at the request of the Joint Committee on Printing (1984). This report summarized responses by depository librarians to questions largely aimed at reflecting the librarians' attitudes toward the management and operational efficiency of the depository library program. The purpose was to obtain information for a review of the effectiveness of the program. However, the study fails in several respects to meet this purpose. There is no clear statement of objectives and no general summary of the findings of the study. There are no citations to other works that relate to any of the questions posed by the survey instrument. The general nature of the questions and possible responses lead to ambiguous results that lack clear meaning. In effect, this study has limited utility for the review and audit purpose for which it was intended and, further, does not build a good foundation for subsequent studies intended to achieve the same purpose. The limitations of the GAO study are common to many of the descriptive studies of the depository library program, and the result is that most have little utility for providing information that can be used for current decision making related to the program.

Collection Development

Until 1982 there was little published literature that viewed collection development for government publication collections as a decision-making process encompassing selection, acquisitions, deselection, and evaluation against stated objectives. The significant research on this topic was a monograph which not only advocated the development of collection development policies encompassing depository collections, but provided examples as well (Hernon and Purcell, 1982). A methodology for obtaining information relevant to collection development decision making was proposed, using the information needs of academic economists as the prototype. Further, by using the GPO's Item Selection File, the authors were able to depict patterns of depository library selection of item numbers. The value of this work is that it shows the need for a documents collection development policy, demonstrates how one can be accomplished, and portrays the patterns of collection development at work within the depository library program. The methodologies used in this research were the survey method to obtain data from both depositories and academic economists, and the analysis of an existing file maintained by the GPO which was used to reflect the distribution of depository items to libraries.

Cataloging

In two important works, Myers (1983, 1985) has examined the quality of GPO cataloging of records on the GPO/MARC tapes, on OCLC, and in the *Monthly Catalog*. Her analysis identifies cost-effective methods of using these records for a library catalog, and is of particular value for decision making by depositories regarding their use of these bibliographic records. For a library to take the records directly from the GPO tapes and load them into a catalog, the records must meet the quality standards which have been set for a library catalog. Her writing represents the state of the art concerning the cataloging of documents collections.

Taking a representative sample of 300 monographs and analyzed serials distributed to depository libraries, Bower (1984) researched each title in the OCLC online system to determine when, how, and by whom depository documents are likely to be cataloged. She found that the overall quality of cataloging is high, that OCLC member libraries may catalog depository documents before the GPO does, and that not all depository monographs are cataloged by the GPO. Clearly, as these three articles illustrate, technical processing of depository documents is starting to receive the attention which it richly deserves.

User/Use Studies

The most significant study of use and users of government publications was that conducted by Hernon (1979), which reported on the use of government publications by academic social scientists in four disciplines. This study, using survey research, built on and expanded a line of research reported earlier by McCaghy and Purcell (1972) and is one of the few examples in documents research of a work that has utilized and expanded on earlier research. The findings of the Hernon study provided a basis for determining those portions of the collection most likely to be used by specific user groups. The work reported in this study set the stage for the research on collection development noted above (Hernon and Purcell, 1982). Neither the Hernon study nor the Hernon and Purcell study has ever been replicated. Therefore, it can be questioned to what extent decision making now can be based on such studies, regardless of their quality.

Two user studies employed citation analysis to obtain information about the way in which government publications are cited in the published literature. Although it is not possible to equate "citation" with "use" on a one-to-one basis, it has been demonstrated that citations do provide some evidence of the use of publications. One study, utilizing the *Social Sciences Citation Index*, found that government publications accounted for only a slight fraction of the citations in writings picked up and cited in this index (Hernon and Shepherd, 1983). Another study examined the frequency with which government publications were cited in doctoral dissertations in several disciplines in the arts and sciences at one institution, at one point in time (McClure and Harman, 1982). These two studies are of interest not only because of their findings, but because of the methodology employed to study the use of government publications.

Quality of Documents Reference Service

Building on a foundation of research studies concerned with the quality of reference service, McClure and Hernon (1983) assessed the ability of academic depository library personnel to respond with correct information to questions posed to them through a process of unobtrusive testing. The most significant finding was that only 37 percent of the questions were answered correctly. The findings of this study are important in that they reflect on the effectiveness of the depository library program in meeting the information needs of the public served by the program. The *Guidelines for the Depository Library System* (1977) specify that the libraries are to provide reference service. The unobtrusive study clearly calls into question such a vague recommendation and suggests that government depository administration should not accept any self-reporting as a true indication of the quality of service provided. The study is also important because it uses a methodology previously unused in the field of government publications, that of unobtrusive testing. Clearly, methods other than survey research can be used effectively for research in the documents field.

Technology

The research literature documents the challenge depository libraries have received from rapid developments in computer technology. The most comprehensive study (McClure, 1981) examined the use of bibliographic databases and other computer-based technology by depositories. His findings indicate that depository libraries have limited access to terminals for searching, and that depository librarians have had limited training in the use of online databases. Although this study, based on a survey and utilizing self-reporting by depositories, is valuable, it covers only one time period and it does not provide longitudinal data that might reflect change. It has not been replicated fully, although data reported elsewhere in this book addresses some aspects of the use of technology in depository collections and services.

There is only one study in the literature that reports extensively on the willingness of academic social scientists to use microformatted government publications. This study (Hernon, 1982) is based upon a survey of academic economists and political scientists from a cross section of institutions. A study like this merits replication and investigation drawing upon more than a self-reporting methodology by the users. Such a study would be useful, given the amount of depository material distributed in a microformat.

Financial Support for Depositories

Several authors have noted the financial burden placed on depositories, particularly regional ones. One study reports on the wide disparity in levels of support provided for libraries in the depository program (Cook, 1982). Although this study is limited to academic libraries that are members of the Association of Research Libraries, it could well serve as the basis for further research which examines a wider range of depositories. The primary finding of this study was that the resources received by the documents department are not correlated to resources available to the library as a whole.

Attempts have been made to view depository status in terms of cost-benefits (Faull, 1980; Bregent, 1979). However, such analyses are hampered by the fact that the depository program lacks formal goals, objectives, and performance measures (see Chapter 1). Further, libraries participating in such studies generally have not gathered data in a similar way to permit comparisons. The authors also make questionable assumptions about the nature and collection policies of libraries. For example, any list of basic titles for inclusion in the collection must take into account the needs, circumstances, and objectives of individual libraries.

Circulation

Studies have explored the use of depository collections based upon an analysis of in-house use and the circulation of federal documents (Sears and Moody, 1984). Since these studies emphasize use at only one institution, they have limited applicability. Further, they do not view collection use and collection development in a subject context. In effect, they do not link collection use to the theory of collection development (Hernon and Purcell, 1982). Another study surveyed academic depositories to determine their policies and practices regarding the circulation of government publications (Yannarella and Aluri, 1976). The findings indicated that 90% of the depositories did circulate documents. However, this study has not been replicated for other types of libraries, nor does it reflect circulation policies over a period of time.

Federal Information Policies

Research concerning the effects of federal information policies on the depository library program has been very limited, even though the topic has generated a great deal of debate in the literature. The attempt by President Ronald Reagan in April 1981 to limit the number of new government publications has prompted two studies on the impact of the president's information policy. A study by Florance (1984) measured the effect of President Reagan's declared moratorium on government publishing on the quantity and nature of documents issued by the Department of Health and Human Services. She found that for this agency differences in publishing before and after the announcement of the president's policy were slight, with the major change being the switch to less costly formats. However, another study which examined the effect of the publishing moratorium on depository libraries found that it had had an important impact on the nature of the information which depositories could make available to the public (Stokes, 1984). Documents found on the Office of Management and Budget's *List of Government Publications Terminated and Consolidated by Agency* were compared with depository library distribution patterns, and the author's finding was that the policy had forced depositories to be increasingly dependent on publishing by the private sector and thereby had reduced or eliminated the availability to the public of some statistical information.

The findings of the latter study are significant for depositories because they document the impact that President Reagan's information policy has had on public access to government information through the depository system. The two studies show the value of the methodology the investigators used to address the issue of federal information policy, and thus provide another research method through which information pertinent to the decision-making process of the depository library program can be obtained. This topic, virtually untouched by empirical research, should be examined further to provide depository librarians with a better understanding of how their services are impacted by such policies.

Bibliographic Instruction and Outreach Programs

Studies have probed the use of current awareness and selective dissemination of information services by faculties of academic institutions that have access to documents collections that are a part of the depository library program (Goehlert, 1980; Moody and Sears, 1982). Such studies commonly base their evaluation of the services upon response to a self-reporting questionnaire, as well as on factors such as amount of staff time involved in the preparation of the service. However, they have not adopted an experimental design and compared alternative methods for generating awareness and enhancing physical access to needed documents. The comparison of different approaches would be useful for library planning and decision making. Further, it would be beneficial for such studies to be ongoing, and thus to reflect the impact of changes in the services provided. It would also be useful for such studies to explore the comparative effectiveness of various marketing techniques used to call attention to public documents.

Research has also explored methods by which students can be instructed in the use of depository publications (e.g., Vertrees and Murfin, 1980). Experimental designs employing the use of control and treatment groups offer a rich opportunity to explore effective methods for teaching and learning. The literature on bibliographic instruction for libraries in general is rich with examples of research easily adaptable to documents librarianship, and should be utilized more fully for models that could be followed.

Looking to the Future

At the beginning of this chapter, observations were made concerning the role and value of research about the GPO depository library program.

Throughout the remainder of this book, some of these points will be reiterated. A central purpose of the book is to report and analyze information compiled by the authors that establishes a body of baseline data about libraries participating in the depository program. This is presented in the hope that it will constitute the beginning of a regular process of collecting similar data and thus provide the basis for longitudinal studies of the depository program.

The value of the research reviewed in this chapter and the research reported in subsequent chapters is ultimately determined by its potential for use as part of a policy-making and decision-making process. Unless the research reported here becomes a part of the knowledge base that is used in the decision-making process by the GPO, the Joint Committee on Printing, and individual libraries that are a part of the depository library program, the value of this book is diminished. Thus, the responsibility for the value rests not with the investigators, but rather with those who are in positions of responsibility to make constructive use of research findings in decision making. The primary thrust of Chapter 7 of this book is the development of a system for providing information to improve the decision-making process for the depository library program. A necessary component of any such program for the provision of information is recognition and use of the knowledge base that already exists.

The accumulated body of research on the depository library program, as evidenced from the studies reported above, is still meager in comparison with the need. It is largely of recent origin and covers only a limited number of aspects of the depository program, and a disproportionate amount of the work has been done by a few persons. The stimulus for much of the other work has also come from the work of these individuals. For the knowledge base to increase at a rate required to address various problems and issues, there must be a greater commitment by organizations centrally concerned with the depository library program, and by individuals with a similar concern.

Empirical research is but one type of scholarly writing needed in the documents field. Additional writings might take research findings and apply them conceptually to such issues as bibliographic control and improved access to government information. By developing its theoretical base, the documents field can place practice in proper perspective and not be consumed by practice. According to Saunders, the

hall-mark of any true profession is a body of general principles, a theoretical framework, which supports and guides the actual practice of that profession. To an individual practitioner this framework, these guiding principles, may become more and more shadowy, may be pushed further and further into his subconscious, with the passage of time and the accumulation of experience on the job. But...this sort of knowledge is an indispensable basis for the practice of his profession. (Saunders, 1971)

Awareness of the role of research, as well as the relationship between theory and practice, will enable documents librarians to better adapt to new environments and situations. At the same time, existing values, beliefs, and practices will be reviewed, evaluated, and challenged.

It is clear that what is needed at this time is a research agenda for government documents librarianship, and particularly for the ongoing study of the depository library program. It is also clear that certain organizations must take the leadership in establishing the agenda and developing a program to implement it. The primary organizations that have an interest in this are the GPO, the JCP, and the Government Documents Round Table of the American Library Association (GODORT). The authors challenge these organizations to co-sponsor a national conference that would bring together the leaders of the documents field, to address directly the need to develop a strong research agenda, and to develop resources for the funding of the needed research. The challenge extends to establishing a coherent body of research topics that are interrelated and that, taken together, would dramatically increase the knowledge base required for intelligent decision making on issues pertaining to the depository library program.

What type of research needs to exist and in what ways is the needed research important to decision making concerned with the depository library program? What issues should be studied? Of what should the research agenda consist? The topics for a research agenda which have been identified elsewhere (Hernon and McClure, 1984, Chapter 20) could constitute the basis for position papers on research needs to be presented at the conference. Areas where additional research is needed are identified below, together with a brief statement about why each is important to the decision making process of the depository library program:

- *identification of what constitutes a "good" system and formulation of goals and objectives for the system.* Research which leads to the identification of the attributes of a good system, and the concurrent establishment of sound goals and objectives for the system is the fundamental first step in determining if decisions regarding the allocation of resources of the program are resulting in improved public access to government information.
- *formulation of precise measures of effectiveness and performance.* The development and use of measures of effectiveness and performance provide a basis for determining whether program objectives are being met, and also a basis for the program to justify its services and demonstrate the benefits it provides.
- *similarities and dissimilarities between goals and objectives of the overall program and the member institutions.* Compatibility among the goals, objectives, and expectations of the depository

library program and the individual member depositories is a necessity for successful planning and policy development. At present there is no research that demonstrates whether or not compatibility exists between the program level and individual libraries.

- *the economic efficiency of the program.* No research exists that demonstrates the relative economic efficiency of the depository library program as a means for the dissemination of public information. Lacking data on economic efficiency of the present program, decision makers in the GPO and the JCP will not have the data to make informed judgments leading to cost-effective changes in the program.

- *formal evaluation of depository marketing.* Research and an ongoing review of efforts by participants in the depository program to inform the public of their right of access to information which depositories collect is necessary to determine the effectiveness of such marketing efforts. No ongoing evaluation of these efforts, nor of those by the GPO, currently exists.

- *the reasons for use and non-use of depository publications by the public, and the degree to which various client groups are aware of, and use depository libraries and collections.* Research is required to expand the knowledge of who uses depositories, for what purpose, and how they become aware of the existence of depositories. Knowledge of the information-seeking behavior of users and non-users of information in depositories provides a basis for decision makers, in both government and individual libraries, to take steps to enhance the public visibility of depositories, and to adapt services to meet information needs of current and potential users.

- *complexion of member institutions.* In order to formulate policies that will maximize the effectiveness of all depositories in the program, the characteristics of various subgroups of libraries in the program must be understood, with the realization that the differences are meaningful and consequently should be taken into account in decisions that affect the depository program.

- *inter-institutional cooperation and effectiveness in document delivery for meeting the information needs of the public.* The patterns of cooperation among depositories have not been subjected to study in a systematic fashion. Of particular importance is the need to determine the extent of cooperation among depositories in close geographical proximity, and cooperation between regionals and selective depositories. Research on patterns of cooperation must study the speed of document delivery and the frequency and nature of the referral of information requests among depositories. Research in these areas is necessary to determine where improvements must be made to develop the depository library program into an effective and efficient system for the delivery of government information to the public.

- *quality of documents reference service.* Additional research is needed to gain further insights into the quality of reference service provided by depositories. Unless the results of the one unobtrusive study (McClure and Hernon, 1983) on the quality of documents reference service is augmented, and the results accepted, improvement in the quality of reference service will not be forthcoming. The results of this type of research are a necessary first step toward developing strategies for the improvement of documents reference service.

- *degree of institutional support (in terms of personnel, facilities, and budget).* In-depth information is needed about the degree of institutional support which libraries of various types provide. The purpose is to determine whether libraries offer a similar level of support for documents and other collections. Decision makers concerned with the depository library program must have this type of information available in order to monitor the importance of the depository collection for the accomplishment of national, state, and local objectives.

- *the impact of changing technology on the program.* Rapid changes in technology, such as the introduction of computer-based systems, will have an increased effect on the depository library program and the nature and format of the services and information offered. In order for program administrators to make sound decisions in response to technological changes, it is essential that there be in-depth longitudinal studies on the impact of various technological changes.

- *staff training.* Research (e.g., McClure and Hernon, 1983) indicates that enhanced training of documents staff is a necessity. It should be incumbent on the depository library program to encourage and facilitate such training to improve the program. However, regular monitoring of the extent of staff training, together with an assessment of its relative success, is crucial if the effort is to result in meaningful improvement.

Inadequate attention has been given to ranking the importance of tasks and responsibilities performed by documents staff. Writings in the field of general reference services have identified the range of tasks performed and have enabled departments to engage in introspection. Similar studies do not exist for the documents field; research is also lacking in such areas as analysis of the types of reference questions asked and user perceptions toward the role and duties of documents librarians (Reeves, Howell, and Van Willigen, 1977; Hernon and Pastine, 1977).

The documents field would be well served by having studies involving the development and testing of models. Such studies depend on prior conducting of descriptive research and on gathering information on the current status of a phenomena, and are directed to determining the nature of a situation as it exists at the time of the study, so that accurate and valid data can be used in model construction and testing. The profession needs to be aware of and to consider a variety of models so that those most appropriate to a given situation, level of funding, political climate, etc., are identified and implemented.

The problem, however, is that often the necessary descriptive research is not in place. As noted in one study,

> given the dearth of reliable information, it is difficult for senior policy makers to determine what should constitute rational standards of service for government publications or a national program for library and information services in this area; nor can front-line practitioners determine where their institution stands in comparison to other depository libraries or to accepted standards. (Richardson, Frisch, and Hall, 1980, p. 464)

Descriptive research is a prerequisite for the development of a national information policy, one pulling together information resources from all levels of government. Because of the size, cost, potential benefit to information seeking, and commitment on the part of libraries and government agencies, the depository library program requires research, experimentation with modeling, and formal evaluation. These activities may well be beyond the responsibilities and expertise of government officials assigned to carry out the depository library inspection program.

The challenge issued by the authors goes beyond developing a national conference and a research agenda. It also includes the allocation of resources that make it possible for the type of research described above to be conducted, and the active participation of additional persons qualified to undertake research to enter into this process. The base of active investigators must be expanded if all of the key issues and problems are to be addressed. The limited number of active investigators is insufficient to do the job in a satisfactory fashion.

This chapter has focused on the identification of research related to the effectiveness and the efficiency of the depository library program and its member libraries. As noted above, there are still a number of topics that have not been addressed. However, there is little evidence to show that the knowledge and insight obtained from existing research have been effectively used to improve the decision-making process in the depository library program, or in most of the member depositories. The great need at this point is for the development and utilization of a decision support system (DSS) to provide decision makers within the GPO, the JCP, and individual depositories with an ongoing resource for obtaining information necessary for informed decision making. The need and the necessary attributes for this type of system form the basis for Chapter 7 of this book.

One of the results of the development of a decision support system that could lead to the improvement of the depository library program is the partial or significant restructuring of the program. Recommendations for the possible restructuring of the program have appeared in the literature (McClure, 1982b; Hernon and McClure, 1984). However, before alternative structures for the depository library program can be explored successfully, it is necessary to know how well the present system is working. There is a need for detailed data on the current structure of the program that reflect the extent to which the present structure facilitates or interferes with the task of the depository library program in providing the public with access to government information. Until data which address this issue can be obtained, restructuring of the program would be based on guesswork, at best. That some restructuring of the depository library program is necessary and desirable would likely receive widespread agreement from the depository library community. However, until a well-designed, effective decision support system is in place, there is no method of determining specifically what changes should be proposed and how the various components of the program interact.

Chapter 3

Overview of Depository Library Characteristics

Given the commitment of both the federal government and the library community to the continuation and expansion of the depository program, as well as the size, cost, and potential value of the program to information seekers, it is surprising that the only current regular statistical profile of member libraries is the *Biennial Survey* administered by the Government Printing Office (GPO). As shown in this chapter, as well as in Chapters 4 and 6, this survey has serious weaknesses inhibiting its value for planning and decision making. It offers only a sketchy glimpse of the depository libraries at a given moment in time.

The needed evaluation and improvement of the depository program is not possible without the collection and analysis of basic factual data about member libraries. With this in mind, the authors assembled a database on member libraries, for the intended purpose of demonstrating to the GPO and other groups the value in constructing and maintaining a similar, ongoing, but more extensive, database of current, factual information on the program. Sorely needed is the ability to compare basic descriptive information over time so that trends can be identified and improvements in the program can be implemented.

This chapter is intended to accomplish four specific objectives:

- to present a composite profile of libraries participating in the program
- to provide background data for the discussion of depository subgroups covered in the next chapter
- to examine a number of key variables descriptive of depository libraries to determine which do or do not have statistical significance
- to relate these findings to those of other selected surveys—governmental and other

To accomplish these objectives, the set of hypotheses identified in Figure 3-1 were developed and tested to determine if they could be supported, based on the findings of this study.

Figure 3-1. Study Hypotheses and Whether or Not They Were Supported

Hypothesis	Status
There is no statistically significant difference between respondents and non-respondents to the survey	Supported
The more populated states contain a larger number of depositories than less populated states	Supported
There is no statistically significant difference between geographical location and the year in which depository status was gained	Supported
Depository libraries tend to be located in cities with populations not exceeding 500,000	Supported
There is no statistically significant difference between type of depository and the size of the city in which the library is located	Not Supported
There is a positive correlation between the number of depositories in a state and the state's population	Supported
Depository designation accords greater emphasis to population density than to geographical region	Supported
Those libraries receiving their depository status before 1900 are the most likely to be located in large population centers	Not Supported
There is no statistically significant relationship between the percentage of items selected and:	
a. volume count	Supported
b. budget	Supported
c. number of library staff	Supported
d. number of documents staff	Supported
e. population of the city	Not Supported
f. geographical region	Supported
g. collection arrangement	Supported
h. collection organization	Supported
Congressional or law designation does not comprise a statistically significant variable in the analysis of depository library characteristics	Supported
There is no statistically significant difference between staffing of the depository collection and:	
a. budget	Supported
b. geographical region	Supported
c. volume count	Supported
There is no statistically significant difference between collection arrangement and:	
a. staffing of depository collection	Supported
b. volume count	Supported
c. geographical region	Supported
d. budget	Supported
e. date on which depository status was gained	Supported
There is no statistically significant difference between collection organization and:	
a. budget	Supported

Figure 3-1. (continued)

Hypothesis	Status
b. staffing of depository collection	Supported
c. volume count	Supported
d. geographical region	Supported
e. date on which depository status was gained	Supported
There is no statistically significant difference between whether depository libraries select microfiche and:	
a. the percentage of items selected	Supported
b. budget	Supported
c. volume count	Supported
d. staffing of depository collection	Supported
e. geographical region	Supported
There is no statistically significant difference between whether a library engages in online searching for government publications and:	
a. budget	Not Supported
b. percentage of items selected	Not supported
c. geographical location	Not supported
There is no statistically significant difference between the use of bibliographic utilities for documents searching and geographical region	Not Supported
There is no statistically significant difference between the size of the library (determined by the number of volumes) and the likelihood that online searching of government documents databases is performed	Not Supported

This chapter is divided into three major sections. The first provides an overview of the study and highlights the methodology, the quality of the data used, a comparison between respondents and non-respondents to the survey, and study findings. The second section compares the findings of this study to selected surveys of the depository program, including those produced by the federal government and those originating in the private sector. The third offers concluding remarks about the lack of comparability among the different studies.

Study Methodology

Government Depository Libraries (GPO, 1982, 1983), an annual committee print from the Joint Committee on Printing, lists existing depository libraries, their addresses, and their identification numbers. The authors used the 1983 edition of this document as the basis for determining the current population of federal depositories. The list was updated with the identification of newly designated libraries reported in *Public Documents*

Highlights (GPO) through September 1983, as well as a telephone call to the GPO in January 1984. In order to gather descriptive data on these 1,373 libraries, the authors considered using three options: (1) they could request that the GPO supply a copy of the latest *Biennial Survey*, in machine-readable format, containing questionnaire responses from individual libraries; (2) they could consult standard reference works providing information on libraries in the United States; or (3) they could survey *all* libraries participating in the depository program administered by the GPO.

The authors contacted the GPO about the availability of the data contained in the *Biennial Survey*. Because the GPO and its legal counsel took eight months to render a decision,[1] the authors concluded that because of the GPO's slowness in making a decision, they had to rely entirely on the two other methods for data collection. These two methods of data collection served both as a substitute for the lack of access to data contained in the *Biennial Survey* and as a mechanism to capture basic information about depository libraries—much of what was not included in the *Biennial Survey*. To reduce expenses, the questionnaire was designed to be brief and capable of being completed in a few minutes. There were nine questions and these elicited information about the number of items selected, depository collection arrangement and organization, the provision of on-line database searching and other uses of technology, the selection of depository microfiche, staffing patterns for the documents collection, and the extent of participation in other depository programs. Appendix B reprints the questionnaire which was used.[2]

In October 1983, the questionnaire was drafted and pretested at ten depository libraries. Based on the comments of the documents librarians, the questionnaire was revised and mailed to all 1,373 depository libraries in November 1983. A stamped, self-addressed envelope was included along with the questionnaire. By April 15, 1984, some 1,101 of the 1,373 libraries had responded; the return rate, therefore, was 80.2%.

In addition to the survey data, descriptive information on the following variables was gathered from standard reference sources:[3]

---

[1] It might be noted that Carl LaBarre, as Superintendent of Documents, supplied gratis and promptly to two of the authors the 1979 *Biennial Survey*, in machine-readable form, for use in the research leading to Hernon and Purcell (1982).

[2] The authors would like to thank Ablex Publishing Corporation and Walter Johnson, its president and publisher, for assuming the cost of conducting this survey.

[3] Descriptive data were gathered from: *The American Library Directory* (1982); National Center for Education Statistics, *Education Directory: Colleges and Universities, 1980–1981* (1981); National Center for Education Statistics, *Library Statistics of Colleges and Universities* (1981); National Center for Education Statistics, *Statistics of Public Libraries, 1977–78* (n.d.); *The World Almanac and Book of Facts 1983* (1983); *Directory of Law Libraries* (1978); *Statistical Abstract of the United States, 1982–1983* (1982); *American Universities and Colleges* (1983); *Barron's Guide to the Two-Year Colleges* (1981); Bureau of the Census, *1980 Census of Population: General Population Characteristics* (1982–1983); and *Directory of Special Libraries and Information Centers* (1983).

- geographical location (see Map 3-1 for a depiction of the regions used by the U.S. Bureau of the Census)
- population of the community in which the depository is situated
- type of library
- year of depository designation
- designation (congressional or "law")[4]
- whether the library is a regional or partial depository
- volume and title counts for holdings of non-government documents
- number of library staff
- library budget (income and staff salaries)

For the academic libraries, additional institutional data were collected on

- the highest degree offered
- control (public or private affiliation)
- number of faculty
- size of student enrollment

The data from the printed sources were than added to those gathered from the survey, converted to machine-readable form, and analyzed, at the University of Tennessee, using *SPSS: Statistical Package for the Social Sciences* (1975).

Percentages were generated, and for the purpose of analysis, the relationships among variables were examined with the chi square test of association. The level of 0.05 was set for the achievement of statistical significance. Because the publication dates of the general reference works varied, and given the categorical nature for most of the data examined (see the section entitled "Quality of the Data"), the authors did not subject the data to more sophisticated methods of statistical analysis.[5]

Quality of the Data

Data Taken from Standard Reference Works

To minimize the intrusion on depository staff, the authors decided to collect certain data from basic reference sources. One purpose of this ap-

---

[4] Law depositories are specifically designated by various acts of Congress and include state agency libraries, land grant college libraries, the libraries of the highest appellate court, federal libraries, and a few miscellaneous designations. Congressional depositories are designated by members of Congress.

[5] For a discussion of the chi square test of association and nonparametric statistical procedures, see Huck, Cormier, and Bounds, Jr., (1974), Chapter 10.

Map 3-1. Regions and Census Divisions of the United States*

U.S. DEPARTMENT OF COMMERCE
Bureau of the Census

* The Midwest Region was designated as the
North Central Region until June 1984

* *Source:* U.S. Bureau of the Census. A similar map can be found in any issue of *Statistical Abstract of the United States* (Washington, D.C.: GPO).

proach was to assess the strengths and weaknesses of the data reported in these sources. This section of the chapter reports on the quality of these data. It is our hope that this analysis will be of value to subsequent studies wanting to rely extensively on similar data given in reference sources.

Geographical Location and Population of Community: The collection of these data posed no problem because of their ready availability through publications of the U.S. Bureau of the Census. Map 3-1, which was produced by the Bureau, depicts geographical location, while the *American Library Directory*, the *Statistical Abstract of the United States*, and the *1980 Census of Population and Housing* report current information on the population of the community.

Type of Library: The *American Library Directory* for 1982 provided current and unambiguous information which enabled the authors to identify libraries by type.

Year of Depository Designation: A list of depository libraries, with the date in which they gained depository status, is available in *Government Depository Libraries*, the committee print issued by the Joint Committee on Printing (GPO, 1982, 1983). In those instances where the year was not provided, one of the authors checked the *Monthly Catalog of United States Government Publications* for those years in which this source listed depository libraries and the year in which status was gained. For those cases in which status was still undetermined, the survey contained one question asking for the year. As a result of these various efforts, the year of depository designation was determined for all but 45 (3.3%) libraries.

Status: The *Monthly Catalog* (any current issue), as well as other sources, lists the libraries currently holding regional status. Thus, there was no difficulty in identifying regional depositories.

Volume and Title Counts: As the subsequent analysis indicates, it was very difficult to obtain this information for all the libraries from sources such as the *American Library Directory* (1982) and the National Center for Education Statistics (1981b). Volume counts were not available for 157 libraries, and title counts were absent for 689 libraries. Because the number of libraries for which data were missing is so large, the subsequent analysis makes only selective use of these two variables.

It is, indeed, unfortunate that more libraries do not report the number of titles that they retain, for this is a more valid indicator of the richness of the collection than a volume count. Volume count does not control for duplicate copies of titles, a phenomenon that is particularly common in large public and academic libraries with branches.

Number of Library Staff: The *American Library Directory* (1982) reports the number of staff members for many libraries. However, reporting procedures vary among libraries. Some include all staff members (professional, paraprofessional, clerical, and student) in their total, while others are more selective in the personnel categories reported. Finding staffing information in other reference sources (e.g., National Center for Education Statistics, 1981a, 1981b, and n.d.; and *Directory of Special Libraries and Information Centers*, 1983) is a time-consuming task, but it produces positive results. After searching the various sources, the number of staff could be located for all but 298 libraries. However, because the number of staff members was unavailable for 21.7% of the depository libraries, this variable was only used selectively in data analysis and interpretation.

Budget (overall and salaries): Budget information was selectively covered in the *American Library Directory* (1982) and other reference sources

(National Center for Education Statistics, 1981a, 1981b, and n.d.; and the *Directory of Special Libraries and Information Centers*, 1983). Therefore, the overall budget for 219 (16%) of the libraries could not be located. The amount spent on salaries was unavailable for 392 (28.6%) of the 1,373 libraries. The variable of budget, therefore, was also used selectively in data analysis and interpretation.

Depository Designation: In only two cases (0.1%) were the authors unable to determine if depository status was derived from federal legislation or as a congressional designation. The previously mentioned committee print from the Joint Committee on Printing provided the information for this variable.

Highest Academic Degree: This information is readily available from the reference sources examined (*American Library Directory*, 1982; National Center for Education Statistics, 1981a); *American Universities and Colleges*, 1983; and *Barron's Guide to the Two-Year Colleges*, 1981).

Institutional Control: This information was also readily available from the same reference sources identifying the highest academic degree.

Number of Faculty: Surprisingly, this information proved difficult to find. Again, institutions varied substantially in their reporting practices. Some of the reported figures combined full- and part-time faculty, while others separated the two. In some cases, administrators were included in the faculty total, while in other instances they were omitted. For these reasons, the authors used the information gathered on the number of academic faculty selectively.

Enrollment: These data were obtained without any problem, using the *American Library Directory* (1982), in combination with other reference works. Where sources vary in the currency of the data reported, the validity of data interpretation can suffer.

Data Derived from the Survey

Certain descriptive information was unavailable in printed sources and therefore was gathered from a survey of depository libraries.

Collection Arrangement: For the most accurate portrayal of this variable, a series of questions should offer a time series demonstrating the ways in which the library has historically handled its holdings of government publications. It must be remembered that libraries will not all answer one question about collection arrangement on the basis of current activity; they may well respond in the context of their historical treatment of government publications. The single question from the survey does not fully address the historical context; however, it does provide an overview.

Collection Organization: For this variable, the authors incorporated questions 25, 26, and 31 of the 1981 *Biennial Survey*. The conditions described by the questions on our survey about collection organization are quite varied. As an example, one survey respondent correctly noted, the collection may be physically separate from other library holdings. Yet various activities (e.g., acquisition, technical processing, and circulation) may be performed elsewhere. "The government documents librarian [at this one institution] acts as a liasion and troubleshooter with staff in other areas of the library." Because of the variety of conditions in depositories, the questions asked do not fully document the system of organization in all libraries.

Use of Technology: The data gathered should be regarded only as a general indicator of the use of technology. It must be remembered that these data were gathered from a self-reporting process and that some respondents may have replied on the basis of future plans and not current practice. Further, the questions do not treat frequency of use. Also, it appears that some respondents confused online bibliographic database searching (e.g., searching from DIALOG) with searching performed on a bibliographic utility (e.g., OCLC).[6]

Number of Items Selected: Unlike previous studies, the authors did not ask survey respondents to check the appropriate predetermined category. Instead, they asked for the actual number selected and instructed respondents to report the number from their latest GPO printout. With this information, the authors created categories reflective of selection practices and then coded respondents in the appropriate category. One advantage of this approach was that the authors could see the range in the actual number of items selected.

Selection of Depository Microfiche: The only problem posed by the two questions was that the one which asked for the location of the microfiche collection assumed that the documents and central microforms areas are not the same.

---

[6] The data derived from the survey suggest the need to investigate all depository libraries about their current and planned use of technology. Such a study should specifically probe use of microcomputers.

Staffing: In some instances, it was obvious that respondents were unfamiliar with the concept of the full-time equivalent (FTE) in staffing, and merely reported the actual number of staff. Further, in some cases, reference staff might also service the documents collection, but they were not listed as part of the FTE reported. However, based on the comments written by respondents and the percentages reported, it would seem that such instances were, indeed, an exception.

Depository for Other Federal Agency Publications Programs: This question, which was taken from the 1981 *Biennial Survey* (question 15), appeared to present numerous problems for the respondents. Apparently many answered the question based on the names of the agencies whose publications they receive on deposit from the GPO. They did not associate the question with their being a depository for other federal agencies. Therefore, the question was not analyzed and the responses are not reported in this book.

The lesson which the authors learned from the inclusion of this question is that it cannot be automatically assumed that the *Biennial Survey* asks questions largely devoid of interpretation and likely to produce reliable and valid responses.

Reliability and Validity of the Data

Whenever researchers collect data, they should attempt to assess the *reliability* and *validity* of the data elements. Reliability, which suggests stability and consistency of measurement, is concerned with the accuracy of the data reported. One criterion for assessing reliability is the representativeness of the questions about the phenomenon that is being measured; the more representative the questions, the higher is the reliability. On this criterion, the data gathered should be reliable; however, this indicator of reliability must take into account the constraints already noted about the specific data elements. Further, all questions presented in the survey, or the data elements taken from standard reference sources, are not unique to this study. They have been used by other investigations into the depository program.[7]

A second criterion of reliability is accurate and consistent coding. The following actions were taken to increase the reliability of data according to this criterion. First, written procedures and a standardized coding form were developed for the gathering and recording of data. One of the authors, with the aid of a graduate assistant, gathered the data from stan-

---

[7] These other studies are identified and discussed in the next chapter.

dard reference works. The assistant went through an extensive training session to assure her understanding of the procedures and the definitions used in coding. Her work was regularly reviewed, and any inconsistencies in coding were corrected. This same author coded all survey responses, while another entered data into the computer. The same two authors then verified that the data entered into the computer were consistent with those listed on the coding sheets. When a discrepancy was found, the error was corrected.

Pretesting a questionnaire enables researchers to avoid the phrasing of questions in ambiguous terms and to ensure that the questions most appropriate to study objectives and hypotheses are asked. Questionnaire pretesting revealed that some of the original questions were open to interpretation and, therefore, they were rewritten.

Since the questionnaire relied on self-reporting, the authors selected ten of the responding libraries with which they were personally familiar and compared the responses to their knowledge of those libraries. After not having found discrepancies in the responses, they telephoned the documents librarian at each institution and reviewed the survey responses. The responses of the librarians were identical to their written responses and conformed with the authors' knowledge of those libraries. Thus, this procedure suggests that the data were, in fact, reliable.

The validity of the data is the extent to which they accurately measure what they purport to measure. *Face validity* refers to an appraisal of whether the content of an instrument corresponds to what it claims to measure. This type of validity requires a representative collection of data and sensible methods of questionnaire construction and administration. The questionnaire drew upon items asked by previous studies and was relatively free of ambiguity, as determined by consultation with several documents and reference librarians. With this, in addition to the fact that the survey was administered according to accepted convention, face validity can be demonstrated.

A possible threat to validity is that some of the data collected from the standard reference works may be outdated and, therefore, comprise a questionable measure. Realizing this, the authors placed all 1,373 libraries in order by their depository identification number and selected 14 libraries using as their sampling base every hundredth library. The libraries, then, drawn from the systematic sample, were telephoned and asked to supply written information about the population of the community, type of library, volume and title counts, and, for academic libraries, the highest degree offered by the institution and the size of the student body. Once received, the responses were compared to the data already collected. There was some variation in actual numbers; however, the variation was confined within the categories which the authors used to collapse the data. This finding suggests that the variation in the age of data reported in different sources did not substantially affect data analysis and interpretation. Further, this finding lends more credibility to the categories used for data analysis and interpretation.

Another criterion of validity is the extent to which results can be generalized to a population as a whole. In the case of this investigation, the authors surveyed the population (the 1,373 depository libraries) and did not draw samples. Because some of the data were gathered from standard reference sources, and because the survey generated a high rate of response (80%), the authors believe that their findings characterize the population.

This assumption can be examined by a comparison of respondents and non-respondents to the survey (see the next section of the chapter); however, it should be noted here that the survey data are representative of the population. To test whether there was a statistically significant difference between respondents and non-respondents to the survey, these two groups were compared on the basis of library type: academic (including law school), public, and other. The chi square test of association did not indicate a statistically significant difference at the .001 level.

Next, the percentage of respondents for each of the three library types was compared to the actual population of libraries comprising that type. In other words,

- academic library respondents totalled 82.9% (755) of the population of academic libraries (911, which includes law school libraries)
- public library respondents totalled 76.3% (212) of the population of public libraries (278)
- the other libraries totalled 72.8% (134) of the population of these depositories (184)

Again, no statistically significant difference emerged with the chi square test. Therefore, survey responses demonstrate external validity, or applicability to the study population.

The above discussion suggests *indicators* that the study obtained data which were both reliable and valid, within the limitations previously defined. The authors utilized data analysis techniques appropriate to the objectives under investigation and did not utilize techniques of analysis which require the making of significant and questionable assumptions. Although a conservative approach to data analysis has been used, the authors believe that the findings are likely to have more validity, given the limitations.

Overview of Non-Respondents to Survey

Because the authors attempted to gather basic information on all 1,373 depository libraries from standard reference works, it is possible to compare respondents and non-respondents to the survey. The characteristics of the two groups, when compared, were essentially the same. The factor of non-response was randomly scattered throughout the population of depository libraries. Given this finding, as well as the high response rate to the survey and the previous discussion of data reliability and validity, the data presented in this chapter (be they gathered from standard reference sources or from the mail questionnaire), as well as data offered in the subsequent chapter, appear to offer a representative profile of libraries participating in the depository program at the time of the survey.

The states with the largest populations and the largest number of depository libraries contributed the most non-respondents. In spite of this, non-response was equally distributed among the census regions depicted in Map 3-1.

Some 121 (44.5%) of the 272 non-respondents were academic libraries, 66 (24.3%) were public libraries, and 35 (12.9%) were law school libraries. The remaining 18.3% was distributed among federal, court of law, state agency, historical, and other special libraries. As is evident, academic and public libraries were most likely not to respond to the survey; however, these two groups comprise a large percentage of depository libraries. As was presented in the previous section, no statistically significant difference was evident between respondents and non-respondents to the survey and library type.

Since the highest degree offered by academic institutions had been determined, this variable was compared to whether or not the academic library responded to the questionnaire. No significant trends were noted; institutional control, the number of faculty, and the size of the student body also did not produce statistically significant differences.

The date in which depository status was gained was unrelated to the willingness of a library to respond to the survey. Because data on the size of the budget, the number of library staff, the overall volume and title counts were missing for many libraries, no comparison was made between respondents and non-respondents for these variables.

In summary, it can be seen that there is no statistically significant difference between survey respondents and non-respondents on the various variables examined. Thus, the data reported in this chapter and the next one can be generalized to the population—1,373 depository libraries.

Study Findings

Date of Depository Designation

The date of designation of depository libraries, individually and collectively, provides an indication of how designations have been distributed

Chart 3-1. Libraries Receiving Depository Status Before and After the
1962 Depository Library Act

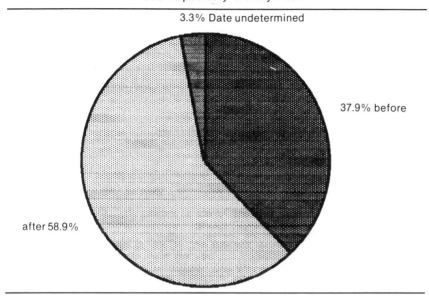

3.3% Date undetermined

37.9% before

after 58.9%

over time. Because changes in public legislation affecting the creation of depository libraries has, since the 1960s, resulted in a substantial increase in the number of depositories (see Chart 3-1), it is of value to know how many have come into existence subsequent to legislation expanding the number of depositories, where they are located, and some characteristics of those relatively new depositories (see Chapter 4 for a discussion of libraries achieving depository designation since 1976).

Table 3-1 shows the historical time period in which the libraries gained their depository status. Approximately one-fourth had achieved their status prior to 1926, while the largest percentage was designated as depositories during the time period after the implementation of the 1962 Depository Library Act. As will be noted in the next chapter, approximately half of those libraries becoming depositories between 1976 and

Table 3-1. Year of Depository Designation

Years	Number	Percentage
Prior to 1900	180	13.1
1900–1925	153	11.1
1926–1950	112	8.2
1951–1975	669	48.7
1976–1984	214	15.6
Date Unavailable	45	3.3
Total	1,373	100.0

1984 belonged to accredited law schools and achieved their designation as part of the 1978 act offering depository status to these libraries.

Population of Community and Geographical Location

Table 3-2 indicates the number of depository libraries by state, as well as the number for those possessions of the United States. It shows that states with the largest populations (e.g., California, New York, Texas, Pennsylvania, and Illinois) contain the largest percentages of depository libraries. In fact, if the states were ranked in two columns (the first showing in descending order the number of depository libraries per state and the second the state population), and if the two columns are statistically compared using the Spearman Rank Order Correlation Coefficient, it results in a correlation that is high; omitting the District of Columbia from the analysis results in over .9 as the correlation. There is a definite relationship between population density and the number of depositories in a state.

Table 3-2. Distribution of Depository Libraries by State

State	Number	Percentage	State	Number	Percentage
Alabama	25	1.8	New Hampshire	9	.7
Alaska	8	.6	New Jersey	43	3.1
Arizona	13	.9	New Mexico	10	.7
Arkansas	18	1.3	New York	91	6.6
California	108	7.9	North Carolina	35	2.5
Colorado	23	1.7	North Dakota	10	.7
Connecticut	22	1.6	Ohio	58	4.2
Delaware	7	.5	Oklahoma	21	1.5
Florida	36	2.6	Oregon	19	1.4
Georgia	28	2.0	Pennsylvania	62	4.5
Hawaii	11	.8	Rhode Island	11	.8
Idaho	10	.7	South Carolina	17	1.2
Illinois	57	4.2	South Dakota	11	.8
Indiana	34	2.5	Tennessee	26	1.9
Iowa	20	1.5	Texas	63	4.6
Kansas	18	1.3	Utah	11	.8
Kentucky	20	1.5	Vermont	8	.6
Louisiana	26	1.9	Virginia	37	2.7
Maine	12	.9	Washington	20	1.5
Maryland	23	1.7	West Virginia	14	1.0
Massachusetts	34	2.5	Wisconsin	29	2.1
Michigan	48	3.5	Wyoming	10	.7
Minnesota	24	1.7	District of		
Mississippi	12	.9	Columbia	48	3.5
Missouri	31	2.3	Guam	2	.1
Montana	9	.7	Puerto Rico	4	.3
Nebraska	14	1.0	Virgin Islands	3	.2
Nevada	8	.6	Panama Canal	1	.1
			Micronesia	1	.1
			Total	1,373	100.0

Chart 3-2. Distribution of Depository Libraries by Census Region

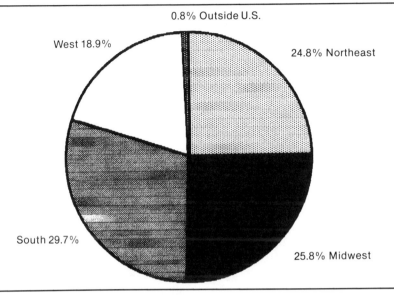

Chart 3-2, which collapses the data from the preceding table into a depiction of depository libraries on the basis of geographical distribution, offers a graphic presentation of the census regions displayed in Map 3-1. It is interesting to note that the South has both a larger number and a larger percentage of depositories than any other geographical region. On the other hand, the West has the smallest percentage of depository libraries. The Midwest and Northeast have similar percentages.

However, the perception of the geographical distribution of depositories is altered if the population of each geographic area is taken into consideration. Table 3-3 shows the number of inhabitants and the percentage of the total population of the United States (including the District

Table 3-3. Distribution of Depository Libraries Compared to Number of Inhabitants by Census Region

Census Region	Number of Inhabitants*	Percentage of Total	Number of Depositories	Percentage of Total	Difference in Percentage
Northeast	49,519,000	21.16	292	21.99	+ .83
Midwest	58,953,000	25.20	354	25.99	+ .79
South	79,539,000	33.99	435	31.94	− 2.05
West	45,970,000	19.65	281	20.63	+ .98
Total	233,981,000	100.0	1,362	100.0	

* Data on the number of inhabitants in the four regions are taken from *Estimate of the Population of States: July 1, 1981 to 1983* (Advance Report). Washington, D.C.: Bureau of the Census, 1984, p. 2 (Bureau of the Census, Series P-25, No. 944).

of Columbia but excluding the territories). It is divided into the four grand regions used by the Bureau of Census. The table also shows the number and percentage of federal depositories in each region. (Because depositories in the territories are not considered, the total number of depositories in the 50 states and the District of Columbia is 1,362 rather than 1,373). These data show that the northeastern, midwestern, and western regions of the United States are each over-represented by depositories, while the South is under-represented, in relation to the population of the region. The difference in representation between the South and the other regions is nearly 3% in each case.

Regardless of geographical distribution, the largest percentage of libraries obtained their depository status in the time period embracing the enactment of the 1962 Depository Library Act. When the geographical distribution of depositories designated between 1951 and 1975 is compared to those designated between 1976 and 1984, a noticeable difference is observed. The South had 31.1% of the new depositories designated from 1951–1975, a percentage which was noticeably higher than any of the other three regions. On the other hand, the Northeast had 33.6% of the depositories designated after 1976. This was considerably higher than the other regions, and especially higher than the 17.8% designated in the West. These findings suggest that there might well have been a "pent-up demand" for new depositories in the South that was met, in part subsequent to the 1962 act. The strong showing of new depositories in the Northeast can be accounted for by the large number of law school and federal libraries in that region. The next chapter provides a more detailed assessment of the "newer" depositories.

Table 3-4 depicts the population of the communities in which depository libraries are situated. Over half (58.7%) are located in communities

Table 3-4. Population of Community in Which Depositories Are Located

Size of Community	Number of Libraries	Percentage
50,000 and under	611	44.5
50,001–100,000	195	14.2
100,001–200,000	166	12.1
200,001–300,000	70	5.1
300,001–400,000	59	4.3
400,001–500,000	55	4.0
500,001–600,000	28	2.0
600,001–700,000	66	4.8
700,001–800,000	22	1.6
800,001–900,000	6	.4
900,001–1 million	12	.9
Over 1 million	81	5.9
Unknown	2	.1
Total	1,373	100.0

of 100,000 or less, while 84.2% of the depositories can be found in cities with populations not exceeding 500,000. At the other end of the spectrum, only 5.9% are situated in cities of over 1 million in population.

One might presume that the older depositories (defined as those designated prior to the end of the nineteenth century) are more frequently located in the larger population centers, while the depositories designated later are found in more widely diversified population centers. When date of depository designation was compared to the size of population, it was observed that of the 180 depositories designated prior to 1900 for which the date of designation was determined, 59 (32.8%) were in population centers of 50,000 or less. Only 42 (23.3%) were in population areas of 400,001 or more. Thus, it cannot be concluded that older depositories are necessarily more likely to be found in larger population centers. Interestingly, far more depositories were designated in large population centers (defined here as areas with a population of 400,001 or more) after 1951 than before that date. The data showing date of designation indicate that numerous depositories located in large population centers became ready for depository status in the post–World War II period, and especially after the implementation of the 1962 legislation. The meaning of the data analyzed here is that for the most part pre–twentieth-century depositories were widely distributed among large and small population centers. On the other hand, many of the depositories designated in the postwar years have been designated in larger population centers, with a result that there is less emphasis on geographical distribution than population density.

Library Type

Table 3-5 depicts the 1,373 participants in the depository program by library type. It might be noted that the two private membership libraries are the American Antiquarian Society and the Boston Athenaeum, both located in Massachusetts.

Table 3-5. Library Types Participating in the Depository Program

Type	Number	Percentage
Academic	765	55.7
Public	278	20.2
Federal	60	4.4
Law School	146	10.6
Court of Law	60	4.4
State Agency	45	3.3
Historical Society	6	.4
Private Membership	2	.1
Medical	3	.2
Other	8	.6
Total	1,373	100.0

The largest percentage of depositories is found in academic libraries. This percentage becomes even more dramatic if general academic libraries are combined with accredited law school libraries. By so doing, it can be seen that academic institutions comprise two-thirds of member libraries. The next largest percentage consists of public libraries. The next chapter will provide a detailed analysis of academic, public, and law school depositories. Together, these three types comprise 86.5% of member depository libraries.

There was a statistically significant relationship between the type of library and the size of the city in which the library is located. Academic depository libraries were more likely than public or other library types to be found in the smaller communities. The next chapter will amplify on this point in regard to academic libraries.

Volume and Title Counts of the Libraries

The authors were unable to locate volume counts for 157, and title counts for 689, of the 1,373 depository libraries. Consequently, for this study, the number of volumes is a more valid indicator of the size of the overall library collection. Table 3-6 indicates that nearly one-fourth of the depositories for which data were available fall between 100,001 and 200,000 volumes. In fact, 41.1% of the libraries have collections of 200,000 or less. If the analysis extends to those libraries having volumes not exceeding 300,000, the percentage increases to 55.6. The implication of these findings is that a large number of depository libraries are small, with volume counts not likely to exceed 500,000.

Table 3-6. Number of Volumes (Non-Government Documents)
Held by Depository Libraries

Number of Volumes	Number of Libraries	Percentage
10,000 and under	76	5.5
10,001–75,000	74	5.4
75,001–100,000	83	6.0
100,001–200,000	336	24.5
200,001–300,000	194	14.1
300,001–400,000	109	7.9
400,001–500,000	50	3.6
500,001–600,000	41	3.0
600,001–700,000	40	2.9
700,001–800,000	27	2.0
800,001–900,000	17	1.2
900,001–1 million	18	1.3
Over 1 million	151	11.0
Undetermined	157	11.4
Total	1,373	100.0

Title counts could be located for 684 (49.8%) of the libraries. It should be noted that for 96 (14%) of these libraries, the count did not exceed 10,000. This finding further indicates that a number of depository libraries maintain small collections. As will be suggested subsequently in this chapter and in the next one, the *Guidelines for the Depository Library System* (1977) suggest a minimum number of titles for depository libraries. It is obvious that a large percentage (at least 14%) fall below the recommended number.

Size of Overall Library Budgets

Of the 1,154 libraries for which the overall budget was determined from standard reference works, half (586, or 50.8%) had budgets exceeding $850,000. For the remaining libraries, the budgets were fairly evenly distributed among the categories ranging from $100,000 or less to $850,000 (see Table 3-7).

Given the number of instances for which the amount of the budget consumed by staff salaries was missing, it can only be observed that at least 86 (6.2%) of all depository libraries provide a maximum of only up to $100,000 for staff, while 305 (22.2%) offer over $1 million. Clearly, the depository program consists of libraries ranging from small to medium and large.

Table 3-7. Amount of Overall Budgets for Depository Libraries

Amount ($)	Number	Percentage
50,000 and under	8	.6
50,001–100,000	24	1.7
100,001–150,000	40	2.9
150,001–200,000	43	3.1
200,001–250,000	53	3.9
250,001–300,000	48	3.5
300,001–350,000	58	4.2
350,001–400,000	47	3.4
400,001–450,000	45	3.3
450,001–500,000	44	3.2
500,001–550,000	28	2.0
550,001–600,000	31	2.3
600,001–650,000	37	2.7
650,001–700,000	18	1.3
700,001–750,000	25	1.8
750,001–800,000	19	1.4
800,001–850,000	24	1.7
850,001–900,000	17	1.2
900,001–950,000	24	1.7
950,001–1 million	22	1.6
Over 1 million	499	36.3
Undetermined	219	16.0
Total	1,373	100.0

Designation (Congressional or Law)

The designation of only 2 (.1%) of the libraries was undetermined. Of the remaining 1,371 libraries, 977 (71.3%) have a congressional designation, while 394 (28.7%) have law designations.

With the exception of the highest appellate court libraries designated under section 1915, Title 44, *United States Code*, all libraries are required to make depository publications available for use of the public. This applies regardless of the method by which depository status was gained. Since only this one library type can discriminate in its services, and since so few depository libraries are affiliated with the highest appellate court, the variable of designation has little practical significance for a study of this type. It merely offers a mechanism by which the number of libraries participating in the program can be increased.

Number of Staff Assigned to Library Collection

With overall staffing information unavailable for over 20% of the depository libraries, the importance of this variable cannot be fully determined. However, it can be noted that 18.2% of the libraries for which staffing data were available have 10 or fewer staff members, while another 18% have between 11 and 20. Some 63% of the libraries have no more than 50 employees, which underscores the fact that many depositories can be characterized as small to medium in size, with limited staff and volume counts.

Staffing of Depository Collection

Some 1,073 libraries (78.2% of the population) supplied information about their staffing of the documents collection. As shown in Table 3-8, regardless of personnel classification, the most typical pattern is to assign a maximum of 1 FTE. There is no statistically significant difference in this finding based on the percentage of items selected, budget, volume count, method of collection organization and arrangement, and geographical location.

Next to professional staff, depository libraries are most likely to assign student assistants, followed by clerical and paraprofessional staff, to the documents collection. If a library employs more than 2 FTEs for the collection, this number is most likely achieved through student assistants.

As mentioned in the table, 74 libraries (5.4% of the population of depository libraries) stated that no professional staff member had documents-related responsibilities. Instead, the collection was under the jurisdiction of clerical or paraprofessional staff, or student assistants.

Table 3-8. Staffing Patterns for Depository Collections
(Expressed in Terms of FTE)

Classification	1.0 or Less	1.1– 2.0	More than 2.0	Total
Professional*	816	115	68	999
	(81.7%)	(11.5%)	(6.8%)	
Clerical	366	58	39	463
	(79.1%)	(12.5%)	(8.4%)	
Paraprofessional	431	86	44	561
	(76.9%)	(15.3%)	(7.8%)	
Student Assistants	410	104	97	611
	(67.1%)	(17.0%)	(15.9%)	
Other**	18	1	1	20
	(90.0%)	(5.0%)	(5.0%)	

* As noted in the text, 74 libraries responding to the survey do not assign professional staff to the depository collection.
** This category includes volunteers, pages, desk aides, and CETA library technicians.

It might be useful to analyze these 74 libraries, although they do not display statistically significant patterns from other depositories. Almost two-thirds of them (48, or 64.9%) were academic libraries, while 14.9% (11) were public libraries, 9.5% (7) law school libraries, 6.7% (5) federal libraries, and the remaining 4% (3) court of law libraries. Only 1 of the 47 libraries employing clerical staff assigned more than 1 FTE to the depository collection. All 29 libraries using paraprofessional staff assigned no more than 1 FTE, while 7 of the 28 libraries using student assistants placed more than 1 FTE in the depository collection.

Of the 70 libraries having no professional assignment for the depository collection and reporting on the number of items selected, 35.7% (25) take 10% or less; 44.3% (31) receive between 11% and 25%; 11.4% (8) select between 26% and 50%; and the remaining 8.6% (6) take more than 50%. Some 80%, therefore, receive a maximum of 25%.

The final point of analysis relates to those 48 academic libraries which do not assign professional staff to the depository collection, and the highest degree program of the institution. Some 18 (37.5%) offer undergraduate programs (either the arts associate or baccalaureate degree), while the remaining 30 (62.5%) have graduate programs (either the master's or doctorate).

Percentage of Items Selected

Table 3-9 highlights the percentage of items selected by the 1,030 libraries reporting the information on the depository survey. Only 13.4% of these

Table 3-9. Percentage of Item Numbers Selected by
Survey Respondents Providing the Information

Percentage Selected	Number of Respondents	Percentage of Respondents
All	52	5.0*
76–99	87	8.4
51–75	115	11.2
26–50	251	24.4
Up to 25	525	51.0
Total	1,030	100.0

* Only 1 of these libraries was not a regional depository.

libraries take more than 50%, while half take fewer than 25%. Chapter 4 highlights the percentages selected by academic, public, and law libraries. It also examines those depositories selecting 25% or fewer items, as well as those achieving depository status between 1976 and 1984.

There is no statistically significant difference between the percentage of items selected and volume count. In effect, a higher volume count is no guarantee that a library will select a higher percentage of available item numbers. Regardless of volume count, libraries are most likely to select no more than half of the items; in fact, some libraries with large volume counts receive 25% or less of the items available for selection. One might assume that as the number of available items and titles increases, libraries may become even more selective in their item choices.

A comparison of the percentage of items selected to the size of the budget and the number of staff also did not produce statistically significant differences. Larger budgets and staffs do not necessarily signify that a library selects more item numbers.

The percentage of depository categories accepted by the libraries was significantly related to the population of the community in which the library was located. Those depositories taking more than half of the items tend to be situated in the larger cities.

Collection Arrangement

Data were absent from 319 (25.2%) of the depository libraries on this variable. The 1,054 libraries reporting on collection arrangement are likely to use either the Sudocs scheme exclusively (515, or 48.9%) or a combination of methods (450, or 42.7%). The remaining libraries arrange the collection by the Dewey (28, or 2.7%), Library of Congress (36, or 3.4%), or another method. This alternative method might be a special classification scheme developed for the legal or medical field, an in-house scheme, the shelving of documents topically, the arrangement of publications alphabetically by agency and then by series, or the arrangement of publications in the sequence received. Generally, those libraries using a combination of methods probably employ the Sudocs system as one method of collection arrangement.

Regardless of the percentage of items selected, the budget of the library, the number of staff assigned to the collection, the volume count, or the geographical location, there is no significant difference in the distribution of method of classification used. The most common methods are either the Sudocs scheme exclusively or a combination of methods.

Collection Organization

Of the libraries responding to the survey and identifying their method of collection organization, the majority (852, or 81.7%) place *most* of their depository publications in a separate collection. Another 113 (10.8%) respondents include *some* of their depository publications in a separate collection. Only 78 (7.5%) libraries indicated that they do not maintain separate collections but either integrate their collections with other holdings or divide their location among different areas of the library system. Of the libraries with separate collections, 702 house some documents (e.g., microfiche and/or maps) separately.

Separate collections prevailed regardless of the percentage of items selected, budget, number of depository staff, volume count, and geographical location. As expected, there is a direct relationship between collection arrangement and collection organization. A separate collection of government publications signifies that library clientele will probably encounter a method of collection arrangement different from that used for the general library collection.

Microfiche Collection

Only 33 of the libraries responding to the questionnaire claimed that they do not receive depository microfiche. Given this small number, there is no statistically significant difference between whether or not a library selects microfiche and the percentage of items selected, budget, volume count, staffing of depository collection, and geographical location.

Arranged in descending order of occurrence, depository libraries reporting on the housing of depository microfiche keep them in the

- documents area (42.7%)
- central microforms area (40.6%)
- both the documents and the central microforms area (8.5%)
- other (8.2%)

The other category might include, for example, other departments of the library, the general reference department/area, or a workroom.

Use of Technology

Of the libraries responding to the survey and reporting on their conducting online bibliographic database searching for government publications, 649 (58.9%) claim that they provide such searching. It merits repeating that the answer was based on self-reporting and that the questionnaire did not probe the frequency with which searching is performed. Undoubtedly the frequency ranges from minimal to heavy.

When asked to identify the location of the terminal(s), the libraries reported it was most likely in the general reference department/area (378, or 58.2%). In descending order of frequency, the other alternatives mentioned include

- technical services department/area (73, or 11.2%)
- separate data search room/area (56, or 8.6%)
- both general reference and documents department (49, or 7.6%)
- a library department such as periodicals, media, or the administrative office (46, or 7.1%)
- documents department/area (28, or 4.3%)
- another library or building such as computer center (10, or 1.5%)
- interlibrary loan (9, or 1.4%)

The questionnaire did not ask about who performed the searching. However, the data on the location of the terminal(s) seem to suggest that non-documents staff are more likely to do the searching of databases, be they government or non-government related.

There was a statistically significant relationship between the use of online database searching and the budget. The larger the budget, the more likely that the library engages in online searching. Libraries with budgets under $500,000 are equally as likely to engage in searching as they are not. Some 75.5% of the libraries with budgets exceeding $1 million engage in online searching.

There was also a statistically significant relationship between the use of online searching and the percentage of items selected. The more items selected, the more likely a library is to do online searching. Those libraries selecting 25% or fewer items either might or might not engage in online searching. Two-thirds of those selecting 10% or fewer items do not perform such searching, while 47.1% of those taking between 11% and 25%, and reporting the percentage received and the use of online searching, do not.

The relationship between online searching of government documents databases and the size of the depository's non-documents collection (as expressed in the number of volumes) was examined. The data show that for libraries with holdings of less than 200,000 volumes, the number of libraries which do not offer online searching is 253, exceeding the 204 which do offer this service. However, in the size category "200,001–300,000 volumes," the number of libraries which offer online searching is 108, compared to 53 which do not. In this size range, the rate of libraries which do offer this service is double that of those which do not. For all the libraries which exceed 200,000 volumes that responded to this question on the survey, the rate is even higher. The number of libraries which offer online searching and have collections exceeding 200,000 is 393 (73.9%), and the number in this size range which do not offer this service is 139 (26.1%). This demonstrates that there is a strong relationship between the size of the library (determined by number of volumes) and the likelihood of the depository offering online searching of government documents databases.

Of the 123 libraries with holdings over 1 million volumes which responded to this question, 14 indicated that they do not offer online searching for government documents databases. This is a surprisingly large number of libraries in this size range, and, further, it is amazing that any library in this size range does not offer this service to its users.

The relationship between the use of online searching and geographical region of the country was also examined. Table 3-10 divides the libraries conducting online searching by census region. For the Northeast, South, and West, the percentage of depositories which offer online searching services for government publications is lower than what might be expected— based on the percentage of distribution of depositories in these regions. However, in the Midwest the percentage is higher. If one examines the differential between the percentages in the distribution of depositories and the incidence of online searching, it can be observed that the regional differences are enough to raise a question about the cause. For example, the West has a −1.70 difference and the Midwest has a +2.50 difference. The reason for these differences cannot be determined from the data compiled in this survey, but it is clear that depositories in the Midwest show

Table 3-10. Percentage of Depositories Offering Online Searching
Compared to Regional Distribution

Census Region	Percentage of Depositories	Percentage of Depositories Offering Online Searching	Percentage Difference
Northeast	24.8	23.9	− 0.9
Midwest	25.8	28.3	+ 2.5
South	29.7	29.5	− 0.2
West	19.9	18.2	− 1.7

more inclination to use online databases in serving users seeking government information than do depositories in other regions.

Some 636 (57.8%) of the libraries responding to the survey and reporting on the use of OCLC do search that database for government publications. However, the two key questions related to this variable are: "How frequently?" and "By whom?" Given the extensive placement of a terminal(s) not in the documents department but in the technical services area, it would seem that many documents staff members are removed from the location where searching is performed. A comparison of the use of OCLC and the percentage of items selected did not produce a statistically significant difference. Apparently, use of OCLC pervades all levels of item selections.

Use of OCLC and the other bibliographic utilities as a resource for searching for government publications does not vary considerably by region. The number of libraries which indicated that they used OCLC, RLIN, or WLN was collected by region and then compared to the number of depositories in the region. Through this, it was discovered that in the Northeast 65.7% of the depositories used one of these three utilities, while in the Midwest the percentage was 57.6, in the West 48.0, and in the South 45.2. Thus, libraries in the South and the West use bibliographic utilities far less often for documents searches than do libraries in the other two regions of the country. This finding, together with the others noted above, suggests that in terms of documents applications, technological advances have had a lesser impact on depository library service in the South and, to some extent, in the West than in the other regions.

Table 3-11 indicates the extent to which the 1,101 libraries reporting on their use of technology make other uses of a computer. The percentages are small—ranging from 1.5 to 5.5. Other than using a bibliographic utility (e.g., OCLC, RLIN, or WLN), a library might generate a computerized documents holding file or a keyword index.

Table 3-11. Other Uses of Technology

Uses	Number	Percentage*
RLIN	60	5.5
WLN	32	2.9
Other bibliographic utilities	31	2.8
Purchase GPO tapes for local use	16	1.5
Use computer to produce keyword indexing	41	3.7
Use computer for documents holding file	48	4.4
Other**	18	1.6

* The percentage is based on the number of libraries reporting the information on the completed questionnaire.

** The other category drew mention of microcomputers; the inclusion of government publications in online, public access, catalogs and COM catalogs; the maintenance of online inventory control systems and online circulation systems; and the production of a specialized index (MEDOC).

Comparison of Findings to Selected Studies

Biennial Survey

The *Biennial Survey* comprises an important means by which the GPO obtains basic information on depository libraries and their willingness to remain in the program. Chapter 6 provides a detailed analysis of the survey and its purpose and utility. The intent of this section is to illustrate the extent to which the survey produces data comparable to those presented in this chapter.

Table 3-12, which provides an indication of the types of questions asked in the *Biennial Survey* from 1975 to 1983, shows that the wording of a question may change over time. This lack of consistency in data reporting inhibits the development of trend data to characterize the program over time.

Table 3-12. The Depository Library Program As Characterized in Responses to Selected Questions Reported in the *Biennial Report of Depository Libraries* (Washington, D.C.) for 1975, 1977, 1979, 1981, and 1983

	Selection*			
	Survey for			
Percentage of Items Selected	1975	1977	1979	1981
all	74 (6.4%)	67 (5.5%)	68 (5.3%)	47 (4.0%)
75–99	176 (15.2%)	169 (13.9%)	116 (9.0%)	90 (7.6%)
50–75	223 (19.2%)	211 (17.3%)	118 (14.6%)	166 (14.1%)
25–50	331 (28.5%)	375 (30.8%)	340 (26.4%)	319 (27.0%)
under 25	330 (28.4%)	381 (31.3%)	562 (43.7%)	549 (46.6%)
no answer	27 (2.3%)	14 (1.2%)	12 (.9%)	—**
Total Response	1161	1217	1216	1218

* This question was not asked on the 1983 *Biennial Survey*. For comparative purposes, the data gathered from the survey reported in this book showed that
 • 52 (3.8%) take all
 • 87 (6.3%) take between 76% and 99%
 • 115 (8.4%) take between 51% and 75%
 • 251 (18.3%) take between 26% and 50%
 • 525 (38.2%) take up to 25%
 • 343 (25.0%) unknown
** The number was not reported. There is great variation among the questions as to the number of respondents. Clearly, there is little data reflecting the population. Some 1,171 libraries reported on the percentage of items selected, while only 1,137 libraries indicated whether they wanted to "continue as a depository" (question 6).

Table 3.12. (continued)

Collection Organization*

Does the documents collection comprise a separate department in the library

	1975	1977	1979
yes	749	811	841
	(64.5%)	(66.6%)	(65.4%)
no	382	385	415
	(32.9%)	(31.6%)	(32.3%)
no answer	30	21	30
	(2.6%)	(1.8%)	(2.3%)

* This question was not asked on the 1983 *Biennial Survey,* while the 1981 *Biennial Survey* asked the question in a manner which cannot be compared to the previous results. Question 25 of the 1981 survey offered response categories a–f; however, the data analysis provided by the GPO reported responses for a "g" category. Clearly, a coding mistake had been made.

Staffing

1975

How many library staff members have documents-related responsibilities?

One: 212 (18.3%)
Two: 380 (32.7%)
Three to Five: 402 (34.6%)
More than Five: 158 (13.6%)
No answer: 9 (.8%)

Does the depository collection have the services of

A full-time documents librarian: 483 (41.6%)
A part-time documents librarian: 486 (41.9%)
Assistance from librarians from other sections: 408 (35.1%)
No one at present: 7 (.6%)
No answer: 17 (1.5%)

1977

How many hours of professional or paraprofessional staff time per week are directly involved with U.S. Government documents?

Less than 10 hours: 136 (11.2%)
10–20 hours: 421 (34.6%)
30–40 hours: 230 (18.9%)
40 hours: 90 (7.4%)
More than 40 hours: 319 (26.2%)
No answer: 21 (1.7%)

1979

How many hours of professional or paraprofessional staff time per week are directly involved with U.S. Government documents?

Table 3.12. (continued)

Less than 10 hours: 138 (10.7%)
10–20 hours: 472 (34.7%)
30–40 hours: 238 (18.5%)
40 hours: 81 (6.3%)
More than 40 hours: 340 (26.4%)
No answer: 17 (1.3%)

How many hours of clerical staff time per week are directly involved with U.S. Government documents?

Less than 20 hours: 559 (43.5%)
20–30 hours: 233 (18.1%)
30–40 hours: 197 (15.3%)
40–60 hours: 123 (9.6%)
More than 60 hours: 154 (12.0%)
No answer: 20 (1.6%)

1981*

Is there a professional librarian directly in charge of processing and servicing depository materials?

a. Yes, for technical services and public services: 876 (74.2%)
b. No, only for the technical services activities: 86 (7.3%)
c. No, only for the public services activities: 35 (3.0%)
d. No, not for any activities: 148 (12.5%)
e. Other: 29 (2.5%)

How long has the person coordinating depository activities been in that position?
a. More than 10 years: 807 (68.3%)
b. 6–10 years: 106 (9.0%)
c. 3–5 years: 87 (7.4%)
d. 1–2 years: 91 (7.7%)
e. Less than 1 year: 79 (6.7%)
f. There is no one in the position: —**

Is there enough support staff...?

a. Yes, there is adequate staff: 429 (36.3%)
b. There is sufficient support staff for public services, but not for technical services: 729 (61.7%)

1983

Is there adequate professional and non-professional staff for the operation and maintenance of the depository collection?

a. Yes, there is adequate staff: 963 (75.1%)
b. Only for the technical services: 30 (2.3%)
c. Only for public services: 89 (6.9%)
d. No: 196 (15.3%)

How many professional staff work with documents?

---

* Reported here are only a few of the questions relating to staffing patterns.
** No numbers or percentages were reported.

Table 3.12. (continued)

Number Responded: 0
Average Count: 0

How many clerical, support staff, and student aides work with documents?

Number Responded: 1
Average Count: 0

How many volunteers work with documents?

Number Responded: 20
Average Count: 0

The percentage of depository libraries selecting under 25% of the available items has increased with each survey. In the time between the conducting and the reporting of the 1977 and 1979 surveys, there was a 12.4% increase. Clearly, as the number of available items goes up, libraries become increasingly selective in the items they decide to receive.

Data on staffing, unfortunately, cannot be compared over time. The questions have varied and may attempt to elicit information on professional and support staff in the same question. Therefore, the data for the *Biennial Survey* provide only a general indicator of the depository program at any two-year interval.

With the 1983 *Biennial Survey* (see Appendix A for a copy of the survey instrument), the GPO substantially changed many of the types of questions asked. Depository libraries, for example, were asked to report information gathered from a monitoring of collection use for a five-day period, as well as their access to computer facilities and terminals.

Eight questions from this survey have potential relevance to this chapter. The first of these, question 13, queried about library type. The GPO developed its own typology for types of libraries. For example, academic libraries could be one of four types: "academic general," "academic law," "academic sci/tech," and "academic medical." Since data were reported on those responding to the survey and a particular question, only 1,281 libraries identified their type. On the other hand, some of the figures and data analysis reported in this chapter, as well as the next one, characterize the population, while others are based on a sample.

Question 12 asked if the library was a regional or partial depository. Some 51 libraries identified themselves as regionals. This is the same number indicated in the study reported in this book (see the next chapter for profiles of regional depository libraries).

Question 14 elicited information about the approximate number of volumes of non-government documents held by the library. However, differences are evident between the data reported in the *Biennial Survey* and those given in this chapter. The analysis of the number of volumes for both studies was based on a similar number of cases. The GPO found 14 libraries reporting 10,000 or fewer volumes, while this chapter identified 76 libraries. The GPO also discovered 25 libraries taking between 10,001 and 100,000 volumes, while this chapter suggests 157; the two studies showed similar volume counts for libraries having more than 100,000 volumes.

The differences between the two studies might be explained from the fact that they derived their information from different sources, the self-reporting of a documents staff member as opposed to data contained in sources such as the *American Library Directory*. Another potential explanation is that neither reported data entirely on the population. Of greater importance than the reason(s) for the difference is "Why is the GPO interested in volume counts?"

According to Title 44, *United States Code* (section 1909), when the Superintendent of Documents

> ascertains that the number of books in a depository library is below 10,000, other than Government Publications, or it [the depository collection] has ceased to be maintained so as to be accessible to the public, or that the Government publications which have been furnished the library have not been properly maintained, he shall delete the library from the list of depository libraries if the library fails to correct the unsatisfactory conditions within six months.

The key point is that this section of the law does not specify either a volume or a title count. In contrast, the *Guidelines for the Depository Library System* (1977), in section 3-4, state that libraries receiving depository status "should possess at least 15,000 titles other than government publications." Here the emphasis is on title counts—15,000 titles. As already noted, volume and title counts are not the same. The GPO should be consistent in what it wants and that clarification should be inserted into Title 44. Further, a more persistent attempt should be made to obtain accurate data from depositories on the number of titles held.

Questions 66–68 attempted to elicit information about the number of FTE professional, clerical, support staff, student assistants, and volunteers assigned to "work with documents." The responses to these questions are analyzed in the next chapter. Suffice to say, the "average count was 0." Since so few libraries responded to the questions, no value, or relevance, can be assigned to this finding. However, it shows that the GPO merely receives and processes returned questionnaires, without following up and eliciting a more complete and accurate representation of the depository program. Chapter 6 will go a step farther and suggest that data derived from the *Biennial Survey* have limited value and utility.

The GPO's 1983 *Biennial Survey* queried about the length of time the person coordinating depository activities had held that position (question

28). Of the 1,277 responding libraries, 942 (73.4%) reported that the person had been in the position for more than 2 years, while 176 (13.7%) indicated between 1 and 2 years and 149 (11.6%) less than one year. For 10 (.8%), nobody coordinated the collection.[8] The question did not specify professional staff.

In contrast, all libraries providing staffing information for the data reported in this chapter indicated that someone coordinated the collection. However, as was already noted, 74 libraries did specify that no *professional* staff members had documents-related responsibilities. The collection was serviced by clerical or paraprofessional staff, or, in some instances, student assistants.

Question 34 of the GPO survey asked if the number of professional and non-professional staff was "adequate...for the operation and maintenance of the depository collection." Although the concept of adequacy was undefined, it is interesting to note that of the responding 1,278 libraries, 963 (75.1%) indicated that staffing was, indeed, adequate. Another 119 (9.2%) qualified their response; it was adequate for either technical or public services. The remaining 196 (15.3%) did not believe that it was adequate.[9]

On the basis of the staffing patterns depicted in this chapter and the next, the answers to question 34 are surprising. It would seem that many depository libraries are satisfied with their present levels of staffing and their current commitment to the depository program administered by the GPO. Based on staffing and other information reported in this chapter, one might question the importance of depository status to some of these libraries, other than as an indication of prestige.

Other Official Surveys

It is interesting to note that other official analyses of the depository program have not subjected the depository program to the type of scrutiny depicted in this, and the following, chapter. Two recent examples illustrate this point.

First, in 1984, the GPO queried depository libraries about their use of GPO/MARC tapes and, in the summary report, identified the number of responses per question. However, the value of the data is weakened by the facts that the survey generated a response rate of only 28.5% (391 libraries), responses were not compared to variables such as library type, and there was no discussion of data reliability and validity (see Chapter 6 for a discussion of these terms).

---

[8] The percentages reported by the GPO total 99.5; 0.5% of the responses are unexplained.

[9] The percentages reported by the GPO total 99.6; 0.4% of the responses are unexplained.

The survey, in general terms, suggests problems which some libraries experience in their use of the tapes sold by the Library of Congress or of the GPO files offered by commercial vendors (BRS, DIALOG, OCLC, RLIN, and others). Some 28 responding libraries use the GPO/MARC tapes, but only 2 of them actually purchase the tapes from the Library of Congress ("Use of GPO/MARC Tapes," 1984). Presumably the others gain access to the tapes through a commercial vendor. In contrast, this chapter identifies 16 libraries claiming that they purchase the tapes.[10]

In the summer of 1983, the General Accounting Office queried depository libraries about the management and operational efficiency of the GPO depository program. The data presentation touched briefly upon the number of libraries serving as regional or selective depositories, the types of libraries participating in the program, the percentage of items which they select, and the number of volumes of non-government publications which the libraries hold (General Accounting Office, 1984).

While the 1983 *Biennial Survey* generated responses from 1,281 libraries, the GAO survey received 1,246 replies. The GAO characterized library types in a manner similar to that used in this chapter. There is some variation in the actual number of libraries per classification type, but the percentages are similar. Information on volume counts for depository libraries cannot be compared among the *Biennial Survey*, the GAO survey, and this chapter. Each used different categories to depict responses.

The GAO discovered that responding partial depository libraries received between 16 and all 5,500 item numbers. "On the average," these libraries selected 1,617 item numbers, (Ibid., p. 2), which comprised 29.4% of what was available. On the other hand, the study reported in this chapter discovered an instance of one library taking 7 items and the average (mean) being less than 1,375—25% of all available items. Chapter 4, which treats subgroups within the depository program, devotes a section to an analysis of those libraries receiving 25% or fewer item numbers. The difference in item selections between the 25% of this book and the 29.4% of the GAO survey must remain unexplained. The GAO did not report the number of libraries providing information on the number of items selected.

An ever increasing amount of government information is electronically generated, processed, stored, and retrieved. With more government information residing in computer systems and unavailable in either paper copy or microformat, much of the populace will not have access to electronic information unless it is provided through the GPO depository library program. Operating on this assumption, the Joint Committee on Printing established an ad hoc committee, in part to determine if depository librar-

---

[10] For a useful discussion of the GPO tapes and the problems in their use, see Myers (1985).

ies have the ability to make use of the new format and "to evaluate the feasibility and desirability of providing access to Federal Government information in electronic formats to the public through the Congressional depository libraries" (Joint Committee on Printing, 1984, p. 4).

The Committee developed a mail questionnaire, which was distributed to all depository libraries. The questions specifically addressed

- the type and size of the libraries
- telecommunications systems used
- cooperative technical processing services used
- types of networks used
- types of charges to patrons
- government research publications used
- computer equipment used
- the most useful of automated databases

By April 1984, a response rate of 93.4% had been achieved. Since a few of the questions have direct relevance to this chapter, the collective responses of depository libraries will be highlighted.

The survey reflected a similar characterization of library types, by actual numbers and percentages, to what was presented in this chapter. Volume counts cannot be compared because different categories were used. Nonetheless, Table 3-13 reprints a table from the report showing the number of volumes held by depository libraries. It is assumed that respondents answered on the basis of volume, rather than title, counts.

Many of the questions about available computer equipment focus on what the library has as opposed to what is actually in, or accessible to, the documents collection. Apparently the assumption is that whatever is available in the library can be used for depository related activities.

Some 74% of the responding libraries belong to one or more bibliographic utility. However, only 9.2% had computer terminals located in the documents department, while 41.6% had terminals located elsewhere and accessible by documents staff. Similar to the study reported in this chapter, the frequency of use was not probed.

The Committee's data analysis did include comparisons on the basis of library type for questions such as those asking about the use of mainframe computers, minicomputers, and microcomputers. Four selective depository libraries (3 academic and 1 public) have mainframe computers in the government documents department, while 1 selective depository (classified as an "other" library type) has a minicomputer in the department. Twenty-one responding libraries placed microcomputers in the department. These libraries can be characterized as: academic (12), public (8), or "other" (1); or as regional (2) or selective (19) depositories.

Table 3-13. Joint Committee on Printing Questionnaire to Depository Libraries. Part A—Questions 6, 7, and 8. Types of Libraries Surveyed Tabulated by Whether Library is a Selective or Regional Depository and Whether Library is Located at a Land Grant or Non-land Grant Institution Tabulated by the Number of Volumes in These Libraries

| | Number of Volumes | | | | | | | | | | | | | | |
| | Less Than 50,000 | | 50,000–99,999 | | 100,000–199,999 | | 200,000–499,999 | | 500,000–999,999 | | 1 to 4 Million | | 4 Million or More | | All Libraries | |
Types of Library	N	%	N	%	N	%	N	%	N	%	N	%	N	%	N	%
Academic	31	4.3	60	8.3	142	19.7	211	29.3	126	17.5	125	17.3	26	3.6	721	100.00
Court	16	29.1	22	40.0	13	23.6	4	7.3	0	0	0	0	0	0	55	100.00
Federal Agency	14	35.0	5	12.5	9	22.5	4	10.0	3	7.5	4	10.0	1	2.5	40	100.00
Law School	2	1.5	7	5.2	59	43.7	57	42.2	9	6.7	1	0.7	0	0	135	100.00
Public	8	3.0	17	6.4	65	24.3	76	28.5	40	15.0	41	15.4	20	7.5	267	100.00
State Agency	2	4.4	4	8.9	5	11.1	15	33.3	6	13.3	12	26.7	1	2.2	45	100.00
Other	3	10.7	7	25.0	5	17.9	8	28.6	4	14.3	1	3.6	0	0	28	100.00
Type of Depository																
Regional	0	0	1	2.0	0	0	4	7.8	9	17.6	30	58.8	7	13.7	51	100.00
Selective	76	6.1	121	9.8	298	24.0	371	29.9	179	14.4	154	12.4	41	3.3	1240	100.00
Type of Institution																
Land Grant	0	0	1	1.8	2	3.5	9	15.8	7	12.3	27	47.4	11	19.3	57	100.00
Non-land Grant	76	6.2	121	9.8	296	24.0	366	29.7	181	14.7	157	12.7	37	3.0	1234	100.00
Totals	76	5.9	122	9.5	298	23.1	375	29.0	188	14.6	184	14.3	48	3.7	1291	100.00

* Source: Joint Committee on Printing. Provision of Federal Government Publications in Electronic Format to Depository Libraries. Report of the Ad Hoc Committee on Depository Library Access to Federal Automated Data Bases (Washington, D.C.: GPO, 1984).

On the basis of the responses, the Committee concluded that a wide array of computer equipment was in place, that many libraries already searched government databases, and that during the present decade most libraries would have the capability to utilize electronic information systems. Two key questions emerge in relation to this conclusion. First, are many documents staff members already engaged in the use of technology, or is the use being made by other departments? Second, what are the implications of the staffing patterns presented in this chapter? The data reported here would seem to be at odds with long-term expectations of the Committee. Will a small number of overworked staff have the time, energy, and ability to extend themselves into a new area—providing bibliographic control and reference service for machine-readable data?[11]

Other Profiles

On occasion, authors have attempted to characterize the types of libraries participating in the depository program, to profile the number of depository libraries by state and congresstional district, and to call for further research into those libraries holding depository status.[12] In 1956, Powell, Duke University Library, and Pullen, University of North Carolina Library, reported to Congress on a survey of 571 depository and 623 non-depository libraries. They profiled responding depository libraries by type, and made a distinction between college and university libraries. They also examined the number of volumes held and identified the percentage of items selected. The two librarians were critical of libraries selecting fewer than 25% of the available item numbers; they questioned if these libraries merely wanted a "convenient method...to receive a small handful of Government publications from a central source" (Powell and Pullen, 1958). Librarians of today would argue that reduced item selections often result in the receipt of more than "a small handful" of public documents.

The value of their survey was that it provided data useful in the reorganization of the depository program. More precisely, Congress and the library community found it of value in formulating the legislation resulting in the Depository Library Act of 1962. It would seem that a more current baseline of data could be of use in revising Title 44, *United States Code*, and in deciding on the formats for depository distribution, the amount of material to be disseminated each year, and the capability of

---

[11] For a useful discussion of numeric databases see Chen and Hernon (1984).

[12] These other studies are discussed in the next chapter. In addition to the two studies highlighted in this section, readers may want to consult Chapters 2 and 4 in this book, or Eastin (1948) and Brock (1962).

depository libraries to provide the public with access to government publications/information.

Based on 1972 and 1979 data, Schwarzkopf, then documents librarian at the University of Maryland, analyzed the types of libraries participating in the depository program. He wrote that "of the 1,080 depositories in 1972, 711 (or 65.8%) were academic libraries; 249 (or 23%) were public libraries; 65 (or 5.8%) were state agency libraries; 9 (or 1.8%) were special libraries; and 27 (or 5.3%) were federal libraries."

By 1979, academic libraries still accounted for approximately the same percentage (65.4); accredited law school depositories comprised 8.6% of the 65.4%. Public libraries had increased slightly in number (277), but they represented a percentage decrease (down to 21.2%) as a library type participating in the depository program (Schwarzkopf, 1982, p. 23). As shown in this chapter, by 1984, public library depositories totaled 278, but now represented only 20.3% of the total depositories.

Viewing his analysis as only general, Schwarzkopf has called for a more detailed analysis of depository libraries, one looking at both the population and the subgroups. It is our hope that both this chapter and the subsequent one provide the type of analysis which he advocated. Further, the GPO, other government agencies, and practicing librarians are now all surveying depository libraries about the extent of staff familiarity with technology, and about the capability of the libraries to exploit technology for collection management and reference service. Such surveys will provide a more realistic view of current practice if they are linked to the type of baseline date reported here. The purpose is to identify and monitor trends, while finding more effective and efficient ways for all depository libraries to take advantage of information-handling technologies.

The Need for Trend Data

This chapter has illustrated problems associated with using the types of questions asked on the *Biennial Survey* and has shown that there is minimal trend data regarding the depository program and its member libraries. The *Biennial Survey*, as well as Chapters 3 and 4 of this book, offer only a "snapshot" view of the depository program at a particular moment in time. The GPO, the Joint Committee on Printing, and the library community should all seek to go beyond this and to produce valid and reliable data relevant to decision making and planning.

Key questions which merit attention include the following:

- what are the characteristics of the participants in the depository program?

- what changes in membership have occurred over time?
- what are the program and library goals and objectives?
- how well is the program meeting its objectives?

It is interesting to note that only the first question has really been addressed from official sources. However, as demonstrated in this chapter, that question cannot be adequately addressed. In regard to the third question, goals and objectives for the program have been reported in various documents, but as shown in Chapter 1, these statements are highly deficient and merit reformulation. The intent should be to produce performance measures, a broad concept encompassing *input* variables (such as an inventory of computer and microform equipment) and *output* (such as a comparison of the number of titles sought to the number found).[13] In the process, the fourth question can be better addressed than through the GPO inspection program as currently constituted (McClure and Hernon, 1983, pp. 161–193).

Succeeding surveys, especially those emanating from the federal government, have an obligation to build from each other and, to some extent, draw upon some similar questions. Clearly, there is a need to develop and pre-test questions which address specific objectives and hypotheses or research questions. The movement toward the development of trend data is critical, otherwise the study reported in this book will merely remain a picture of the depository library program from November 1983 to April 1984.

Although "pictures" of the depository library program are useful, they are only as useful as the degree to which they provide clear and sharp images of the depository libraries they are intended to represent. As shown in this chapter, the "pictures" of the depository library program from the various surveys examined vary in quality and typically offer their views from different angles, thereby limiting the degree to which they can be directly compared. Until there is a centralized, coordinated, and competent national reporting system for descriptive depository library data, librarians, government officials, and others interested in the program will be at a significant disadvantage when making decisions or attempting to plan and evaluate depository library activities.

---

[13] See Hernon and McClure (1984) for a discussion of performance measures aimed at government documents collections and services.

Chapter 4

Depiction of the Depository Library Program by Selected Subgroups

Most previous analyses of the depository library program, including the *Biennial Survey*, have merely surveyed the depository community and reported responses to questionnaire items in a manner similar to that in Chapter 3. The purpose of this chapter is to go beyond this type of data reporting and to analyze the characteristics of selected subgroups within the depository library program. By discussing these subgroups, the chapter clearly demonstrates that the depository program consists of a diverse array of member libraries. In addition to offering a profile of each subgroup, the objectives of this chapter are to

- identify possible relationships among the variables depicted in the previous chapter
- compare the impact of these variables among the subgroups
- compare the findings of this chapter to data generated by selected other studies

The first two objectives highlighted above can be translated into corresponding hypotheses, which guided the collection, analysis, and reporting of data. Figure 4-1 compares various variables under study among subgroups, while Figure 4-2 lists specific hypotheses addressed in the chapter, indicating whether a given one is, or is not, supported.

This chapter, specifically, highlights the following:

- academic library depositories
- public library depositories
- law school depositories
- regional depository libraries

- those depositories selecting 25% or fewer item numbers
- those libraries becoming depositories since 1976[1]

It also examines interrelationships among the subgroups and compares the findings of this study to selected other studies. The conclusion emphasizes key issues generated from the analysis of the data reported for the sub-groups. For example, by comparing study findings to those of other sur-veys, it is evident that little trend data exist for the depository program. This finding serves as a foundation for Chapter 7, which calls for the crea-tion and maintenance of a national database for depository library plan-ning and decision making.

The type of information presented in this chapter has value to members of the Government Printing Office and the Joint Committee on Printing, and the U.S. Congress, in administering the depository program and in developing a program to enhance public access to government publica-tions/information. The information is also of value to librarians, or any-one, interested in the depository program, because individual libraries can see where they fit in the larger context of the program. Further, the discussion of recent patterns and trends (e.g., those libraries selecting a maximum of 25% of the available items and the types of libraries gaining depository status since 1976) enables a better understanding of the current nature of the program.

As with Chapter 3, analysis of the data collected from the standard reference sources and the survey (see Appendix B for a copy) was per-formed with *SPSS: Statistical Package for the Social Sciences (1975)*. The chi square test of association was used to test for significance of relation-ships between variables. For testing purposes, the level of significance re-mained at 0.05. Nonstatistically significant relationships were also identi-fied, and certain ones are presented in this chapter.

Academic Depository Libraries

Overview

Some 765 depository libraries are part of academic institutions; these libraries comprise 55.7% of the total membership of the depository pro-gram. With the inclusion of the accredited law school libraries, the num-ber increases to 911 and the percentage becomes 66.3. This section of the

---

[1] The analysis of these subgroups updates and enlarges that presented by Whitbeck, Her-non, and Richardson (1978).

chapter provides descriptive information about the 765 academic libraries, while a subsequent section profiles the law school libraries.

Date of Depository Designation

As shown in Table 4-1, 38.2% of the academic libraries obtained depository status prior to 1950. The majority of them (414 or 54.1%), however, became depositories after 1962, as a direct result of the Depository Library Act of that year; see Chapter 1 for a discussion of this act.

Population of Community and Geographical Location

Most typically, academic depository libraries are located in communities with populations of 100,000 or less (72.2%) or 100,001 to 500,000 (17.7%). As Table 4-2 indicates, therefore, 89.9% of the academic libraries are situated in communities with populations not exceeding 500,000.

The single largest percentage of academic depositories is located in the South (268, or 35%). The remaining percentages are distributed among the Midwest (207, or 27.1%), the Northeast (164, or 21.4%), the West (120, or 15.7%), and the possessions of the United States (6, or .8%). For a useful depiction of the geographical distribution see Map 4-1.

Table 4-1. Year in Which Academic Libraries Gained Depository Status

Time Period	Frequency	Percentage
19th Century	91	11.9
1900–1925	110	14.4
1926–1950	91	11.9
1951–1975	422	55.2
1976–	49	6.4
Date Unknown	2	.3
Total	765	100.1

Table 4-2. Population of Community by Library Type

Library Type	Population of Community				
	100,000 or Less	100,001– 500,000	500,001– 1 Million	Over 1 Million	Unknown
Academic	552	135	40	37	1
n = 765	(72.2%)	(17.7%)	(5.2%)	(4.8%)	(.1%)
Public	156	95	17	10	—
n = 278	(56.1%)	(34.2%)	(6.1%)	(3.6%)	
Law School	43	59	20	24	
n = 146	(29.5%)	(40.4%)	(13.7%)	(16.4%)	—

Map 4-1. Distribution of Depository Libraries by Census Regions*

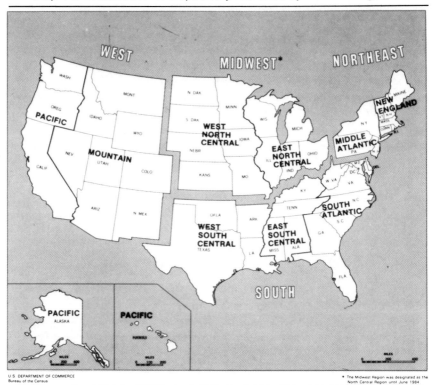

U.S. DEPARTMENT OF COMMERCE
Bureau of the Census

* The Midwest Region was designated as the
North Central Region until June 1984

Academic Libraries		Public Libraries		Law School Libraries		Regional Libraries	
South	35.0%	Midwest	28.8%	South	28.8%	South	33.3%
Midwest	27.1%	Northeast	25.9%	Midwest	26.0%	West	29.4%
Northeast	21.4%	West	24.5%	Northeast	25.3%	Midwest	25.5%
West	15.7%	South	19.8%	West	19.2%	Northeast	11.8%
U.S. Possessions	0.8%			U.S. Possessions	0.7%		

* *Source of Map:* U.S. Bureau of the Census.

Highest Degree Offering and Institutional Control

Table 4-3 depicts academic depositories by both highest degree offering and institutional control (public or private). Sixty percent of the institutions are public and almost 40% are private. The largest percentage (72.2) of academic institutions offer graduate programs; more public than private institutions have graduate programs. As reflected in the table, community college depositories (these are the ones depicted as offering the arts associate degree) tend to be part of public institutions, while baccalaureate depositories are more likely affiliated with private institutions.

Table 4-3. Academic Depository Libraries by Highest Degree Offered and
Institutional Control

		Highest Degree			
Control	Arts Associate	Baccalaureate	Master's	Doctorate	Total
Private	67	32	182	182	463
	(14.5%)*	(6.9%)	(39.3%	(39.3%)	(60.8%)
	(93.1%)**	(22.9%)	(63.4%)	(69.2%)	
Private	5	108	105	81	299
	(1.7%)	(36.1%)	(35.1%)	(27.1%)	(39.2%)
	(6.9%)	(77.1%)	(36.6%)	(30.8%)	
Total	72	140	287	263	762***
	(9.4%)	(18.4%)	(37.7%)	(34.5%)	

* Row percentage.
** Column percentage.
*** Data unavailable for 3 libraries.

The Number of Faculty

The number of faculty employed in an institution was ascertained for all but 19 (2.5%) cases. Almost half of the institutions (363, or 47.5%) employed under 100 faculty members. Over one-fifth of the institutions (205, or 26.8%) had between 200 and 600 faculty, while 84 (11%) had between 601 and 1,000 faculty, and 94 (12.3%) had over 1,000 faculty.

Enrollment

Another indicator of size of the institution is student enrollment. As shown in Table 4-4, more than half of the academic institutions (55.2%) have enrollments of 5,000 or less. On the other hand, 113 (14.8%) of the institutions have enrollments exceeding 15,000. Given the distribution of institutions by enrollment, an appropriate comparison relates to highest degree and enrollment. None of the baccalaureate institutions have enrollments exceeding 5,000, while 16 (22.2%) of the community colleges have enrollments ranging from more than 5,000 to over 20,000. The majority of master's-granting institutions (179, or 62.4%) have enrollments under 5,000, but only 46 (17.5%) of the doctoral institutions have the lesser enrollment.

This portrayal indicates that institutions with degree programs no higher than the master's tend to have smaller enrollments than doctoral institutions. Although one might arrive at this conclusion intuitively, this finding nevertheless serves as a reminder that academic libraries serve

Table 4-4. Enrollment of Academic Depository Institutions

Range	Frequency	Percentage
1,000 and under	92	12.0
1,001–2,000	144	18.8
2,001–5,000	186	24.3
5,001–10,000	147	19.2
10,001–15,000	81	10.6
15,001–20,000	43	5.6
20,001–25,000	32	4.2
Over 25,000	38	5.0
Undetermined	2	.3
Total	765	100.0

higher education and the specialized population of their institution. It also suggests that the information needs of certain segments of the academic population may be served through the depository program better than the needs of others.

Volume and Title Counts of the Libraries

Information about the volume counts for 10.3% of the academic institutions was missing, while data on title counts were unavailable for 41.7% of the libraries. These large percentages inhibit the identification of trends. However, it can be noted that 16.7% of the libraries for which data were available have volume counts of 100,000 or less; in fact, 5.1% of these libraries hold 10,000 or fewer volumes (see Table 4-5). On the other hand, 13.1% have more than 1 million volumes.

Size of Overall Library Budgets

Information on the size of the budget was available for all but 56 (7.3%) institutions. More than one-third of the institutions (36.1%) have budgets of more than $1 million. A similar percentage (37.3%) have budgets of $500,000 or less, and the remaining percentage (26.6) have budgets between $500,001 and $1 million. There is substantial variation among the 765 academic depository libraries in relation to the size of their budgets. Since salary information for library staff in general was unavailable for 141 (18.4%) libraries, trends cannot be noted and comparisons cannot be made to budgeting and the assignment of staff to the depository collection.

Number of Staff Assigned to Library and Documents Collection

Since the total number of library staff could not be determined for 116 (15.2%) libraries, this variable remained unanalyzed. However, the

Table 4-5. Volume Counts by Library Type

Library Type	100,000 or Under	100,001– 300,000	300,001– 1 Million	Over 1 Million	Undetermined
Academic	127	288	171	100	79
n = 765	(16.6%)	(37.7%)	(22.3%)	(13.1%)	(10.3%)
Public	23	105	83	39	28
n = 278	(8.3%)	(37.8%)	(29.9%)	(14.0%)	(10.1%)
Law School	21	91	20	2	12
n = 146	(14.4%)	(62.3%)	(13.7%)	(1.4%)	(8.2%)

Table 4-6. Staffing Patterns at Responding Academic Depository Libraries (Expressed in Terms of FTE)

Classification	None*	Less than 1.00	1.00	1.01– 2.00	More than 2
Professional	48	229	244	60	30
n = 611	(7.9%)	(37.5%)	(39.9%)	(9.8%)	(4.9%)
Paraprofessional	—	86	132	47	25
n = 290		(29.7%)	(45.5%)	(16.2%)	(8.6%)
Clerical	—	123	123	53	24
n = 323		(38.1%)	(38.1%)	(16.4%)	(7.4%)
Student	—	189	102	100	90
n = 481		(39.3%)	(21.2%)	(20.8%)	(18.7%)
Other**	—	4	0	1	1
n = 6		(66.6%)		(16.7%)	(16.7%)

* This category only applies to the professional classification.
** The "Other" category includes graduate assistants, desk aids, pages, and volunteers.

number of staff assigned to the depository collection was identified in the survey, and 611 libraries provided the information (see Table 4-6). Of these libraries, 521 (85.3%) assign no more than 1 FTE professional staff to the depository collection and services. In fact, 48 (7.9%) of the responding academic libraries did not assign any professional librarians. Five of these libraries placed students in charge of the collection, while the rest depended on paraprofessional and clerical staff. According to the comments written by the reference coordinator of one library, clerical staff service the collection and handle all daily tasks. If a matter of policy or a situation requiring a major decision arises, she will investigate the issue and render a decision. However, her role is limited to the time she can devote at home—outside of her normal work responsibilities!

In more than half of the responding libraries, a maximum of 1 FTE per support staff classification is assigned to the depository collection. Data on staffing were compared to the percentage of items selected, the highest degree, and the size of the student body. The hypothesis considered that the number of staff would increase if the institution offered graduate programs, if a larger percentage of items were selected, or if the enrollment became larger. None of these variables supported the hypothesis. The overwhelming majority of libraries, regardless of the variable probed, assign a maximum of 1 FTE classification group to the collection. Using the data reported by the responding libraries, the number of professional staff typically does not increase as the collection becomes larger. If more staff members are added to the collection, they are likely to be from a support classification, in particular student assistants.

Percentage of Items Selected

As shown in Table 4-7, 42.1% of the libraries responding to the survey and providing information about the percentage of items selected take a maximum of the 25% stipulated in the *Guidelines for the Depository Library System* (1977), while less than one-third (28.2%) of the respondents take more than 50%. There is a statistically significant relationship between highest degree and the percentage selected. First, the higher the degree, the less likely that an academic library will select 10% or fewer items. Second, libraries affiliated with institutions offering master's or lesser degree programs are more likely than libraries at doctoral institutions to take between 11% and 25% of the available items. Third, libraries whose institutions offer graduate programs are the most likely to select 51% or more of the items. And finally, the 29 academic regional libraries (profiled in a subsequent section) are affiliated with either master's (1) or doctoral (28) institutions.

In brief, libraries associated with institutions offering no higher than a baccalaureate degree generally take a maximum of 25% of the available items; this is true for 84.9% of the responding community colleges, and 78.9% of the baccalaureate institutions. Of the 225 responding master's-granting institutions, 38.7% (87) take 25% or fewer items, while the

Table 4-7. Percentage of Item Numbers Selected by Responding Library Type

| | Percentage Selected | | | | |
Library Type	10 or Less	11–25	26–50	51–75	Over 75*
Academic	85	157	171	95	67
n = 575	(14.8%)	(27.3%)	(29.7%)	(16.5%)	(11.7%)
Public	41	62	61	12	19
n = 195	(21.0%)	(31.8%)	(31.3%)	(6.2%)	(9.7%)
Law School	41	54	7	1	—
n = 103	(39.8%)	(52.4%)	(6.8%)	(1.0%)	

* Regional depositories have been omitted this category.

largest number (93, or 41.3%) select between 25% and 50% of the items; 37 (16.4%) take between 51% and 75% of the items, and the remaining 8 (3.6%) select a larger percentage.

There is also a statistically significant relationship between the percentage of items selected and the size of the student body. In fact, enrollment appears to be a better indicator of selection than highest degree offered. Libraries whose institutions have enrollments of 5,000 or less infrequently select more than 50% of the items; only 15 (4.6%) of the 330 libraries whose institutions have enrollments in this range select a larger percentage. The largest number of libraries in this category (211, or 63.9%) select 25% or fewer items, while the remaining 104 (31.5%) take between 25% and 50%. As a generalization, it is evident that more than half of the 104 libraries taking between 25% and 50% of the items are affiliated with institutions having enrollments of 2,000 to 5,000.

Of the 245 libraries whose institutional enrollment exceeds 5,000, the largest number (84, or 34.3%) select between 50% and 75% of the items; 29 (11.8%) select 25% or fewer items, 65 (26.5%) take between 25% and 50%, and 67 (27.4%) take a larger percentage. Viewed differently, 94 (38.4%) of the libraries with enrollments over 5,000 select a maximum of half of the available items. If the comparison of enrollment to the percentage of items selected is based upon the actual enrollment figure, and not on a regrouping of figures into broad categories, it is evident that the larger the enrollment, the more likely that the library selects a minimum of 50% of the item numbers.

The examination of the data reported above gives rise to a key question: "Is the size of the student body related to the willingness of a library to select more than 75% of the available item numbers?" When regional depositories are excluded from the analysis, this finding emerges: as the enrollment of the institution becomes higher, an academic library is almost equally as likely to select between 50% and 75% of the items as it is to select a larger percentage. Therefore, a negative answer to the question indicates that size of the student body is not related to a greater willingness to exceed the 75% mark in the selection of item numbers.

Collection Arrangement

Predominantly, academic libraries responding to the survey classify their depository publications by the Sudocs system (341, or 52.3%) or by a combination of methods (270, or 41.4%). Those using the combination of methods most likely use the Sudocs system along with the Library of Congress (LC), or another, method. Some respondents wrote that their library arranges depository microfiche by the Sudocs method and the paper copy publications by LC. The remaining 6.3% of the responding academic libraries used exclusively the Dewey scheme (14, or 2.1%), the LC scheme

(16, or 2.5%), or a locally developed system (11, or 1.7%), which might involve the arrangement of depository publications by item number.

Complicating data analysis is the fact that responding libraries answered the question in the context of the way in which they have historically treated their holdings of government publications. For example, the collection might have been predominantly arranged by the Sudocs system since 1960. Prior to that time, government publications might have been arranged differently; perhaps they were grouped by issuing agency, or by another method. The decision was made that anything received after 1960 would be placed in the Sudocs collection, and it was hoped that eventually there would be sufficient time, money, and staff to convert the historical collection to the Sudocs system so that all the government publications could be located together. This aspiration still has not been achieved; government publications remain in different locations, and the response of a "combination of methods" best describes the situation.

The method for classification does not vary according to highest degree or the other variables investigated. This finding lends support to the assumption that the way in which government publications have been classified historically is probably the most important factor.

Collection Organization

Use of the Sudocs scheme suggests that academic libraries most frequently place many, or perhaps all, of the depository publications in a separate collection. In fact, most (552, or 84.7%) of the 652 academic libraries responding to the survey and the question about the housing of depository publications maintain separate collections containing most of the government publications. The remaining libraries integrate most of the depository publications with the general collection (20, or 3.1%), or place them in different areas of the library or in branches of the system (80, or 12.2%).

Microfiche Collection

Of the 634 libraries reporting on their selection of depository microfiche, 13 (2%) do not receive any. It is interesting to note that 5 of these libraries are associated with institutions offering master's or doctoral programs.

Most typically, academic libraries keep depository microfiche in the documents department, or area, (308, or 49.6%), a central microforms area (199, or 32%), or both locations (65, or 10.5%). The remaining responding libraries place depository microfiche elsewhere:

- the documents department, or area, in combination with another library department or branch library (30, or 4.8%)
- several library departments, none of which, however, includes the documents department, or area (10, or 1.6%)

- the central reference department, or area (5, or 0.8%)
- branch libraries (3, or 0.5%)

Use of Technology

Some 645 of the libraries responding to the survey reported data about their use of technology. First, over two-thirds (445, or 69%) of these libraries claim to engage in at least "some" online bibliographic database searching.[2] Overwhelmingly (276, or 62%), of these libraries have the computer terminal in the general reference department, or area. Only 16 (3.6%) place the terminal used for locating government publications in the documents department, and not the general reference area. Some 33 (7.4%) have terminals in both the documents and general reference departments. As a result, only 11% of the libraries reporting online bibliographic database searching actually conduct the searching in the documents department, or area. The remaining libraries have the searching performed in the general reference department or in another department or building.

When staff at an academic depository use a bibliographic utility, it is most likely OCLC (395, or 61.2%); 23 (3.6%) depository libraries tap the RLIN database, while 18 (2.8%) use WLN and 23 (3.6%) consult another bibliographic utility. The percentage of libraries claiming other uses of technology is small. The largest percentage (7.2, or 32 libraries) generates computerized holdings files.[3] It might be noted that 29 (6.5%) libraries produce computerized keyword indexes, that 9 (2%) purchase the GPO tapes for local use, and that 13 (2.9%) have other uses for technology. For example, they obtain census data in machine-readable form and, when applicable, manipulate these tapes to produce printouts relevant to the information request.[4] Customized searching results in the availability of data not highlighted in paper copy or microfiche publications or in the reformatting of data for easier use by client groups. Other uses might also include the representation of government publications in an author/title, in-house database; the maintenance of an item selection file, with the inclusion of Sudocs numbers, on a diskette for computer manipulation; or the placement of depository publications in an online public access catalog or an online circulation system.[5]

A statistically significant relationship among responding libraries is that those associated with institutions offering graduate programs are

---

[2] A qualification must be inserted at this point. It seems that some survey respondents equated online searching with both bibliographic database searching and OCLC searching. Therefore, the results of this analysis must be viewed as providing only a very general indicator.

[3] For an example of one libraries using such a system see Morton (1981).

[4] For an example of one library doing this see Pope (1984).

[5] It might be noted that only 2 respondents specifically mentioned the current use of microcomputers for depository collections and services. However, 5 suggested that microcomputers were on order.

most likely to engage in online bibliographic database searching; 79% of the libraries whose institutions offered graduate programs claimed that they performed at least "some" online database searching. On the other hand, half (52.1%) of the responding libraries from baccalaureate institutions, and less than one-fourth (22.8%) of those affiliated with community colleges, did. Concerning OCLC, over 60% of the responding libraries from baccalaureate, master's, and doctoral institutions make at least "some" use of this bibliographic utility. However, only 29% of the community colleges did. A similar pattern prevailed for the use of other bibliographic utilities or technology in general.

Summary

If a composite profile of the "typical" academic depository library were constructed, it would show that the library gained its depository status after the passage of the 1962 Depository Library Act. This library is located in a community, with a population not exceeding 100,000, perhaps in the southern or midwestern region of the United States. The library has a budget greater than $500,000. The institution itself would offer graduate programs, have an enrollment of 5,000 or less, and employ fewer than 100 faculty members.

Concerning the depository collection, it would be staffed by a maximum of 1 FTE professional, assisted by no more than 1 FTE per support staff classification. No more than half of the available item numbers would be selected; in fact, the library would probably select 25% or fewer items. The depository holdings would be placed in a separate collection arranged by the Sudocs system. Depository microfiche would be taken and retained in the documents department, or area. Finally, the library would make "some" use of technology for government publications, perhaps only for online database searching or consultation with OCLC. However, the frequency of use is open to question, and may well be minimal.

Public Library Depositories

Date of Depository Designation

Twenty percent (278) of the 1,373 depositories comprise public libraries. Similar to the group of academic libraries, the largest percentage obtained their depository designation in the time period embracing the Depository Library Act of 1962; almost half of the libraries became depositories during this time. On the other hand, as shown in Table 4-8, almost one-fourth of the public library depositories can trace their designation back to the previous century.

Table 4-8. Time Periods in Which Public Libraries Gained Depository Status

Time Period	Number	Percentage
19th Century	66	23.7
1900–1925	39	14.0
1926–1950	15	5.4
1951–1975	135	48.6
1976–	20	7.2
Date Unknown	3	1.1
Total	278	100.0

Perhaps the most important observation from the table is that only 7.2% of all public library depositories gained their status in the years since 1975. Apparently, either the depository library program as currently constituted offers few opportunities for public libraries to apply for a congressional designation, or the large public libraries already participate. In the case of smaller communities, an academic or other library type might possibly extend its services to the broader community. The key questions, though, are "Does this library type extend its services to the broader community?" and "To what extent?" These questions, however, cannot be answered from the data collection for this study.

Population of Community and Geographical Location

Over half of the public libraries are located in communities with populations of 100,000 or less (see Table 4-2). The next largest percentage can be found in communities with populations of 100,001 to 500,000; in fact, 207 (74.5%) of the public library depositories are situated in communities of 200,000 or less.

Excluding the 3 public libraries located in possessions of the United States, the largest number of public depository libraries is located in the Midwest (80, or 28.8%), followed by the Northeast (72, or 25.9%), the West (68, or 24.5%), and the South (55, or 19.8%); see Map 4-1 for a pictorial depiction of these percentages. The major difference in distribution patterns between academic and public library depositories is that the largest percentage of academic libraries is situated in the South, while this region offers the smallest number of public libraries. Clearly, the depository program in the South is better developed for academic, than for public, libraries.

Volume and Title Counts of the Libraries

Over two-thirds of the public libraries hold between 100,001 and 1 million volumes of non-government publications (see Table 4-5). More specifically,

137 (49.3%) have volume counts ranging between 100,001 and 400,000. By including the 23 libraries having less than 100,000 volumes, the percentage of public libraries with 400,000 or fewer volumes becomes 57.6. It is interesting to note that 4 libraries hold fewer than 75,000 volumes; one of these even has less than 10,000.

All 129 public libraries for which title counts could be determined have more than 15,000 non-government publications. However, since title counts were unavailable for 149 (53.6%) or the public libraries, the extent of their compliance with recommendation 3-4 of the *Guidelines for the Depository Library System* (1977), which specifies that a depository library "should possess at least 15,000 titles other than government publications," cannot be ascertained.

Size of Overall Library Budgets

Budgetary data were available for all but 6 public libraries. Over half of the rest (160, or 57.6%) had budgets exceeding $1 million; at the other end of the spectrum, only 15 (5.4%) had budgets of $200,000 or less. If the budgets for the remaining libraries were arranged in categories, each of which was incremental by $50,000, the median budget would encompass the category "$550,001–$600,000." The large numbers of missing data for the size of salary allocations inhibit the identification of any patterns, other than the fact that at least 104 (37.4%) libraries expend more than $1 million per year in salaries. It might be inferred that budgets of this size have implications for the size of a staff; in effect, the larger the expenditures for salaries, the larger is the number of personnel. Again, the number of cases for which data are missing prohibits comment, except to note that at least 85 (30.6%) libraries have more than 100 personnel.

Number of Staff Assigned to Library and Documents Collection

More revealing than the overall number of library personnel is the actual number of FTE staff assigned to the depository collection. As shown in Table 4-9, 9 (4.4%) of the libraries reporting data on staffing do not have any professional staff with depository-related responsibilities, while 169 (83.3%) have 1 or fewer FTE professionals working with the collection. Similarly, regardless of category for support staff, the typical pattern is to assign 1 or fewer FTE to the depository collection. It might be noted that the responses to the "other" category encompass volunteers, pages, and CETA technicians.

Percentage of Items Selected

Table 4-7, which displays the percentage of item numbers selected by library type, indicates that over half (103, or 52.8%) of the 195 respond-

Table 4-9. Staffing of Depository Collections in Public Libraries
(Expressed in Terms of FTE)

Classification	None*	Less than 1.00	1.00	1.01– 2.00	More than 2.00
Professional	9	75	85	17	17
n = 203	(4.4%)	(36.9%)	(41.9%)	(8.4%)	(8.4%)
Paraprofessional	—	28	33	6	5
n = 72		(38.9%)	(45.8%)	(8.3%)	(6.9%)
Clerical	—	58	40	17	11
n = 126		(46.0%)	(31.8%)	(13.5%)	(8.7%)
Student	—	29	7	3	5
n = 44		(65.9%)	(15.9%)	(6.8%)	(11.4%)
Other**	—	12	1	2	—
n = 15		(80.0%)	(6.7%)	(13.3%)	

* It is most meaningful only to report the number of public libraries not assigning direct responsibilities to professional staff.
** This category encompasses volunteers, pages, and CETA technicians.

ing selective depositories take 25%, or fewer, of the currently available 5,500 item numbers. On the other hand, only 9.7% take more than 75% of the items. With the inclusion of the 5 public libraries serving as regionals, the percentage of responding libraries taking a minimum of 76% of the items becomes 12.

It might be tempting to hypothesize that the larger the population of the community, the more likely a public library will be to select more item numbers. However, since many public libraries are situated in communities having populations of 200,000 or less, and since some libraries with populations larger than 1 million select fewer than 25% of the available item numbers, such a hypothesis is not supported. The number of items selected is also unrelated to the size of the budget and the volume count. Undoubtedly, factors such as the mission of the library, the composition of the community, and the perceived importance of government publications in relation to other types of holdings have an important effect on the number of items selected.

Collection Arrangement

Of the 212 responding libraries, 102 (48.1%) classify their depository collection by a combination of methods, while 95 (44.8%) rely exclusively on the Sudocs scheme, 13 (6.1%) on the Dewey scheme, and 2 (.9%) on another system.

Collection Organization

Three-fourths (161, or 75.9%) of the public libraries responding to the survey maintain separate documents departments, or areas, while 42

(19.8%) primarily integrate their depository publications into the general collection. The remaining 9 (4.3%) distribute a large percentage of their documents to different areas in the library system.

Microfiche Collection

Of the 198 libraries reporting on the collection of microfiche, 86 (43.4%) retain them in the documents department, or area, while 70 (35.4%) keep them in a central microforms area. Some 14 (7.1%) keep depository microfiche in both locations, and 17 (8.6%) place them in another department, one other than the general reference department. The remaining 4 (2%) libraries keep some microfiche in the documents department, or area, and others in another department or branch library. As is evident, 104 (52.5%) of the libraries reporting on their collection of microfiche place at least some of them in the documents department, or area.

The response of one library merits special note. The staff store depository microfiche wherever there is a cabinet with extra space. Instead of pulling the collection together and assigning a particular cabinet or cabinets to depository microfiche, the practice is to split the collection and let available space dictate holding location.

Use of Technology

In contrast to the other subgroups highlighted in this chapter, public libraries are the least likely to offer online bibliographic database searching; 79 (37.3%) of the survey respondents did, while 133 did not. The same 212 public libraries also provided information about their other uses of technology. Some 89 (42%) consult OCLC for the government publications contained in the database; although respondents were not probed about the type or extent of use, some volunteered that use was minimal. Other bibliographic utilities were infrequently used: 7 (3.3%) use RLIN and 3 use (1.4%) WLN. Few public libraries make other uses of technology; 3 (1.4%) purchase GPO tapes for local use, 3 (1.4%) use a computer to generate a documents holdings file, 1 (.5%) uses a computer to produce a keyword index, and 1 (.5%) incorporates depository publications into an online circulation system. Clearly, the technological revolution for depository collections and services in public libraries is something of the future, not the present.

Summary

The "typical" public library obtained its depository status in the time period embracing the passage of the Depository Library Act of 1962. This library is probably located in a community of 100,000 or less, perhaps in the Midwest or Northeast. Further, it has between 100,001 and 400,000 volumes of non-government publications and a budget exceeding $1 million.

Similar to the "typical" academic library, it assigns a maximum of 1 FTE professional, and 1 FTE per support staff classification, to the depository collection and services. However, unlike its academic library counterpart, the public library classifies its depository collection by either a combination of methods or the Sudocs system. Either way, government publications typically are placed in a separate collection. The library selects depository microfiche and locates them in the documents department, or area.

Two other differences between the academic and public library depositories relate to the percentage of items selected and the use of technology for government publications. The "typical" academic library selected a maximum of 50% of the available items, while the public library counterpart takes a maximum of 25%. The academic library made selective use of technology; however, the public library counterpart probably does not use technology at all for its documents collection. If by chance it does, the library consults OCLC for government publications but does not engage in online bibliographic database searching.

Law School Depository Libraries

Overview

Law school libraries, a subgroup of academic libraries, have been accorded separate treatment in this chapter because they are designated by a separate public law and because they comprise a significant percentage of libraries participating in the depository program administered by the Government Printing Office—10.6%.

Date of Depository Designation

The majority of the 146 accredited law school libraries (105, or 71.9%) received their depository status since the implementation of the 1978 legislation permitting their participation through a law designation (Public Law 95-261, 92 *Stat.* 199). Of the remaining 41 libraries, 39 (26.7%) achieved their designation in the period 1951–1975; one obtained its status in the nineteenth century and the other in the period 1900–1925.

Population of Community and Geographical Location

Over two-thirds of the law school libraries (102, or 69.9%) are situated in population centers of 500,000 or less. Of the library types depicted in

Table 4-2, law school depositories are more likely than academic or public library depositories to be in communities of 100,001 or more; however, they are the least prevalent in communities under 100,000.

The largest number of law school depositories is located in the South (42, or 28.8%). The remaining libraries are distributed among the Midwest (38, or 26%), the Northeast (37, or 25.3%), the West (28, or 19.2%), and a possession of the United States (1, or 0.7%). Again, see Map 4-1 for a depiction of the percentages by geographical region.

Volume and Title Counts of the Libraries

Table 4-5, which depicts the number of volumes held by library type, indicates that only 2 law libraries have volume counts exceeding 1 million, while 112 (76.7%) have fewer than 300,000 volumes. The largest percentages of libraries falls into the range of 100,001 to 300,000.

Of the libraries for which title counts were available, 2 have fewer than 10,000 non-government publications. One of these libraries obtained depository status in the early 1970s and the other in the early 1980s. The small number of holdings for the one library achieving depository status after implementation of the *Guidelines* (1977) definitely conflicts with the previously identified section 3-4 of that document.

Size of Overall Library Budgets

Since data were missing for more than one-third of the libraries, data analysis was not performed.

Number of Staff Assigned to Library and Documents Collection

Data on the number of library staff also were unavailable for more than one-third of the libraries. However, data were gathered on the staffing of the depository collection. Of the 106 libraries providing information, 7 (6.6%) reported no professional assignment to the collection, while 89 (84%) have 1 or fewer FTE professionals working with depository documents. Only 10 (9.4%) assign more than 1 FTE professional to the collection.

Support staff are also selectively used in the depository collection. Sixty-four (60.4%) of the 106 libraries reporting personnel information employ clerical staff to handle government publications; 58 (90.6%) of these libraries assign 1 or fewer FTE, while the other 6 (9.4%) have more than 1 FTE. A similar pattern prevails for the use of student assistants and paraprofessionals. Fifty (90.9%) of the 55 libraries using student assistants assign 1 or fewer FTE of this classification to the depository collection; 5 (9.1%) use more than 1 FTE. Only 37 of the libraries have paraprofessional staff working with government publications; 33 (89.2%) assign 1 or fewer FTE, and 4 (10.8%) use more than 1.

Percentage of Items Selected

As was shown in Table 4-7, law school depositories are most likely to select no more than 25% of the available item numbers. In fact, 41 (39.8%) of the 103 libraries supplying the percentage of item numbers selected take 10% or less, while only 8 (7.8%) select more than 25%. Law school depositories, as one might expect, are indeed highly selective in the number of items taken.

Collection Arrangement

One survey question concerned the classification scheme used for the depository collection. Of the 110 libraries for which data are available, 30 (27.3%) use the Sudocs scheme exclusively, 53 (48.2%) rely on a combination of methods, and 21 (19.1%) arrange their documents by the LC system. The 6 remaining libraries use either the Sudocs scheme, in addition to a local system (4, or 3.6%), or exclusively a scheme developed for the legal field (2, or 1.8%). The libraries employing a combination of methods might also use a specialized scheme.

Collection Organization

More than half (64, or 55.2%) of the 116 libraries reporting information about their collection place at least 41% of their depository holdings in a separate department, or area. Another 38 (32.8%) libraries place a lesser percentage in a separate collection, while 14 (12.1%) libraries mostly integrate their depository publications with other holdings.

Microfiche Collection

All of the survey respondents reporting on the selection of depository microfiche include this information resource in their collection. About three-fourths of them (80, or 75.5%) keep the microfiche in a central microforms area, while 18 (17%) store them in the documents department, or area, and 7 (6.6%) place them in both a central microforms area and the documents department, or area; 1 (0.9%) responding library stores microfiche in a workroom.

Use of Technology

Another survey question asked about the use of online bibliographic database searching. Some 116 (79.4%) libraries provided data on this; over half of the respondents (65 or 56%) claim that they provide online database searching for government publications. Further, 79 (68.1%) suggest that they make at least "some" use of OCLC for the depository collection. Some libraries may use another bibliographic utility; 22 (19%) use RLIN

and 5 (4.3%) use WLN. Any other uses of technology for the depository
collection are minimal. None of the respondents purchase the GPO tapes
for local use, while 1 (.9%) uses a computer to generate a keyword index
and 4 (3.4%) use a computer to produce a documents holdings file.

Summary

Since the "typical" library for an accredited law school gained its depository status as a result of the 1978 legislation, it has a law, rather than a
congressional, designation. The library is situated in a community with a
population of 500,000 or less, and this community has a probability of
being located in the South, Midwest, or Northeast. The library perhaps
has between 100,001 and 300,000 volumes of non-government publications, and places depository publications, at least in part, in a separate
department, or area, arranged by a combination of methods or the Sudocs
system.

Unlike its academic and public library counterparts, the law school
library keeps its depository microfiche in a central microforms area, not
the documents department, or area. Similar to the "typical" academic
and public library depository, the law school library assigns a maximum
of 1 FTE professional, and 1 FTE per support staff classification, to the
depository collection and services. Like the "typical" public library depository, the law school library selects a maximum of 25% of available
item numbers. Since it may make "some" use of technology for government publications, it is more like the academic, than the public, library
depository in this respect.

Comparison by Library Type

Thus far, this chapter has highlighted individual library types and offered
comparative observations in each "summary" section. The purpose of this
section is to present a comparison among academic, public, law school,
and other depositories. No statistically significant differences prevailed
between library type and budget, volume count, number of staff assigned
to the depository collection, the percentage of items selected, collection
arrangement, and collection organization. Use of technology for government publications was statistically significant, but the trends have already
been noted. Consequently, this section will only emphasize three variables
(the year of depository designation, population of the community, and
geographical location), whose analysis enhances the previous discussion.

Date of Depository Designation

"The main purpose of the Depository Library Act of 1962 was to increase
the number of non-federal depositories" (Schwarzkopf, 1982, p. 21).

Clearly, this goal has been achieved. The largest percentage of academic and public libraries gained depository status since 1962. Public law 95-261 (92 *Stat*. 199), which became effective in 1978, authorized the designation of accredited law schools as depository libraries. Therefore, more than any other library type, law schools have accounted for the largest number of depositories since 1976.

Population of the Community and Geographical Location

There is a statistically significant difference between the type of library and the size of the community in which it is located. Academic and public libraries tend to be situated in smaller communities (populations under 100,000), while law school and other depositories were found in larger communities.

Given the dominance of academic libraries in the depository program, it can be hypothesized that these libraries account for the largest percentage distribution per geographical region. In fact, this is not the case. As shown in Table 4-10 (which is basically a representation of Map 4-1), there is substantial variation among geographical regions. The method for establishing depository designation focuses on availability in a congressional district or state, or the willingness of a library meeting the requirements for a "law" designation to apply for the status. The larger the population of the state, the more depositories are located there (see Chapter 3). However, the number does not indicate distribution with a state. Depository status is linked to individual states and their characteristics. It does not take into account a larger geographical base—the region.

Regional Depository Libraries

Overview

Regional libraries comprise another subdivision of the depository program administered by the Government Printing Office, for which separate data analysis was performed. The 51 libraries fitting this category comprise 3.7% of the entire depository population (1,373 libraries) and can be found in 41 states.

Table 4-10. Percentage of Library Types by Geographical Region

Library Type	Northeast	Midwest	South	West	Outside the U.S.
Academic	21.4%	27.1%	35.0%	15.7%	.8%
Public	25.9%	28.8%	19.8%	24.5%	1.1%
Law School	25.3%	26.0%	28.8%	19.2%	.7%
Other	36.9%	15.8%	23.4%	23.4%	.5%

The 51 regionals are distributed among the following library types:

- academic (29, or 56.9%)
- state agency (15, or 29.4%)
- public (5, or 9.8%)
- historical society (1, or 2%)
- other special (1, or 2%)

The "other special" refers to the Nebraska Library Commission. These statistics indicate that over half of the regionals are located in academic institutions, that only 1.8% of the public library depositories serve as regionals, and that 3 of every 10 state agency libraries hold regional status.

Date of Depository Designation

Since libraries designated as regionals must previously have been selective depositories, it can be assumed that on the whole these 51 libraries have held depository status for a number of years. Examination of the year in which the libraries gained their status supports this hypothesis. Some 15 libraries (29.4%) can trace their depository status back to the nineteenth century; on the other hand,

- 19 (37.2%) gained it between 1900 and 1925
- 1 (2%) acquired it between 1926 and 1950
- 5 (9.8%) received it after 1950

The year in which 11 (21.6%) gained their status was not reported in either the *Monthly Catalog of United States Government Publications* or *Government Depository Libraries* (Washington, D.C.: GPO). However, it might be assumed that since neither the individual libraries nor the GPO could identify the year in which status was gained, this is a indication that they have held their status for a number of years and that pertinent records have long ago ceased to exist. At any rate, over two-thirds (68.6%) of the libraries received their status prior to 1950; by deducting the 11 for which records are unavailable from the 51, and then recalculating the percentage, it is evident that 34 (85%) have held depository status prior to 1926.

Population of Community and Geographical Location

Using the characterization developed by the U.S. Bureau of the Census, as explained in the previous Chapter, 17 of these libraries are located in the South (33.3%), while 15 (29.4%) are in the West, 13 (25.5%) in the Midwest, and 6 (11.8%) in the Northeast; see Map 4-1 for a depiction of the distribution. According to Title 44, *United States Code*, two regionals are authorized per state; as well, regionals can be situated in the Commonwealth of Puerto Rico and the Virgin Islands. However, 9 states, in addition to the two possessions of the United States, do not contain a regional depository. Further, only 10 states have the prescribed two regionals.

Volume and Title Counts of the Libraries

The number of volumes held was available for all but 3 libraries. As shown in Table 4-11, there are 11 (21.6%) regionals which do not have volume counts exceeding 500,000. In fact, 8 (15.7%) libraries have between 75,001 and 300,000 volumes; five of these are state libraries and the remaining 3 are academic libraries. Another 8 (15.7%) hold between 500,001 and 1 million volumes, while 26 libraries have over 1 million volumes. While the largest percentage (51) has sizable collections of other than government publications, 2 libraries are much more modest in their holdings—having between 75,001 and 100,000 volumes of non-government publications.

Size of Overall Library Budgets

The size of the budget allocation for libraries serving as regional depositories was collected from the sources identified in the previous chapter; the information for only 1 library was unavailable. For 47 regional depositories (92.2%), the budget was over $1 million; 2 of the remaining 3 had budgets between $800,001 and $850,000, and the third had one falling in the range of $400,001 to $450,000.

Table 4-11. Volume Counts for Regional Libraries

Number of Volumes Held	Frequency	Percentage
75,001–100,000	2	3.9
100,001–200,000	3	5.9
200,001–300,000	3	5.9
400,001–500,000	3	5.9
500,001–600,000	3	5.9
600,001–700,000	5	9.8
700,001–800,000	1	2.0*
900,001–1 million	2	3.9
Over 1 million	26	51.0*
Undetermined	3	5.9
Total	51	100.1

* Percentages have been rounded to nearest whole number.

As for the budgetary allocation for staff salaries, data were available for all but 3 libraries (5.9%). Almost three-fourths of the libraries (38, or 74.5%) spent over $1 million in salaries for the fiscal year. Some 7 libraries (13.7%) provided between $650,001 and $900,000 in salaries. The remaining 3 libraries (5.9%) reflected the most variation; 1 spent between $550,001 and $600,000, 1 between $400,001 and $450,000, and 1 between $100,001 and $150,000.

Number of Staff Assigned to Library and Documents Collection

Data on the number of overall library staff were unavailable for 8 (15.7%) of the regional depositories. For the remaining 43, the number reflects considerably variation. Some 30 (69.8%) employ over 100 staff members, while 8 (18.6%) have between 51 and 100 employees. The remaining 5 (11.6%) libraries have between 21 and 50 staff members; one of these (a historical society) has between 21 and 30 staff members, and another (an academic library) has between 31 and 40 personnel.

The survey of the 1,373 libraries obtained data about the assignment of staff to the depository collection. Table 4-12, which expresses staffing patterns in terms of FTE, identifies patterns for the four personnel categories. Of the 44 regional libraries providing data on staffing, 34.1% assign a maximum of 1 FTE professional, while over two-thirds (68.2%) have 2 or fewer professional staff engaged in depository-related activities. Some 5 libraries provide 4 FTE professionals for the collection, and 1 has 4.5.

Of the three categories for support staff, clerical personnel are the most prevalent; they are used in 33 libraries. Over half (54.6%) of these libraries assign 2 or fewer FTE clerical staff to the depository collection, while

Table 4-12. Staffing of Documents Collections
at Regional Depository Libraries (Expressed in Terms of FTE)

Classification of Staff	Maximum of 1.00	1.01–2.00	2.00	2.01–4.00	4.00 or More
Professional	15	6	9	8	6
n = 44*	(34.1%)	(13.6%)	(20.5%)	(18.2%)	(13.6%)
Paraprofessional	13	2	6	7	1
n = 29	(44.8%)	(6.9%)	(20.7%)	(24.1%)	(3.5%)
Clerical	9	3	6	13	2
n = 33	(27.3%)	(9.1%)	(18.2%)	(39.4%)	(6.1%)
Student	10	6	2	9	4
n = 31	(32.3%)	(19.3%)	(6.5%)	(29.0%)	(12.9%)

* Forty-four of the 45 responding regional libraries supplied data about their staffing patterns.

two libraries have 4 and seven use between 2.01 and 4.0 such staff. Student assistants are used in 31 of the responding 44 libraries. Over half (58.1%) of these libraries assign 2 or fewer student FTEs to the depository collection, while, at the other end of the spectrum, one has 7.0, two have 5.0, and one has 4.0. Almost three-fourths (72.4%) of the responding libraries which assign paraprofessional staff to the depository collection have a maximum of 2 FTE paraprofessionals in these positions.

As is evident, regardless of staff category, the number of personnel which regional libraries assign to depository collections is small—a maximum of 2 FTEs. Some of the respondents, obviously, reported on the survey the number of staff assigned and did not convert these numbers into the appropriate FTE. Therefore, Table 4-12 may itself represent an inflated picture of staffing in regional library collections.

Microfiche Collection

Since regional libraries presumably receive whatever is eligible for depository distribution, they all receive microfiche on deposit. Of the 42 libraries reporting on the location of the microfiche collection, 27 (64.3%) place it in the documents department, or area. Five (11.9%) keep depository microfiche in a central microforms area, while 4 (9.5%) retain them in both the documents department, or area, and a central microforms area. The remaining 6 (14.3%) libraries retain them in the central reference department, or area, in branch libraries, or in the documents department, or area, in combination with another library department or a branch library.

Academic Regionals

The following sections further highlight regional depositories. Coverage of these academic regionals and the use of technology in regional depositories rounds out the discussion of the community of libraries holding regional status.

Highest Degree Offering and Institutional Control. Only 1 of the 29 academic libraries serving as a regional depository is part of a private institution; clearly, public institutions dominate the landscape. Again, only 1 offers the master's degree as its highest offering, while the remaining 28 are doctoral-granting institutions.

Volume Counts. Over half (55.2%) of the academic regionals have volume counts of 1 million or more; with the exception of the 1 library for which data were unavailable, the remaining libraries held volumes ranging from the category "75,001–100,000'" to that of "900,001–1 million."

Size of Overall Library Budgets. Overwhelmingly, academic regionals have budgets over $1 million (27, or 93.1%). One has a budget between $400,001 and $450,000, and the other between $800,001 and $850,000. The majority (21, or 72.4%) expend over $1 million for salaries. Two provide less than $450,000 in staff salaries, while 5 offer between $650,001 and $900,000; data for 1 library were unavailable.

Number of Staff Assigned to Library and Documents Collection. Over half (15, or 51.7%) of the academic libraries are affiliated with institutions employing over 1,000 faculty, while another 34.5% (10) have between 400 and 1,000 faculty. One institution (3.4%) has between 100 and 200 faculty and the remaining 2 (6.9%) have between 200 and 400 faculty; data were unavailable for 1 institution. Staffing for the depository collection is similar to the picture already presented; there is no statistically significant difference. Regardless of staffing category, the maximum number, in general, was 2 FTEs.

Collection Arrangement. Similar to the general population of academic libraries, academic regionals either employ the Sudocs classification scheme or a combination of different systems; the only exception relied on a local system.[6] The combination method takes into account the various ways in which the library has handled its documents collection over the years.

Collection Organization. With one exception, academic regionals have a separate department, or area, for their depository collection, while over half (51.7%) house some document types or formats (e.g., maps and microfiche) separately, and almost one-fourth (24.1%) place a large percentage of depository publications in branches of the library system.[7]

Use of Technology

Some 45 of the 51 regional depositories provided information concerning their use of technology. Overwhelmingly (88.9%), these libraries claim that they provide "some" online searching of bibliographic databases containing government publications; only 5 (11.1%) do not appear to provide such database searching. Undoubtedly there is great variation among those libraries engaged in online searching concerning the frequency with

---

[6] Data about use of a classification scheme were unavailable for 4 libraries.

[7] Data on the method for housing government publications were unavailable for 4 libraries.

which that searching is performed. Most often (62.5%), the searching is done in the general reference department. In the remaining 15 libraries, 5 offer online searching in the documents department, or area; 4 in both the general reference and documents department, or area; and the other 6 in another location (interlibrary loan, technical services, or another department).

Next to online bibliographic database searching the largest percentage of responding libraries suggested their use of technology was related to a bibliographic utility, in particular OCLC; 29 (64.4%) of the 45 responding libraries claimed that they use this one utility. Four libraries use RLIN and the same number consults WLN; 2 libraries make use of other bibliographic utilities. Undoubtedly the use of any utility, for a regional depository collection, varies from seldom to often, depending on the particular library.

Table 4-13 identifies other uses of technology. The response to the "other" category includes the placement of government publications in an online circulation system or a COM catalog. Clearly, the application of technology to the depository collection is limited at this time. In the future, the diversity of use of technology may well increase. For now, it cannot be stated that regional libraries are leaders in its use.

Summary

The "typical" regional library is part of a public, academic institution that offers graduate programs culminating in the doctoral degree. The library is probably located in the South or West, and there is already another regional in the same state. The "typical" regional has held depository status since 1925 or before, maintains a collection of more than 1 million non-government publications, and has a budget well over $1 million.

Table 4-13. Other Uses of New Technology by Regional Depository Libraries

Uses	Frequency	Percentage
Purchase GPO tapes for local use	4	8.9
Use a computer to produce keyword indexes to the documents collection	5	11.1
Use a computer to produce a documents holdings file	5	11.1
Other	3	6.7

The library places depository publications in a separate department, or area, arranged by the Sudocs classification system, or by a combination of methods. A maximum of 2 FTE professionals, and support staff classification, have depository-related responsibilities. This number does not differ significantly from academic and public libraries serving as selective depositories. Given the size of the collection and the responsibilities associated with regional status, this is a surprising finding.

The library engaged in "some" online bibliographic database searching for government publications; however, the terminal is probably located in a general reference department, not the documents department, or area. To some degree, the staff consult OCLC for government publications. Clearly, the "typical" regional does not differ from the "typical" academic, selective depository in its use of technology.

Depositories Selecting 25% or Fewer Items

Overview

Contrary to the recommendation contained in the *Guidelines* (1977), a substantial percentage of depository libraries in fact select fewer than 25% of the available item numbers. As Table 4-14 indicates, 525 (38.2%) of the responding libraries take no more than this minimum account. Almost half of these libraries are academic, while approximately one-fifth are public. The data displayed in the table can be viewed from another perspective. In addition to examining the number of libraries selecting a maximum of 25% in relation to the number of libraries comprising membership in the depository program, there can be a comparison between these highly selective depositories and the extent to which they encompass each library type. As a result, it can be seen that a maximum of 25% is selected by at least

Table 4-14. Library Types Selecting 25% or Fewer Item Numbers

Library Types	Frequency	Percentage of Libraries Selecting 25%	Percentage of all Libraries in that Category
Academic	245	46.7	32.0
Public	103	19.6	37.1
Federal	29	5.5	48.3
Law School	93	17.7	63.7
Court of Law	37	7.1	61.7
State Agency	10	1.9	22.2
Other	8	1.5	42.1
Total	525	100.0	

- 32% of the academic depository libraries
- 37.1% of the public libraries
- 48.3% of the federal libraries
- 63.7% of the law school libraries
- 61.7% of the court of law libraries
- 22.2% of the state library agencies
- 42.1% of the remaining depositories

These data indicate that at least 1 in every 3 academic and public library depository selects a maximum of 25%, while almost 2 of every 3 law school libraries take fewer than the recommended percentage.[8]

The libraries selecting 25% or fewer item numbers were compared to the various variables identified in the previous chapter, for which data were collected. No statistically significant difference emerged between the percentage selected, on the one hand, and geographical location, type of depository designation (congressional or law), the year in which depository status was received, classification scheme employed, or collection arrangement, on the other. The number of libraries for which data were missing inhibits valid generalizations concerning volume counts, budgets, and the number of general library staff.

Microfiche Collection

Of the 503 libraries selecting 25% or fewer items and reporting about whether they receive depository microfiche, 5% do not take GPO microfiche. These 25 depositories comprise academic (10), public (8), federal (2), court of law (3), military (1), and private membership (1) libraries. Overwhelmingly, those taking depository microfiche place them in a central microforms area (269, or 56.3%); the documents department, or area, (138, or 28.9%); or in both locations (40, or 8.4%). Some 13 (2.7%) place them in both the documents department, or area, and another library department or a branch library. The remaining 18 (3.8%) libraries keep the microfiche in the reference department, a workroom, or a branch library.

Number of Staff Assigned to Depository Collection

Table 4-15 indicates the number of FTE staff assigned to the depository collection. For 59 (11.9%) of the libraries selecting 25% or fewer items

---

[8] It is important to keep in mind that the percentages reflected in Table 4-14 and the subsequent analysis in this section of the chapter are based on a response to a question on the survey. Some 353 libraries (25.7% of the participants in the depository program) did not furnish information about the percentage selected. Therefore, both the overall percentage of libraries selecting 25% or fewer item numbers, and the depiction of these libraries by the type of library which they represent, may well be larger than the percentages reported here.

Table 4-15. Staffing of Depository Collections for Libraries Selecting 25%
or Fewer Item Numbers (Expressed in Terms of FTE)

Classification	No Professional	Less than 1	1	1-2	More than 2
Professional	59	236	162	27	14
n = 498*	(11.9%)	(47.4%)	(32.5%)	(5.4%)	(2.8%)
Paraprofessional	—	96	63	8	5
n = 172		(55.8%)	(36.6%)	(4.7%)	(2.9%)
Clerical	—	132	85	16	6
n = 239		(55.2%)	(35.6%)	(6.7%)	(2.5%)
Student	—	131	52	19	7
n = 209		(62.7%)	(24.9%)	(9.1%)	(3.3%)
Other	—	6	0	0	2
n = 8**		(75.0%)			(25.0%)

  * Some 27 libraries supplying data on the percentage of items selected did not answer the question relating to staffing.
  ** The other category includes volunteers, pages, desk aids, and CETA library technicians.

and reporting data on staffing, no professional librarian had responsibility for the documents collection. Overwhelmingly, 91.8% of the 498 libraries represented in the table assign 1 or fewer FTE professional. The distribution of responses for support staff also indicates that the typical pattern is to assign a maximum of 1 FTE to the collection.

A chi square test did not indicate a statistically significant difference in staffing between those libraries selecting 25% or fewer item numbers and those selective depositories taking a larger percentage. Regardless of the percentage received, the typical pattern is to assign a maximum of 1 FTE professional and support staff classification to the depository collection and services.

Use of Technology

When polled about their use of technology, less than half (224, or 42.7%) of the 525 libraries engage in online bibliographic database searching. In this regard, there is a statistically significant difference between those libraries selecting a maximum of 25% of the available items and those taking a larger percentage.

Over half (275, or 52.4%) have used the OCLC database at least to some minimal extent; only 44 (8.4%) libraries use RLIN, WLN, or another bibliographic utility. Some 43 libraries claimed other uses of technology:

- generation of computerized keyword indexes for the documents collection (20, or 3.8%)
- maintenance of a computerized documents holdings file (18, or 3.4%)

- purchase of GPO tapes for local use (3, or .6%)
- production of a local computerized index or inclusion of collection in online circulation system (2, or .4%)

Clearly, the smaller collections make only selective use of technology. The central issue relates to the extent to which these libraries make use of technology in their other operations.

Academic Depositories

The final set of analyses of the libraries selecting less than the percentage recommended in the *Guidelines* (1977) relates to those situated in academic institutions. Law schools naturally offer law degrees and typically have enrollments not exceeding 1,000. Therefore, Table 4-16 depicts the 245 academic institutions, but does not include law school libraries; readers interested in law school depositories are encouraged to consult the section of this chapter on them. Over half (55.5%) of the academic institutions offer undergraduate degrees. Some 9% of the depository libraries taking a maximum of 25% of the available items are affiliated with institutions offering the doctorate as their highest degree. An important issue relates

Table 4-16. Academic Libraries Selecting 25% or Fewer Item Numbers

	Frequency	Percentage
Highest Degree		
Arts Associate	44	18.0
Baccalaureate	92	37.5
Master's	87	35.5
Doctorate	22	9.0
Total	245	100.0
Control		
Public	110	44.9
Private	133	54.3
Undetermined	2	.8
Total	245	100.0
Enrollment		
1,000 and under	67	27.4
1,001–2,000	75	30.6
2,001–5,000	73	29.8
5,001–10,000	25	10.2
10,001–15,000	3	1.2
15,001–20,000	1	.4
Over 25,000	1	.4
Total	245	100.0

to which subject areas these institutions, as well as the master's-granting institutions, offer. It is obvious that government publications have more value to some subject areas (e.g., political science and economics) than to others (e.g., art and music).

There is no statistically significant difference between the percentage of items taken and those libraries whose institutions are public and those which are private. Public institutions are as likely as private ones to select the lesser percentage. Enrollment is a more revealing variable; 87.8% of the institutions have enrollments of 5,000 or less. Over one-fifth of the percentage (27.4%) consists of institutions with enrollments of 1,000 or less, while 30.6% has a student body of 1,001 to 2,000; the remaining 30% has between 2,001 and 5,000 students.

Summary

The data presented in this section suggest that many of the variables explored may well not explain the selection patterns of the libraries. Perhaps the two most revealing variables relate to staffing of the depository collection (especially the number of libraries not assigning professional staff to the depository collections) and the enrollment of the academic institutions. Undoubtedly, the critical factors explaining the number of items selected relate to the amount of annual publication eligible for depository distribution, the perceived importance which staff attach to these publications, and the ability of libraries to manage and service these publications.

As for the profile of the "typical" library selecting a maximum of 25%, half of the 525 libraries reporting that they select within this percentage are part of an academic institution. The institution offers undergraduate programs and has an enrollment of 5,000 or less.

If the 525 libraries are viewed within the context of the library type they represent, the "typical" depository would be a law school library. Whether it is an academic or law school library, the "typical" depository assigns a maximum of 1 FTE professional, or support staff classification, to the documents collection and services. The library probably does not engage in online bibliographic database searching, but consults the OCLC database for government publications, at least to some minimal extent.

Libraries Receiving Depository Status between 1976 and 1984

The Depository Library Act of 1962, which was discussed in the first chapter, has exerted a major influence on the composition of the depository program. As shown in Chapter 3, a substantial number of libraries have gained their depository status since the enactment of this legislation. Further, legislation of the late 1970s provided depository status for accredited law school libraries. Given the impact of federal statutes on the depository program since 1962, the authors decided that a comparison of libraries gaining depository status before and after 1962 or 1976 would not be productive. It is more important to profile those libraries newly entering the depository program.

Overview

Some 214 of the 1,373 libraries (15.6%) have gained depository designation between 1976 and 1984. Since the date when 45 depository libraries received depository status could not be determined, the 214 represents 16.1% of all the libraries whose date of depository designation is known.

Almost half of the 214 libraries are those of accredited law schools (105, or 49.1%), receiving their depository status as a result of a public law, rather than by congressional designation. The other recipients of depository status during these years were

- academic libraries (49, or 22.9%)
- court of law libraries (21, or 9.8%)
- public libraries (20, or 9.3%)
- federal libraries (17, or 7.9%)
- state agency libraries (2, or .9%)

Clearly, special libraries (law school, court of law, or federal government) dominate the number of new designations. Only the 71 (33.2%) academic, public, and state agency libraries could be regarded as serving a broader constituency—a college or university campus, city, county, or state. The 49 academic libraries may well serve a narrower constituency than the public and state libraries.

Table 4-17 indicates the geographical location, by library type, for the recipients of depository status since 1976. With the exception of the state libraries, and the academic libraries where two geographical areas tied for first position, the Northeast has accounted for the largest number of new members in the depository program. The District of Columbia, however, is responsible for the skewing of data. Thirteen of the federal libraries, 2 court of law libraries, and 1 academic library are located there. If the data in the table are compared to Map 4-1, which depicts the geographical distribution of academic and public library depositories, the Northeast is better represented among the post-1975 depositories. Interestingly, no southern public library has gained depository status since 1976.

Table 4-17. Geographical Region of Those Library Types Receiving
Depository Status Between 1976 and 1984*,**

	Northeast	Midwest	South	West	Outside U.S.
Academic	14	12	14	7	2
n = 49	(28.6%)	(24.5%)	(28.6%)	(14.3%)	(4.1%)
Court of Law	8	2	4	7	—
n = 21	(38.1%)	(9.5%)	(19.1%)	(33.3%)	
Public	8	6	—	6	—
n = 20	(40.0%)	(30.0%)		(30.0%)	
Federal	14	—	2	1	—
n = 17	(82.3%)		(11.8%)	(5.9%)	
State	—	—	2	—	—
n = 2			(100.0%)		

* The geographical designations are based upon a categorization developed by the U.S. Bureau of the Census. See Map 4-1 for a depiction of what states are encompassed by a geographical designation.
** Law school libraries are excluded from the depiction because of the impact of the federal legislation of the late 1970s according them a "law" designation.

Academic Depositories

Perhaps it might be useful to highlight the academic libraries briefly. First, 13 (26.5%) comprise community colleges, while 10 (20.4%) offer the baccalaureate as the highest degree, 16 (32.7%) are master's-granting institutions, and 10 (20.4%) have doctoral programs. Second, 31 (63.3%) are public institutions and 18 (36.7%) are private. And, third, 36 (73.5%) have enrollments of 5,000 or less; 9 (18.4%) have enrollments between 5,001 and 10,000; and 4 (8.2%) have student bodies of 10,001 to 20,000.

Volume Counts

Data on volume counts for 32 (15%) of the libraries were unavailable. Over one-fifth of the libraries for which data were available (58, or 27.1%) have 100,000 or fewer volumes of non-government publications, while 46.7% (100) possess between 100,001 and 200,000 volumes. The remaining 24 (11.2%) libraries have volume counts ranging from 300,001 to over 1 million; 5 of the libraries in this range hold more than 1 million volumes.

Size of Overall Library Budgets

Data were unavailable for the overall budgets of 72 (33.6%) libraries and for staff salaries of 103 (48.1%) depositories. Therefore, no valid inferences could be drawn in either instance.

Number of Staff Assigned to Library and Documents Collection

Information about the number of personnel for 68 (31.8%) libraries was unavailable. This large percentage, by itself, inhibits the drawing of firm conclusions about overall staffing. It can be noted that 105 (49.1%) have 30 or fewer staff, while 32 (15%) have between 31 and 100, and 9 (4.2%) have more than 100.

Through the survey of the depository library community, the authors were able to collect data on staffing patterns for 151 (70.6%) of the 214 libraries. Eight (5.3%) of these libraries do not have any professional staff assigned to the depository collection. Most typically, these libraries have less than 1 FTE professional (64, or 42.4%) or 1 FTE professional (66, or 43.7%) responsible for the depository collection. Only 13 (8.6%) assigned more than 1 FTE professional to the collection.

Of the support categories, clerical staff was the most prevalent. They could be found in over half (78, or 51.7%) of these libraries. However, only 8 (10.3%) of these libraries assign more than 1 FTE of clerical personnel to the collection. Some 61 (40.4%) of the libraries made use of student assistants. The typical pattern was to assign 1 or fewer student FTE to the collection; only 9 (14.8%) libraries use more than 1 FTE. For the final category, 46 (30.5%) libraries make use of paraprofessional staff. However, only 3 (6.5%) assign 2 or more to the depository collection.

Regardless of personnel category, the new depository libraries most typically assign 1 or fewer FTE to the depository collection. Given this finding, a key issue relates to the number of depository items selected. Presumably, smaller collections require fewer staff. However, this conclusion ignores the fact that 8 libraries place clerical personnel in charge of the collection and reserve professional staff for other library responsibilities.

Collection Arrangement

Over half of the responding libraries reporting on collection arrangement (81 or 51.9%) place most of their depository publications in a separate department, or area. The remaining percentage either integrates depository publications with other library holdings or scatters the publications among different parts of the library.

Collection Organization

The depository collections of these libraries are most often arranged by a combination of methods (68, or 43.6%) or solely by either the Sudocs scheme (50, or 32.1%) or the Library of Congress system (25, or 16%). Two (1.3%) libraries rely on the Dewey scheme and 11 (7%) employ a specialized classification system.

Microfiche Collection

Only 3 (1.9%) of the 154 libraries reporting on the selection of depository microfiche do not take any. Two-thirds (99, or 66%) of the libraries receiving microfiche retain them in a central microforms area, while 37 (24.7%) keep them in the documents department, or area; 9 (16%) split the collection between a central microforms area and the documents department, or area. The remaining 5 (3.3%) libraries place microfiche in the documents department, or area, and a branch library, or a library department other than the documents or central microforms.

Percentage of Items Selected

Table 4-18, which shows the percentage of item numbers selected by the newer depository libraries, indicates that regardless of library type, the pattern is to select fewer than the 25% recommended in the *Guidelines to the Depository Library System* (1977). Excluding the 1 library which switched its designation from a selective to a regional, only 17 (11.8%) of the 144 libraries select more than 25% of the available item numbers.

Table 4-18. Percentage of Item Numbers Selected
by the Newer Depository Libraries (Status Gained 1976–1984)*

| Library Type | Percentage of Items Selected | | | | |
	10 or Fewer	11–25	26–50	51–75	76–
Academic	13	15	7	—	—
n = 35	(37.1%)	(42.9%)	(20.0%)		
Public	6	2	5	1	—
n = 14	(42.9%)	(14.3%)	(35.7%)	(7.1%)	
Federal	6	4	—	—	—
n = 10	(60.0%)	(40.0%)			
Law School	36	33	3	—	—
n = 72	(50.0%)	(45.8%)	(4.2%)		
Court of Law	9	1	—	1	—
n = 11	(81.8%)	(9.1%)		(9.1%)	
State	—	1	—	—	1**
n = 2		(50.0%)			(50.0%)

* The data in this table are based upon survey responses; some respondents did not provide the percentage of item numbers selected.
** This library changed its depository status from a selective to a regional depository.

These libraries were academic (41.2%), public (35.3%), law school (17.6%), and court of law (5.9%).

Clearly, there is widespread disregard for the recommendation in the *Guidelines* concerning the minimum percentage of item selections. This finding provides another indication that points in this document do not all reflect current practice or a goal to which libraries will aspire.

Use of Technology

The libraries gaining depository status since 1976 make limited use of technology. Of the 156 libraries reporting data, 75 (48.1%) do not engage in online bibliographic database searching for government publications, while 81 (51.9%) do. Slightly more than half (88, or 56.4%) use OCLC for access to government publications; 15 (9.6%) consult RLIN and 5 (3.2%) use WLN. Any other use of technology for government publications is insignificant.

Summary

The "typical" library receiving depository status since 1976 is part of an accredited law school. Therefore, the profile is similar to that presented in the section on law school depositories. This library is highly selective in the percentage of items selected and the number of professional, and support staff classification, assigned depository-related responsibilities. The library may engage in online bibliographic searching for government publications or consult OCLC for documents; however, the use of technology for government publications should not be regarded as a given.

Comparison of Patterns among Subgroups

Figure 4-1 highlights the prevailing patterns, for each variable under consideration, for six subgroups. The data presented in the figure reinforce the summary section given for a subgroup, where the "typical" depository was profiled.

Further investigations will have to elicit the missing data elements from the individual depositories so that all gaps in the figure can be filled in and an even more extensive examination of the interrelationships among variables can be completed. As indicated in Chapter 3, more attention should be given to title (not volume) counts so that the extent of compliance with the *Guidelines* can be documented and appropriate action taken as necessary. In addition, any future survey should be expanded to permit greater analysis of budget allocations, staffing, and the use of technology.

Figure 4-1. Identification of the Most Prevalent Patterns Among Subgroups*

Variables	Subgroups					
	Academic	Public	Law School	Regional	Taking 25% or Fewer Items	Status Gained 1976–1984
Geographical Location**	South	Midwest	South	South	South	No Pattern
Population	100,000 or less	100,000 or less	500,000 or less	200,000 or under	500,000 or less	500,000 or less
Year of Depository Designation	Time span of 1962 Act	Time span of 1962 Act	1976–1984	1925 or earlier	1976–1984	—
Volumes	—	100,001–400,000	—	Over 1 million	—	—
Titles	—	—	—	—	—	—
Number of Library Staff	—	—	—	—	—	—
Budget	—	$1 million	—	—	—	—
Percentage of Items Selected	Up to 50	Up to 25	Up to 25	100	—	Up to 25
Staffing of Documents	Up to 1 FTE	Up to 1 FTE	Up to 1 FTE	Up to 2 FTE	Up to 1 FTE	Up to 1 FTE
Collection Arrangement	Sudocs	Combination or Sudocs	Combination or Sudocs	Combination or Sudocs	Sudocs	Sudocs
Collection Organization	Separate	Separate	Separate	Separate	Separate	Separate
Use of Technology	Some online searching	None	Some online searching	Some online searching	Perhaps some online searching	Some online searching
Highest Degree	Graduate	—	Graduate	Graduate	Undergraduate	No difference
Control	Perhaps Public	—	Perhaps Private	Public	No difference	Public
Number of Faculty	100 or less	—	100 or less	Over 1,000		
Enrollment	5,000 or less		5,000 or less	Over 5,000	5,000 or less	5,000 or less

* In certain instances, the absence of many data elements inhibits the identification of trends, or the presentation of a trend would be inappropriate. The purpose of this figure is to highlight the major trends and to encourage subsequent research to round out the picture and the interrelationship among variables.

** Map 4-1 depicts geographic distribution by library type.

Once an enlarged database has been constructed and researchers are certain that the data gathered are both reliable and valid (see Chapter 6 for a discussion of these terms), data analysis can go beyond frequency counts and testing by chi square. The intent should be to examine the interrelationships among variables, by using analysis of variance and other more powerful statistical procedures.

Figure 4-2 summarizes the hypotheses specifically addressed in this chapter. Again, having a more complete database would offer an opportunity to expand the number of hypotheses and to reconsider the ones explored here.

Figure 4-2. Status of Hypotheses Specifically Addressed in This Chapter

Hypothesis	Status
Academic Libraries	
1. There is no statistically significant difference between the number of staff assigned depository responsibilities and	
a. whether or not the institution offers graduate programs	Supported
b. percentage of items selected	Supported
c. enrollment of the institution	Supported
2. The more items selected, the higher the degree program	Supported
3. The more items selected, the larger the enrollment of the institution	Supported
4. There is no statistically significant difference between the method of classification used for the depository collection and the highest degree (or the other variables identified in Figure 4-1, for that matter)	Supported
5. There is no statistically significant difference between whether or not the library keeps its depository publications in a separate collection and	
a. the highest degree of the institution	Supported
b. the percentage of items selected	Supported
6. There is no statistically significant difference between the highest degree of the institution and the use of technology	Not Supported
Public Libraries	
1. The larger the population of the community, the more items selected by the library	Not Supported
2. There is no statistically significant difference between the percentage of items selected and	
a. the size of the budget	Not Supported
b. volume count	Not Supported
Library Types (General)	
1. Regardless of geographical location, academic libraries comprise the largest percentage of depository type	Not Supported
2. There is no statistically significant difference between library type and	
a. year of depository designation	Supported

Figure 4-2. (continued)

Hypothesis	Status
b. population of community	Not Supported
c. budget	Supported
d. volume count	Supported
e. number of staff servicing depository collection	Supported
f. percentage of items selected	Supported
g. collection organization	Supported
h. collection arrangement	Supported
i. use of technology	Not Supported

Regional Libraries

1. Regionals have held depository status for a number of years (at least prior to the 1962 act)	Supported
2. Regionals typically have budgets larger than $1 million	Supported
3. There is no statistically significant difference between regionals and other depositories as to the number of professional and support staff assigned depository-related responsibilities	Not Supported
4. There is no statistically significant difference among academic regionals according to	
a. institutional control	Supported
b. highest degree of the institution	Supported
5. Regionals have more than 1 million volumes of non-government publications	Not Supported
6. Regionals make more use of technology than other depositories	Not Supported

Depositories Selecting 25% or Fewer Items

1. There is no statistically significant difference among these libraries as to	
a. library type	Not Supported
b. geographical location	Not Supported
c. volume counts	Not Supported
d. budgets	Not Supported
e. number of library staff assigned depository responsibilities	Not Supported
f. the year in which depository status was received	Not Supported
g. the classification scheme employed	Not Supported
h. collection arrangement	Not Supported
2. There is no statistically significant difference between those libraries selecting a maximum of 25% of the items and those taking a larger percentage as to	
a. the number of professional staff assigned to the depository collection	Not Supported
b. the use of technology	Not Supported
3. Academic depositories taking 25% or fewer items are only a part of institutions offering undergraduate degree programs	Not Supported
4. Academic depositories taking 25% or fewer items have enrollments not exceeding 5,000	Supported

Figure 4-2. (continued)

Hypothesis	Status
5. There is no statistically significant difference between academic depositories selecting 25% or fewer items and the type of their institutional control (public or private)	Not Supported
Libraries Receiving Depository Status between 1976 and 1984	
1. There is no statistically significant difference among these libraries as to	
a. geographical location	Supported
b. the percentage of items received	Supported
c. whether depository status was "law" or "congressional"	Not Supported
2. There is no statistically significant difference between those libraries receiving depository status during this time period and those gaining it in previous years as to	
a. the percentage of items received	Supported
b. the number of staff assigned depository duties	Supported

Comparison of Findings to Selected Other Studies

This section relates the findings of this chapter to those of selected previous studies. Comparisons, however, are imprecise due to differences in research design (investigating a sample or the population) and objectives (e.g., the collection of descriptive data about the characteristics of depository libraries, the analysis of user groups and patterns of use by library and institutional variables, or an examination of the ability of documents staff to answer pretested reference questions correctly and a comparison of their performance to related library and institutional characteristics). Other complicating factors include differences in the time periods in which data were collected, dissimilar questionnaire emphasis and phraseology, and the type of data reported. Still, certain similarities among the findings of various studies are evident. For example, as Richardson, Frisch, and Hall observe, the use of technology by depository libraries, on the whole, is "modest" (1980, p. 471). Also, in this study, as in the other studies, a large number of the variables investigated have not demonstrated statistical significance.

1983 *Biennial Survey* Conducted by the GPO (1984)

As part of its analysis of the 1983 *Biennial Survey*, the GPO has summarized data for 31 (of the 76 questions) by library type (*Depository Library Biennial Survey for 1983: U.S. Summary by Library Type*, 1984). The library types depicted in this report include

- general academic
- academic law
- academic sci/tech
- academic medical
- historical society or museum
- court
- federal agency/department
- public
- state library agency
- other

For the purpose of data reporting, each type has been subdivided into three groups: "small," "medium," and "large." The difference among these groups is based on the number of volumes held by the library: "small" libraries had volume counts between 10,000 and 100,000; "medium" libraries held between 100,001 and 500,000 volumes; and "large" libraries had more than 500,000 volumes. For each question, the number of total responses and the "average response" or "average count" is given. This average is the median, not the mean.

One might expect that five questions relating to staffing and the use of technology are pertinent to this chapter. The first three elicited information on staffing. Question 66 queried about the number of professional staff working with government documents and instructed depository libraries to "add all the hours librarians spend with documents in a week and divide by 40 to arrive at a full-time equivalent number, e.g., 1.5." Questions 67 and 68 probed the number of clerical, support staff, student aids, and volunteers assigned to government documents. Surprisingly, regardless of question, the average number for responding libraries was 0; apparently many libraries did not answer the questions, and GPO staff rounded down responses of 0.05 or less to 0.

Another curious point is that general summary data (part 1) placed the number of academic general libraries at 696 and the number of public libraries at 258. However, the section summarizing data by library type gives the population of academic general libraries as 694 and that for public libraries as 256.

For the 1,100 responses to question 46, the number of database reference searches conducted in a five-day period, the "average count" was 3.5. Five library types completed more than the average:

- academic medical (medium), 23
- academic law (large), 18
- general academic (large), 10
- academic sci/tech (large), 9
- public library (large), 4

Key issues concerning these findings become "Which databases were searched?," "How reliable are the "average counts?" (see Chapter 6 for a discussion of reliability), and "What is the significance of these findings?" Clearly, sampling based merely on a five-day period does not provide further clarification about the frequency by which depository libraries search databases for government publications.

The final question (number 72) elicited data about the number of computer terminals "available to documents users and/or staff for searching files relating to documents." The "average count" for the 1,228 responding libraries was 3.8. Only five library types had counts large than this overall average:

- academic law (large), 35
- academic sci/tech (large), 8
- academic general (medium), 7
- academic medical (medium), 6
- academic general (large), 4

For reasons similar to those raised for question 46, no significance can be attached to these findings.

As is evident, data generated for the 1983 *Biennial Survey* and displayed on the basis of library type cannot be compared to those reported in this chapter. The GPO has developed its own unique depiction of library types and did not compare types and subdivisions by the chi square test of association or other basic methods of statistical analysis. Key questions become "Is this a valid depiction of library types?," "Is there a statistically significant difference among library types and subdivisions?," and "Would the type of variables reported in this chapter have had a statistically significant impact upon the GPO's library types and the questions explored in the *Biennial Survey?*"

Chapter 6 extends the analysis of the *Biennial Survey* and finds much of the data gathered from it inaccurate, misleading, and inappropriate as a means both to describe depository libraries and to assist the GPO and individual depository libraries in decision making and planning. The chapter also offers specific recommendations by which the *Biennial Survey* can be better designed, administered, and analyzed.

Whitbeck, Hernon, and Richardson (1978)

In the winter and early spring of 1977, the three authors surveyed the depository library community about basic characteristics of collection organization, arrangement, and staff. They achieved a response rate of 86.8%. In their article, they highlighted three subgroups: academic libraries, regional depositories, and those libraries selecting fewer than 25% of the item numbers.

Their characterization of academic depository libraries by highest degree and institutional control is similar to that presented in this chapter. In both studies, the largest number of depositories was associated with institutions offering graduate programs. In the 1978 article, the variable of highest degree offered was significantly related to the percentage of depository items received, and a statistically significant relationship was found between enrollment and the percentage of items selected.

Certain differences between the terminology used in that study and this one complicate comparisons. For example, in the earlier study, the options for collections arrangement were confined to: "entirely separate," "totally integrated," "partially integrated," and "mixed." As reported in this chapter, entirely different terminology was used to describe collection arrangement. Another difference between the two studies relates to staffing. For the 1978 article, respondents were asked to identify the number of persons assigned to duties in the documents division, while the study behind this chapter sought more precise information—the number of FTEs assigned to depository collections and services. In spite of the differences, both studies have shown that the "typical" depository is staffed by a maximum of 1 professional, assigned on either a full- or part-time basis. As is evident, staffing has not changed in the seven-year period between the two studies.

The distribution of regional depositories by library type was similar in both studies. Other similarities relate to collection organization and arrangement. Easily the most striking discovery from both studies is the small number of staff working with a regional depository collection.

Close to 30% of the libraries replying to the 1978 survey took less than the recommended 25% of available items. By the time of the survey reported in this chapter, the percentage had increased to at least 38.2. It should be noted that in the time period between the two studies, the number of items distributed had increased. However, the distribution of libraries taking a maximum of 25% does not differ remarkably between the two studies. Further, both surveys discovered that some academic libraries whose institutions offered doctoral programs were taking less than the recommended percentage.

Hernon (1979)

In an investigation of social scientists from midwestern academic institutions, the author found no statistically significant difference between the frequency of documents use and the method of collection organization or collection arrangement, the percentage of items selected, the percentage of government publications entered in the public catalog, and the number of staff members servicing government publications. The most important criteria for predicting the frequency of documents use by social scientists were probably institutional mission, the commitment of individual faculty members to research, and the perceived value of government information to their information needs. For those social scientists using the library collection of government publications, all library variables become secondary considerations.

Since this study examined use of government publications in academic depository libraries, exact comparisons to the investigation reported in this chapter are not possible. It is important, however, to note that the overwhelming majority of hypotheses generated for academic libraries (see Figure 4-2) were supported. There is a statistically significant relationship between the number of items selected and the degree program, the percentage of items selected and the size of the student enrollment, and the highest degree of the institution and the use of technology.

Richardson, Frisch, and Hall (1980)

In 1979, the three authors surveyed the depository library community about the number and type of staff assigned documents responsibilities, the size and arrangement of the documents collection, and the methods used to provide descriptive and subject access to depository publications. They received 737 usable questionnaires, for a response rate of 60.5%.

From their survey, the authors discovered that regardless of library type, "a government documents collection is not likely to have even a full-time librarian." As they note,

> this staffing pattern supports the conclusion that depository libraries view documents as not requiring or deserving high levels of professional attention. The same generalization holds for other levels of staffing. . . . All of this suggests that most libraries think documents are not particularly unique or as deserving of attention as books, and that they require no more than simple maintenance (i.e., shelving). (p. 475)

The authors draw certain conclusions about staffing which are not supported by this chapter. For example, it cannot be stated that at this time, public libraries are more likely than academic or special libraries to assign 2 or more professionals; viewed in terms of FTE, public libraries assigned professional staff members in smaller units of time than did academic libraries (p. 469). The differences between the studies may be that they were conducted five years apart and that the study here includes a much larger pool of responding libraries.

McClure (1981 and 1982)

McClure, who surveyed a sample of depository libraries from each of the fifty states about the nature and extent of online database searching which they performed for government publications, received completed questionnaires from 156 academic and public libraries, as well as 15 other depositories. He discovered that academic depositories assigned an average of 1 FTE professional staff member to the documents collection, while for public libraries the average was 1.1. As did the study reported in Chapters 3 and 4, he discovered "much disagreement as to a precise meaning" of such terms as online searching and online bibliographic database searching. The result may have been "confusion" and an equating of online bibliographic database searching with OCLC searching. Therefore, there may be less than a totally accurate picture of the extent and type of online searching which responding libraries perform for government publications (1981, p. 248). As has already been noted, a similar confusion probably prevailed for this study.

McClure's data suggest that responding academic and public depository libraries are little involved in online database searching for government publications, have limited access to online terminals (including those for gaining access to the OCLC database), have received little training in the use of online databases, and acquire virtually no microformatted government publications online. His study also shows that library online searching is not the same as depository department online searching and that the vast majority of documents librarians do not have departmental access to online services. Online searching is performed outside the sphere of influence of documents staff.

A similarity between the McClure study and the data reported in this chapter is that the terminals are frequently located in other than the documents department, or area. It can be hypothesized that online searching of bibliographic databases is still, most likely, performed by staff of the general reference department, or a separate search room, and that online searching of OCLC, or another bibliographic utility, is done by technical service staff.

On the surface, it would seem that the study reported in this book suggests that more libraries are now involved in the online searching of bibliographic databases or a bibliographic utility for government publications. However, such a conclusion is premature. Although it was outside the scope of this study to probe the frequency of computer searching, or the specific databases searched, a number of responding libraries volunteered the information that searching was infrequently done or that the library had just begun offering database searching for government publications. Perhaps the most important conclusion to be drawn is that the McClure study merits replication.

McClure and Hernon (1983)

In their unobtrusive investigation of the quality of reference service provided by a sample of seventeen academic depository libraries in two geographical regions of the United States, the authors compared the distribution
of correct answers to a variety of variables. They discovered that the number of correct answers was not statistically related to highest degree offered
by the institution, the number of staff members assigned to the documents
department, the size of the budget, the percentage of items selected, or
the number of volumes held.

Since this study focused on staff performance, it does not offer an exact
comparison to the investigation reported in this chapter. However, of the
variables explored in the McClure and Hernon study, only the highest
degree offered and the percentage of items selected indicated significant
relationships in this study.

Key Issues

Information-Handling Technologies

The analysis of subgroups has disclosed several trends and possible concerns relating to the depository program as it moves into the mid-1980s.
First, it would appear that many depositories, including state agency and
academic libraries, make either no use or minimal use of information-
handling technologies to increase integration of, and access to, depository
publications. If technology is used, it is most likely for online bibliographic
database searching or use of a bibliographic utility, in particularly OCLC.
Even these uses may be infrequent and carried out through a department
other than the one responsible for the depository collection.

If the use of information-handling technologies is viewed in the context
of library types, public libraries make much less use than academic and
law school depositories. With the increase in the production of government information in machine-readable formats, libraries which fail to
provide access to these sources will be less able to meet the current and
future information needs of their users and to apply technology to the
development and maintenance of depository collections and services. If
depository libraries do not offer the public the benefits of technology to
meet information needs, many depository collections may become less
relevant to the information needs of an increasing segment of the population. Users in the future will likely show a preference for those parts of the
collection under the control of technology (e.g., an online catalog).[9] As

[9] For a pertinent discussion about the use of online catalogs see Matthews, Lawrence, and
Ferguson (1983).

they do so, government publications may be perceived as less relevant to their information needs.

Public Library Depositories

Given the intent of the depository program to provide the public with access to government publications, the role of public libraries in the depository program must be reevaluated, and possibly extended. Public libraries represent a decreasing percentage of the total membership in the program, while law libraries, or "law" designations, account for a larger proportion of the newer depositories. In theory, only the libraries of the highest appellate court can limit access to their collection to their immediate clientele. In practice, it has been shown that other depositories discriminate in their provision of service and access to the documents collection (Armstrong and Russell, 1979; McClure and Hernon, 1983). A key issue, therefore, becomes whether the very composition of libraries participating in the depository library program inhibits public access.

Depositories Selecting a Maximum of 25% of Available Items

A comparison of Table 3-12 to Table 4-14 indicates that the number of depository libraries selecting 25% or fewer items has dramatically increased since the results of the 1975 *Biennial Survey* were reported. At least 38.2% of the libraries participating in the depository program select a maximum of 25%. It would seem that as the number of publications distributed through the depository system increases, libraries will tend to reevaluate their selection profiles and become even more selective.

If this trend continues, it means that as the number and types of source material (print and nonprint) entering the depository program increase, more depository libraries will not select larger percentages of item numbers. Further, one might question the ability of regional depositories to absorb all the publications into their collections and services.[10] Perhaps more selectivity should prevail in the distribution of government publications to depository libraries.

The *Guidelines for the Depository Library System* (1977) are outdated and too general in their recommendation for a minimum percentage for all depositories to select. Variations should be possible by library type and perhaps in other ways as well. Further, the *Guidelines* provide a weak foundation from which to build an inspection program. As the final two chapters will suggest, the *Guidelines*, an inspection program, and state plans will not improve the effectiveness and efficiency of the depository

---

[10] For a discussion of the issues and problems confronting regional depositories, see Faull (1985).

program until formal goals and objectives are developed, performance measures implemented, and a meaningful database to support planning and decision making established. Of course, the depository program can continue to function without the establishment of goals and objectives, but it cannot become a dynamic network, central to meeting the information needs of a diverse range of the public.

The GPO, in cooperation with the Joint Committee on Printing and the library community, needs to rewrite the basic documentation intended for use as administrative law. The purpose of this rewriting should be to foster an environment based on planning and looking toward the future. At the same time, Congress itself must review the depository program and Title 44, *United States Code*, and develop a coordinated, comprehensive, and realistic view of the production and dissemination of government publications/information.[11] Libraries themselves must regard depository status as integral to their mission and goals, as well as increase the institutional resources devoted to their documents collections and services. Depository librarians must work toward the integration of government publications in their own library's collections and services.[12]

Staffing of Depository Collections

The number of staff working with government publications, in many cases, is small; too many libraries assign from "0" to a maximum of 1 FTE professional to the collection—even libraries serving graduate programs, where the institution has an enrollment over 5,000, and where the percentage of items selected exceeds 25%. Cook, who surveyed academic libraries belonging to the Association of Research Libraries (ARL) in 1980, discovered that 29 (43.3%) of the 67 responding libraries assign a maximum of 1.99 professionals to the collection, while another 29 have between 2 and 3.99 professionals. The number of support staff, including student workers, is also minimal (Cook, 1982, p. 462).

It would seem that a number of ARL and other libraries view depository status as a means of free access to titles which they otherwise might have to purchase. Further, where the number of staff is small and the work load and responsibilities are large, both professional and support staff are likely candidates for fatigue and work-related "burnout"—"a syndrome characterized by certain physical symptoms and emotional conditions that affect job performance" (Ferriero and Powers, 1982, p. 274).

The observation about "burnout" applies to personnel of both selective and regional depositories. Where a small number of staff are charged with maintaining a regional collection and services, these individuals may find

---

[11] For a discussion of issues associated with revision of Title 44 see McClure (1984d).

[12] For a complete discussion of collection integration see Hernon and McClure (1984).

it both difficult and emotionally taxing to fulfill their responsibilities to their institutions as well as to assist "selective depositories with reference questions, interlibrary loan and photocopies," and to contribute "to the effectiveness of the depository network through workshops, training sessions and consultative services within their region" (Section 12-2, *Guidelines*, 1977).

The findings relating to staffing patterns, the high number of depositories selecting 25% or fewer item numbers, and the selective use of information-handling technologies are not new. They have been documented by Whitbeck, Hernon, and Richardson (1978); Richardson, Frisch, and Hall (1980); and McClure (1981 and 1982). What should be of concern is that the situation has not improved since these studies were conducted.

Chapter 5

Defunct Depositories

Perusal of the annual reports issued by the Public Printer of the United States, from the inception of the GPO to the present, indicates that, upon occasion, depository library status has been terminated. For years, at the beginning of every new session of Congress, members of that body could withdraw depository status and reassign it to another library. However, as was pointed out in Chapter 1, an act of 1913 made all designations permanent unless a library volunteered to relinquish its designation or failed to comply with existing law.

These annual reports never disclosed the reasons for termination of status. In fact, the Superintendent of Documents, Government Printing Office, did not begin to keep a record of these libraries until fiscal year 1970. This record, however, merely comprises a listing of those libraries relinquishing status each fiscal year; there is neither an identification of the reasons for termination of status nor an analysis of trends. A library, upon checking a questionnaire item in the *Biennial Survey*, can terminate its depository status. There is no formal attempt in the questionnaire to ascertain the reasons behind the decision.

The purpose of this chapter is fivefold: (1) to fill a gap in the published literature on the GPO depository program; (2) to develop a profile of the libraries relinquishing their status; (3) to identify prevailing patterns among these libraries; (4) to identify factors contributing to the termination of depository status; and (5) to bring the topic of defunct depository libraries before the library community for further consideration. It is hoped that the subsequent information will better enable the depository community to anticipate which libraries might terminate their status and identify some fundamental issues meriting consideration in the professional literature.

The Superintendent of Documents supplied a list of the depository libraries relinquishing depository status between January 1970 and September 1983. Using this list as the study population, descriptive data were collected on these libraries from the same published sources used to elicit data on those libraries currently holding depository status (see Chapters 3 and 4), and a survey of these libraries was then conducted in October 1983.

Study Population

From January 1970 until September 1983, 51 libraries have been officially recorded as having terminated depository status. However, the numbers reported by the GPO for fiscal year 1982 are misleading. One library listed as having relinquished its depository status was accepted as a member of the depository community, but for some unspecified reason terminated its status before the service had actually begun. Another library did not actually terminate its status. Rather, according to the librarian at that institution, the main college library never held depository status, but it "piggy-backs" on the depository status of the law school library. During the GPO depository inspection of 1982, the inspector recommended that the law school library change its depository status from a congressional appointment to that of a law designate; accredited law school libraries comprise one type of law designation. The library did not experience "any break in its tenure as a depository library or in the service as such." The advantage of the change in designation was that it "freed one slot in the congressional district for an additional depository library."

Through the survey of the currently existing depository libraries (described in the two preceding chapters), it was discovered that 3 libraries were in the process of informing the GPO that they intended to relinquish their depository status. Incidentally, one of these libraries was part of an academic institution which had recently ceased to exist. Thus, Figure 5-1, which is based on the 49 libraries covered by the GPO records and the 3 libraries identified through the survey of the current depository libraries, depicts the number of libraries relinquishing depository status by fiscal year.

Overview

Examples of defunct depositories can be found in 30 states and the District of Columbia; 15 were located in the Midwest, 16 in the Northeast, 13 in the South, and 8 in the West.[1] The population of the communities in which the defunct libraries were situated ranged from 669 to 3,005,072. Some 31 (59.6%) had populations under 50,000; in fact, 13 libraries were situated in communities with fewer than 10,000 people. Eight libraries were in communities with populations over 200,000 and the remaining libraries were situated in communities with populations over 50,000 but under 200,000.

---

[1] The terminology used for categorizing a state as part of a particular region was developed by the U.S. Bureau of the Census. See Map 3-1 for a depiction of these regions and the states comprising each.

Figure 5-1. Number of Libraries Relinquishing Depository Status
by Fiscal Year

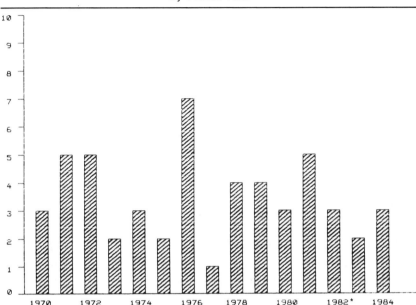

* Note: As explained in the text, three libraries, rather than the five suggested in
GPO records, relinquished depository status in 1982.

The defunct depositories encompass the following types of libraries:

- academic (23, or 44.2%)
- public (18, or 34.6%)
- court of law (3, or 5.8%)
- law school (academic) (1, or 1.9%)
- other special library (7, or 13.5%)

The other category encompasses military, state, government, and assorted
other special cases. Interestingly, 12 (23.1%) of the 52 defunct depositories have either ceased to exist or have merged with another library,
thereby, one assumes, changing the mission of the institution and the need
to collect government publications on an extensive or regular basis. These
libraries either were academic (9) or fell within the "other special library"
group (3). In at least four cases, the academic institution itself had gone
bankrupt and ceased to function.

Six of the 52 libraries were part of an academic library system, with
campuses in other localities; another campus library retained depository

status. The total number of volumes and titles held by the libraries relinquishing depository status was difficult to determine. Of the two, volume count was easier to find; however, these data were available in only 32 instances. Given the large number of libraries for which data were unavailable, meaningful conclusions based on either volume or title counts cannot be derived. Suffice to say, only 3 libraries for which data were available held more than 200,000 volumes.

The date of receipt for depository status was located for all but 2 of the 52 libraries. Knowing this information, as well as the year in which status was relinquished, the duration of participation in the depository program can be calculated. The duration ranged from 2 to 120 years, with 29 libraries holding status for 10 or fewer years and 11 libraries being depositories between 11 and 17 years; the remaining 10 libraries held status considerably longer—29 to 120 years. Just those libraries ceasing to exist or merging with other libraries were examined for statistically significant patterns. None prevailed; the number of years that depository status was retained ranged from 3 to 111 years.

Similar to the main study, additional data were collected about the academic depositories; the one law school library has been included in this analysis. Fourteen institutions offered baccalaureate or arts associate degrees, 6 offered the master's, and 2 the doctorate, as the highest degree.[2] Further, 9 of the academic institutions relinquishing depository status had enrollments under 1,000 and 4 had enrollments under 2,000; 3 had enrollments between 2,000 and 5,000, while the remaining 5 had enrollments between 5,000 and 15,000.[3]

Again, with the inclusion of the one law school library, nearly two-thirds of the 24 academic libraries were affiliated with private institutions (15, or 62.5%). Focusing on these private institutions, over half (8, or 53.3%) offered the baccalaureate as the highest degree, while 4 had the master's degree, and 1 the doctorate, as the highest degree.[4] Nine private institutions had enrollments under 1,000; on the other hand, only 2 had enrollments greater than 2,000.[5,6] Further, 8 of the 9 academic institutions which have either ceased to exist or merged with other institutions were private institutions offering the baccalaureate (6) or the master's degree (2) and typically had enrollments under 1,000; only 1 private school had an enrollment between 1,000 and 2,000 students. At one time, the one public institution offered a master's degree, but it now shares facilities with a college whose library currently maintains depository status.

---

[2] The highest degree offering for 2 institutions could not be determined.

[3] The enrollment for 3 institutions could not be determined.

[4] Data on 2 institutions were unavailable.

[5] Enrollment data for 2 institutions could not be determined.

[6] Data on the number of faculty employed were typically unavailable for the institutions relinquishing depository status.

Survey of Defunct Depositories

Excluding the 12 libraries ceasing to exist or merging with other libraries, the population of libraries remaining to survey was 40. These libraries were sent a brief mail questionnaire to elicit information about the percentage of item numbers selected at the time that depository status was terminated, the number of staff servicing the collection, whether depository publications were still retained in the collection, and the reason(s) for having relinquished depository status (see Appendix C). It should be remembered that the responses and subsequent analysis are based on self-reporting by the library directors. The responses, therefore, may *not* fully reflect any actions or input from depository library inspectors, other members of the GPO, or the staff of the JCP.[7]

Some 32 of the library directors responded, for a return rate of 80 percent. Three directors did not complete the questionnaire because their libraries no longer retained the necessary records and the entire staff had changed in the intervening years. Therefore, the following analysis is based on 29 responses. Twelve (41.4%) took fewer than 24% of the item numbers available at the time depository status was relinquished, while 5 (17.2%) took between 25% and 54% and 4 (13.8%) selected between 55% and 84%; eight directors (27.6%) no longer had information on the percentage taken.

Only 4 of the 29 responding libraries employed a full-time documents librarian. When queried about what had become of that position, 2 libraries responded that the person had been reassigned to the reference department. The documents librarian at the third library had transferred to the regional headquarters, which then became the depository library. The fourth library had eliminated the position because of a severe reduction in local funding. At the other 25 libraries, depository-related responsibilities were handled by clerical staff or professional staff assigned on a part-time basis.

The number of staff servicing the depository collection, prior to termination of depository status, ranged from 0 to 6, with the mean of 1 person. Clearly, documents and the depository library program were not high priorities for these libraries. Perhaps at the time depository status was gained, government publications were more of a priority; if this were so, the value of these publications to the collection, and the attainment of library goals and objectives, had greatly diminished. Still, a fundamental,

---

[7] As noted in Chapter 1, libraries not abiding by the appropriate statutory and administrative law may be placed on probation and subsequently removed from the depository library program if the violations are not rectified. The questionnaire did not probe whether a library had been placed on probation and, if so, the impact of this on the decision to drop out of the depository program. This line of inquiry was not probed because the authors perceived a possible validity problem—will libraries admit that they had, in fact, been placed on probation?

but unanswered, question relates to why these libraries ever sought depository status.

The directors were asked to specify the reason(s) for their libraries having relinquished depository status. Ranked according to frequency of mention, the following six reasons were suggested the most (respondents could identify as many as applicable):

- the publications were seldom utilized (23)
- we thought that another library in the area was a better choice for depository status (21)
- we had severe space limitations (20)
- we lacked the professional staff to maintain the status (12)
- we lacked the support staff necessary to maintain the status (11)
- participation in the depository program was a financial burden (6)

According to 2 respondents, the decision was based, in part, on the fact that their libraries could not select a minimum of the 25% of the item numbers recommended in the *Guidelines for the Depository Library System* (1977).

Two respondents explained that severe reductions in local funding required their public library to rethink its collection and service priorities. As one of them noted,

> Severe budget restraints imposed by Massachusetts' Proposition 2½ forced our hand. In addition, we are in a concentrated metropolitan area with numerous academic depository libraries in close proximity. Fifteen years ago, we perceived ourselves as a "noble experiment" to bring government documents to the people through a public library . . . We had to recognize the failure of the experiment and the need to discontinue depository status.

The comments of another director are noteworthy and merit quoting in their entirety. According to his reference librarian,

> Prior to my coming in 1971 the only previous professional reference librarian was almost 10 years before. In between, one junior library clerk opened the mail and tried to put materials into a subject classification scheme developed in-house years before. The collection was not publicized and was located on the third floor; no catalog existed except in the clerk's head. A new director wanted the space for improvements—remodeling a 1905 Carnegie building with 10,000 square feet total building area. He informed me that, among other things, I was in charge of the 76-year accumulation of documents—no weeding was ever done! One of my first recommendations was that we drop depository status and encourage the new four-year college in the area to become a depository. This was done and many of our documents were transferred there.

Another director explained that there had been a seventy-year accumulation of documents; these were basically unorganized and selected at random by an elderly non-professional hired under a previous director. Since the reference librarian was charged with overseeing the documents collection, as well as reorganizing and staffing the reference department, which was on another floor, it was very difficult for her even to find time to open the depository shipments or the mail. The building provided no additional space, and the prospect of more staff was unlikely. The reference professional decided, with the director's approval, to relinquish depository status to a state college in the congressional district, "where these valuable resources could be widely used and properly organized."

The response from one other library should be highlighted. According to the director, "space was at a premium... and the government publications collection was housed in a trailer." When a new library was built in the same congressional district and designated as regional headquarters, depository status was relinquished so that the new library could be designated as a depository, and the government publications collection and services were transferred there.

The final question asked if the library still retained publications which had been received on deposit; interestingly, 13 of the libraries do. The brief survey did not follow up on the retention policies governing these publications. The *Instructions to Depository Libraries* (1977) outlines the general procedures to follow for the recovery or continued use of official publications when a library terminates depository status. These procedures and the existing literature on the GPO depository library program suggest what should happen, rather than what has actually occurred.

With these comments in mind, several questions, each of which merits scrutiny, can be posited governing the status of publications still technically classified as property of the United States government. First, when an institution ceases to exist, what in fact becomes of the depository collection? Second, when a library discards documents received on deposit, were the prescribed procedures followed? Section 5 of the *Instructions* specifies that libraries served by a regional are supposed to seek that library's guidance in the disposition of depository publications. The Office of the Superintendent of Documents provides guidance for libraries not served by a regional. With permission from a regional or the Superintendent of Documents, and assuming that the publications are, in fact, not selected by another depository library, the library relinquishing its status may retain publications received on deposit.

Third, if depository publications were sold, what became of the monies; were they returned to the government? Fourth, when a library surrenders depository status, but still retains depository publications in its collection, are restrictions placed on their use? And, lastly, what actions have regional depository libraries, the GPO, and the JCP actually taken when depository status is surrendered?[8]

In summary, defunct depositories comprise a small percentage of the population of depository libraries. These libraries are frequently located in population centers of under 50,000 people; may have encountered financial problems or a change in institutional mission; may have been part of a private academic institution; may have a depository collection which was seldom used and have needed the space for other purposes; or may have given the documents collection low priority and have understaffed it. Frequently, defunct depositories have not had any professional staff assigned to the official collection. It is possible that libraries which are part of small academic institutions and which have minimal professional staff are high-risk depositories. Another characteristic of the defunct group is that the staff may have believed that another library in the congressional district was a better choice for depository status. If this were so, an interesting question becomes, "Was their belief in fact correct?" Are members of that congressional district better served from another library, in terms of staff, space, finances, or extended hours for the depository collection and reference services?

Challenge to the Future

Although the number of libraries relinquishing depository status for any given year is small, the numbers accumulate over time—52 such libraries between January 1970 and January 1984. Many of the libraries currently participating in the depository program, as has been shown in the two previous chapters, operate on limited budgets, assign a minimal number of staff to the depository collection (in some cases, no professional staff members have been given documents-related responsibilities), and select far less than the 25% of item numbers recommended in the *Guidelines for the Depository Library System* (1977).

Presumably, many of these same libraries also encounter space problems. It can be hypothesized that depending on institutional goals, these and perhaps other libraries are potential candidates for relinquishing their depository status. Additional support for this hypothesis is given by Carol Watts, former Classification Specialist for the Library Division of the GPO and former Depository Library Inspector, who claims that " . . . one-fifth of the depository libraries are either unwilling or unable to per-

---

[8] The authors attempted to elicit from the GPO a detailed response about what actions are taken when depository status is surrendered. Unfortunately, the Office of the Superintendent of Documents did not want to make such information available.

form their responsibilities and should be evaluated more completely by the GPO" (Watts, 1982, p. 61).[9]

On the basis of such considerations, a logical question becomes, "How important is it that the number of defunct depositories does not dramatically increase, either for a given year or over time?" The answer focuses on issues of cost-benefit and whether the program should remain relatively static or fluid in its composition. An impression from monitoring the number and types of libraries becoming depositories in the past decade (as well as from noting the lack of previous attention to defunct depositories in the published literature) is that the membership is meant to be fluid, with libraries each year entering and exiting the program.

Since library goals and objectives may change over time, government publications may lose their importance to a library in fulfilling its mission. To the credit of some libraries, they have apparently realized that they are no longer the best suited, in that congressional district, to represent the depository program and have, therefore, relinquished their membership.

Factors such as these should be balanced with those of costs and benefits so that the depository program represents the best interests of the government, the library community, and residents within a congressional district. As is evident, all the relevant factors should be identified and incorporated in the decision-making and planning process.

Recognizing the need for better coordination of the depository program in each state, the GPO and the Depository Library Council to the Public Printer have encouraged states to develop state plans. A number of draft and final plans have now been produced. These plans vary significantly in the topical areas covered; some, for example, address the purpose of the program in the state, the authority of the GPO, the responsibilities of participating libraries, staffing, technical services, selection, resource sharing, bibliographic access to depository holdings, public relations, continuing education of depository staff, and financial obligations (Hernon and McClure, 1984, p. 294). These plans should include another category —the likelihood of participating libraries to remain in the program for a specified time period. The purpose would be to anticipate which libraries might relinquish depository status and the implications of their exiting the program. The loss of member libraries should not disrupt resource sharing and the operation of the program in a state.

Excluding costs related to the classification and cataloging of publications for inclusion in the *Monthly Catalog*, it costs Congress "an average of $11,000 per year for each library in the depository program" (*Federal Government Printing and Publishing,* 1979, p. 42). Since this figure represents an average, the actual cost, in many instances, is either higher or

---

[9] See also Chapter 1 of Hernon and McClure (1984).

lower. Although for any given year the amount is undoubtedly insignificant, expenditures compound over time and the investment becomes more substantial.

Cost-benefit issues could be raised, especially since a number of these libraries have held depository status for a long time and presumably have received numerous government publications. Instead of looking on these libraries as merely part of the historical record, every effort should be made to examine existing depositories, as well as those libraries applying for depository status, with the overview presented in this chapter in mind. This is critical since the survey of currently existing depository libraries disclosed 3 libraries in the process of relinquishing depository status. Clearly, the depository inspection program and the *Biennial Survey* should explore to a much greater extent than they apparently do the ability of a library to remain in the program for a certain length of time.

The GPO and the library community should scrutinize libraries applying for depository status and collect more data than those specified in section 3 of the *Guidelines for the Depository Library System*. Any data collected should be useful for analyzing a specific objective—predicting the ability of a given library to participate in the program for a specified number of years. The GPO and the JCP would be best advised to explore models showing interrelationships among data elements and the use of regression analysis to make such predictions. Modeling has greater utility than vague, *subjective*, pronouncements that "the library should have the interest, resources and ability to provide custody of the documents and public service" (section 3-3). Further, what is the predictive value of knowing such factors as the size of the student body of an academic institution or the "size and character" of a library's collection (section 3-7)? Clearly, there is substantial variation among the libraries comprising the depository program and the *Guidelines* are vague and open to interpretation.[10]

Section 3-7 of the *Guidelines* also specifies that libraries seeking depository status should "apply to the state library authority for evaluation and recommendation." However, neither the GPO nor the JCP have developed guidelines governing the nature and scope of the evaluation. These guidelines should go beyond the general points provided in section 3-8. Further, libraries of independent agencies and the executive branch may be designated as "depositories upon certification of need according to the provisions of *44 U.S.C.* 1907"; a precise and measurable definition of "need" should be advanced.

Tabulation of the data required for the *Biennial Survey*, or suggested in the *Guidelines*, results in a descriptive profile of the depository program rather than serving as a component of the planning process, where goals and objectives are set and the ability of member libraries to accomplish

---

[10] See McClure and Hernon (1983); and Hernon and McClure (1984).

shared and individual objectives is measured in an objective manner. Further, as will be discussed in the next chapter, the descriptive data gathered by the GPO are not reported back to depository libraries in a meaningful manner.

The brief survey reported in this chapter suggests that perhaps the factors most likely affecting the ability and willingness of a library to continue as part of the depository program relate to institutional funding and the financial solvency of the institution; to the goals and objectives of the institution and the degree to which government publications assist a library in accomplishing its objectives; to the extent of commitment to the depository library program, and to whether the library is part of a branch of a larger system. Indeed, these and other factors merit exploration and inclusion in an appropriate model, as well as full coverage in the *Biennial Survey* and the inspection program.

Instead of merely asking if a library wants either to continue or to discontinue as part of the depository program, the *Biennial Survey* should be restructured to accomplish specific objectives, one of which should relate to predicting the circumstances under which a library might relinquish depository status. Making predictions, however, requires trend data and the asking of a full range of pertinent questions. The point is that the GPO, the JCP, and the library community should not be caught unaware of a library's decision to discontinue its association with the depository program. Instead, institutional decisions should be anticipated so that a congressional district receives high-quality and uninterrupted service.

Now is the time for the GPO and the JCP to review all the documentation governing the depository library program, as well as the inspection program. They should act aggressively by commissioning research, hiring consultants, and seeking widespread support to establish objectives for the depository program (the points listed in the *Guidelines* as "objectives" are goals; there are no formally stated objectives governing the program), performance measures, and output measures.[11] The next two chapters of this book elaborate on these and other points, while suggesting an agenda for action. The development and implementation of such an agenda could lead to change and substantial improvement in the quality of the existing depository program.

In conclusion, the analysis of defunct depository libraries shows the difficulty of assessing aspects of the program from an empirical basis and the limited ability of either GPO officials to make informed decisions about methods to improve the program or depository librarians to use available information for decision making in their particular library. Data available from the *Biennial Survey* do not adequately address the reasons for terminating membership in the program. Further, the GPO has made available

---

[11] Ibid.

minimal follow-up information which analyzes defunct depositories and which serves as a basis to provide libraries applying for depository status, and depository librarians as a whole, with a projection of the likelihood of these libraries making active, and long-term, contributions to the depository program.

Indeed, the data collected about defunct libraries only whets one's appetite for additional information. As it is, a meaningful model of factors which contribute to depository termination cannot be stated; such a model must go beyond the identification of factors and demonstrate interrelationships. Additionally, one wonders why there was no "early warning system" of information from the official surveys or inspection program which identified, monitored, and dealt with libraries where "materials had not been put on the shelves for 70 years." Such situations should not have persisted for so long and decry the need for a valid inspection process. Clearly, this chapter demonstrates a decision support system which is inadequate to meet the needs of government officials, librarians, and researchers, as well as to develop strategies to better resolve the information needs of depository library clientele.

Chapter **6**

The Biennial Survey *as a Basis for Depository Library Program Decision Making and Planning**

If decision making is defined as the conversion of information into action, a decision maker's access to accurate, timely, and understandable information takes on great importance. Indeed, the *quality* of available information used as input into the decision-making process has a direct relationship to the resulting effectiveness of the decision (Janis and Mann, 1977). In short, the quality of data must be constantly maintained and enhanced if decision makers are to understand and resolve complex issues.

Linking quality information to the decision-making process is a key issue for a number of reasons. First, it assumes that decision makers recognize the importance of having accurate and timely information as a basis for decision making. Second, it assumes that the formal collection and analysis of information can serve as a basis for improved decisions. Third, it suggests that value, or benefit, is derived from a database of information that supports decision making. Information, therefore, becomes an essential resource for decision making only in those situations in which decision makers chose to make use of information and integrate it into the decision-making process (Harrison, 1981).

The cast of decision makers related to the depository library program is large and includes the GPO, the JCP, other Congressional committees and executive agencies, librarians and information specialists in the various depository and non-depository settings, library educators, researchers studying the depository library program and its relationship to larger

---

* Most of this chapter was previously published by McClure, under the title "An Assessment of the 1983 *Biennial Survey*," *Government Information Quarterly*, 2 (1985), 79–111.

issues (e.g., access to government information and federal information policy), and citizens and other interested individuals and groups attempting to influence decisions related to the depository program. All of these groups require valid, reliable, and timely information which, when considered in light of political, personal, or other factors, provides a basis for decision making.

The availability of a reliable, valid, and timely database of information describing the depository library program is essential if decisions are to be made and strategies developed to improve its effectiveness. For years, various attempts have been made to collect and analyze information about the depository library program. Best known, of course, are the Biennial Surveys conducted by the GPO, but other agencies and individuals have also conducted surveys that describe depository libraries.

For instance, in the years 1983 and 1984 alone, four major surveys were conducted: *Depository Librarians' Views Concerning GPO's Depository Library Program* (General Accounting Office, 1984); *Provision of Federal Government Publications in Electronic Format to Depository Libraries* (Joint Committee on Printing, 1984); the GPO *Biennial Survey* (*Biennial Report...*, 1983); and the one reported in Chapters 3 and 4 of this book. Given the amount of time, money, personnel, and other resources committed to these efforts, one must assume that collecting survey data which describes either characteristics of the depository library program and individual depositories or attitudes and opinions of depository librarians about the program is believed to be important for planning, decision making, and evaluation of the depository library program.

Planning, decision making, and evaluation are all critical activities if the depository library program as well as individual depository library collections are to increase overall effectiveness.[1] Without adequate information, decision making, planning, and evaluation will not be effective and attempts to *improve* the performance of the depository library program and individual depository libraries are not likely to be successful. Thus, it is within this context of improving the basis for planning, decision making, and evaluation that the information generated by the Biennial Surveys will be assessed.

If the Biennial Surveys are to be used for improved decision making, planning, and evaluation a number of questions should be considered:

- why is it important to have collected the data?
- to what extent are the data trustworthy and useful?
- what is the ultimate purpose of the data collection process?

---

[1] See Hernon and McClure (1984, pp. 183–207 and 275–298) for a detailed discussion of planning, evaluation, and decision making as they relate to the depository library program.

- why have specific data elements been collected and for what (if any) decisions are they to be used?
- are the results made available and reported in such a fashion that they can be integrated into decision making, planning, and evaluation?

Examination of such questions is important because data collection for the sake of data collection has little utility and less impact on policy, decisions, and planning.

The purpose of this chapter is to discuss these and other questions related to the data collected, and the information provided, from the *Biennial Survey*. The quality of the information provided from the *Biennial Survey* will be assessed, specific examples will be identified as a means of illustrating various weaknesses with the current *Biennial Survey* data collection process, and suggestions will be made for its improvement. Throughout the chapter, the importance of developing data collection instruments and reporting mechanisms that enhance decision making will be stressed. Further, it is essential for the GPO to improve the process by which the Biennial Surveys are developed, administered, analyzed, and reported.

Quality of Survey Data

Currently, the GPO gathers descriptive data about the depository library program largely through survey instruments.[2] Of the various research designs available, ones that rely exclusively on self-reported surveys are the *least* likely to provide reliable, valid, and useful data because (Sellitz, Wrightsman, and Cook, 1976)

- responses are *self*-reported by participants
- questions can be widely interpreted by participants
- many surveys are not carefully pretested
- response rates can be low
- the degree to which the results can be generalized to other subpopulations can be limited
- analysis is typically limited to frequency counts, percentages, and averages
- specific measures and variables may not be identified

---

[2] In addition to the *Biennial Survey* (to which all depository libraries are legally expected to respond), numerous survey instruments are attached to the *Daily Shipment List* and *Administrative Notes*, as well as distributed separately. All of these represent a *sample* of libraries in the depository program because they produce less than 100% response.

Thus, for such surveys to be credible, specific techniques must be implemented to insure the data have reliability, validity, and utility. Administrators of such surveys must be accountable for the quality of such surveys and have a responsibility to demonstrate that the data do, in fact, meet these criteria.

Reliability

This criterion seeks to determine the degree to which the data are consistent; consistency is the extent to which the same results are produced from different samples of the same population (Katzer, Cook, and Crouch, 1981, p. 91). Thus, if a question seeks to determine the number of microfiche held by a depository library, one would expect the answer to be the same if asked three different times or three different ways at a specific point in time. If two librarians at the same depository were asked, "How many microfiche do you have?" and one said 8,546 and the second said 5,687, data related to microfiche holdings are not likely to be reliable. Unreliability, then, is where the data or the instrument will not produce the same results twice.

Reliability can also be injured if two respondents interpret a question differently. For instance, if a librarian at one depository interprets the question "How many microfiche do you have?" as how many within that department and a librarian at another library interprets the question to mean how many microfiche are in the entire library, the resulting data are not likely to be reliable.

Inconsistent coding and inappropriate analysis of data also can cause reliability problems. Such problems typically occur either when the researcher has to interpret "open-ended" questions and categorize them for analysis, or simply when coding errors occur (e.g., when a response that should have been coded as a "1" was coded as a "2").

Vagueness and lack of clear definitions for key terms in questions contribute to unreliable data. For instance, question 31 on the 1983 *Biennial Survey* asks, "Does the library have adequate facilities and equipment to serve handicapped library patrons?" Responses to this question are likely to be unreliable because the degree of adequacy is open to individual interpretation. Rewording the question, for example, to ask "Can patrons in wheelchairs physically have access to materials in the documents collection?" is more specific and is also likely to produce reliable data about access to the collection by the handicapped.

Validity

Validity, which is the extent to which the instrument accurately measures what it purports to measure, can be further examined in terms of *internal validity* and *external validity* (Kerlinger, 1973, pp. 456–459). Internal validity simply asks for survey items which do, in fact, measure what is being studied. For instance, question 21 on the 1983 *Biennial Survey* asks, "Does the library have enough shelf space to house the volume of paper copy documents it will select from GPO during the next two years?" The internal validity of data resulting from this question is limited because answers must be based on the assumption that (1) respondents know the volume of paper copy documents they will select in the next two years; (2) "shelf space" will be measured similarly by the various respondents; and (3) the librarian does not exaggerate or minimize the estimate for other motives, e.g., to obtain additional space.

Internal validity also asks if the researcher has the correct *interpretation* of the findings, or, if there have been factors, variables, or conditions that have not been considered or acknowledged. For example, question 69 of the 1983 *Biennial Survey* asks, "How many seats are available for users of documents?" Obtaining a result that there are 18 seats for users in a specific documents collection cannot be interpreted as either "good" or "bad" unless there is also information about the need for such seating, about the degree to which the goals and objectives of the collection encourage in-house use, or about whether a specific area for documents seating has, in fact, been designated. Producing results from data is a different process from *interpreting* the meaning of those results.

The external validity of an instrument is the degree to which the data can be generalized to the larger population or to other sub-populations. This degree of generalizability is largely dependent on the sampling process, the selection of study sites, and the characteristics of the participants in the study. In order for a study to have external validity, the characteristics of the study participants (be they depository libraries, depository librarians, or whatever) must be similar to the characteristics of the population as a whole.

If, for instance, the group of study participants in a survey is 56% male, with an average age of 32, and the characteristics of all respondents in the population show this latter group to be only 23% male with an average age of 51, the results are not likely to be generalizable. Most surveys of depository libraries or depository librarians are samples; however, for surveys of the entire population, i.e., all depository libraries in the program, external validity should be high. But if the reliability and internal validity of the data are limited, so too is the degree to which the findings can be generalized.

Utility

For data to have utility, they must be both reliable and valid. But the utility question includes the following (Paisley, 1969, p. A-3):

- what are these findings good for?
- what decisions in the real world can be affected by them?
- how are theories or other knowledge affected by the findings?
- what can be learned from the study, or can the study be dismissed with the comment "so what"?

The utility criterion is one having to do with applications, impact, and usefulness of the findings and presupposes that one of the broader purposes for the data collection was to affect policy or decision making.

For much of the survey data available about the depository library program, the question "so what?" appears to be hard to answer. The utility criterion assumes that for each question on the *Biennial Survey*, answers to the following can be obtained:

- what is the purpose of having this question on the survey?
- how can information from this question assist in decision making, by the GPO, JCP, other government agencies, librarians, or other information specialists?
- can the results from this question be tabulated and summarized so that they can be understood by decision makers and *related* to other data from the questionnaire?

Thus, the utility criterion calls for careful consideration and justification for questionnaire content and the development of analysis techniques and reporting strategies which encourage the use of the data. Clearly, such does not appear to be the case with data from the various Biennial Surveys.

Interrelationship Among Reliability, Validity, and Utility

The overall value of the data resulting from such surveys, then, is dependent on the degree to which the data are reliable, valid, and useful. Indeed, a graphic presentation of their interrelatedness is given in Figure 6-1, which suggests that the criteria build upon each other. If the data are not reliable, the degree to which they can be valid is significantly reduced; if the findings are not valid, the degree to which the study has utility also is injured. While all survey research cannot be "perfectly" reliable, valid, and useful, these criteria must be kept in mind during the development of the instrument, its pretesting and administration, the analysis of data, and the reporting of the results.

Developers of survey research, especially, have a responsibility to inform readers of the study about the *degree* to which the data are reliable

Figure 6-1. Criteria for Quality Data*

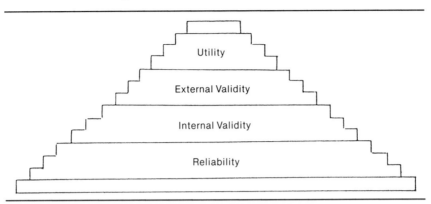

* Source: William J. Paisley, *Behavioral Studies on Scientific Information Flow: An Appendix on Method* (New London, NH: Gordon Research Conference on Scientific Method, July 14–18, 1969), p. A-4.

and valid.[3] However, results from the recent *Biennial Surveys*, the 1984 GAO study, or the JCP study on provision of government documents in electronic format have not provided readers with such information. Thus, the degree of *confidence* that users can place in such data is limited at best. Further, since an analysis of instruments such as the 1983 *Biennial Survey* identifies numerous weaknesses, the *value* of information resulting from such surveys is limited.

Evaluating Information from the 1983 *Biennial Survey*

Understanding the basic concepts of reliability, validity, and utility is essential, but additional attention must be given to producing information from such surveys that has "value." This concept of information value is complex; Figure 6-2 provides a useful overview of criteria to assess information reported from the *Biennial Survey.*

The criteria suggested in Figure 6-2 represent areas where users of information reported from the Biennial Surveys can assess the value of that information. Each of the five broad areas—relevance, reliability, understandability, sufficiency, and practicality—will be discussed and appropriate examples from the 1983 *Biennial Survey* provided (see Appendix A

---

[3] Specific approaches, tests, and scales to assess reliability and validity have been developed and are discussed in, for example, Isaac and Michael (1971); Carmines and Zeller (1979); and Kerlinger (1973).

150

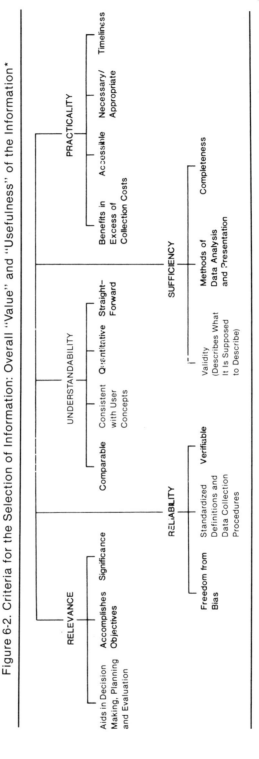

Figure 6-2. Criteria for the Selection of Information: Overall "Value" and "Usefulness" of the Information*

* Adapted from William R. King, *Marketing Management Information Systems* (New York: Petrocelli/Charter, 1977), p. 43.

for a copy of the survey). The criteria listed on Figure 6-2 are interdependent, and frequently, information that fails to meet criteria for practicality, for example, tends to have limited relevance. Thus, the following discussion examines the criteria separately, but overall information value results from a merging of these criteria. Nonetheless, an examination of each of these criteria suggests areas where improvements can be made.

Relevance

The first, and perhaps most important, criterion to consider is the degree to which the information provided from the instrument meets the goals and objectives of the project. The purposes for the 1983 *Biennial Survey* were given in one source as to (*Administrative Notes*, no. 7, 1983, p. 2)

- provide GPO with a picture of conditions in depositories
- provide depositories with meaningful statistics which will enable them to draw conclusions about services in their libraries

However, different purposes are stated on the cover page of the actual 1983 *Biennial Survey* instrument:

- to determine whether the publications are being used to the best advantage of the American public
- to obtain other information which would be helpful in administering the depository library program
- to conduct on-site inspections of depository libraries

In addition to the problem of having different stated purposes for the *Biennial Survey*, they are not accompanied by specific objectives (measurable, time-limited, challenging, and specific guides to action) to what was intended to be accomplished by the process. Without study objectives or research questions one should not be surprised that there have been few tangible products or impacts resulting from the Biennial Surveys.

As an example, given the purposes provided above, the following objectives might have been stated:

- to present summary information to individual depository libraries within six months of collection that could be used as input for decision making
- to establish a national database of information by 1987, accessible online by appropriate government officials and depository librarians

- to develop six national performance measures by which the effectiveness of the depository libraries could be determined[4]
- to assess, within one year of the publication of the findings, the degree to which depository libraries are meeting the *Guidelines for the Depository Library Program* (1977)

These, of course, are just examples and are intended to be neither comprehensive nor representative of GPO's actual expectations.

The point, however, is that no one knows specifically the expectations of the GPO regarding such surveys since there are no detailed objectives that explain

- *why* the survey is being done
- *how* the information is expected to be used
- *who or what* is expected to use the resulting data

Given such vagueness, the effectiveness of the *Biennial Survey* cannot be meaningfully assessed, since effectiveness is the degree to which the survey accomplishes stated objectives. Further, the lack of specific objectives suggests that the GPO does not have clear intentions about how the data will be used or what they intend to accomplish by conducting the survey. In short, the relevance of the *Biennial Survey* is severely injured and its overall value is vague at best.

The relevance of the survey data and its findings must be considered from the perspective of both the GPO and the library community. An assessment of how the data are used by the GPO for decision making and planning is difficult to make, but indicators such as the following suggest that the data are not fully exploited for GPO decision making:

- summaries of the surveys are made available on computer printouts providing no interpretation of the data
- data from the surveys are not integrated with results from similar surveys or data
- to date, there is no decision support system (DSS) at the GPO from which such data can be organized and accessed by appropriate decision makers[5]

---

[4] Examples of such performance measures can be found in Hernon and McClure (1984, pp. 286–293).

[5] A decision support system (DSS) is an information system designed to meet the individual information needs of various users for improved decision making; it tends to be an interactive system, decentralized, and adaptive (McClure, 1984, p. 3). Chapter 7 of this book discusses DSS in more detail.

From the vantage point of the librarians, the relevance of the data is limited because of the following:

- a number of the questions on the survey have little importance or significance for *internal* library decision making
- no summary data are presented on a library-by-library basis; e.g., individual depository collections do not receive a "customized" profile of their depository *relating* various data to each other
- overall analysis of the data for the various libraries is limited at best; e.g., no long-term trend data are provided, data are not presented in the context of performance measures, and correlations among the data elements are not provided

Given these indicators, the degree to which the data are relevant for library and GPO decision making appears to be limited. Although clearly there is a *potential* for these data to become more useful, currently their usefulness has not been exploited.

In addition, data from a number of the questions are not relevant because they do not provide enough information to take action. For example, question 29—"Does the documents staff need more training in the handling of documents and their use?"—is answered only by a "yes/no" response. If the question had asked the respondents to rank or compare existing knowledge/competencies to those needed to acquire specific skills related to the "handling of documents" or "their use," the data would at least provide assistance to the GPO and local librarians developing continuing education programs by providing a sense of the training areas which respondents *perceive* as needed.

Figure 6-3 shows a different approach to obtaining information about perceived training needs. By comparing the structure and wording of the question, as shown in Figure 6-3, to the question as currently asked on the *Biennial Survey*, it is clear that the former is much more specific, provides clearly defined training areas, and allows an analysis that, if correlated to an earlier question having to do with type of depository library answering the survey, could rank which training areas are perceived as most important for specific types of library settings.

Support for the notion that the data are not seen as relevant for most depository librarians is evident in the state plans produced between 1982–1984. A quick perusal of these plans shows that the data from the Biennial Surveys are seldom mentioned as input for decision making and planning, or as a basis for needs assessment. The fact that the data in the Biennial Surveys have been ignored in the state plans is a message to the GPO about the data's perceived relevance.

Figure 6-3. Example of a Question Which Provides Information
That Assists in Decision Making

Circle the number that corresponds to your staff's *existing* and *desired* skill levels for each of the following skills/competencies.*

	Existing Skill Level			Desired Skill Level		
	High	Adequate	Low	High	Some	Low
1. Ability to operate OCLC terminals for cataloging	1	2	3	1	2	3
2. Ability to operate OCLC terminals for public services	1	2	3	1	2	3
3. Initiation of Information and Referral Services (I&R)	1	2	3	1	2	3
4. Awareness of new U.S. government reference sources	1	2	3	1	2	3
5. Ability to organize and extend bibliographic control over vertical files	1	2	3	1	2	3
6. Ability to search government document online bibliographic databases such as CIS, ASI, and *Monthly Catalog*	1	2	3	1	2	3
7. Ability to develop a formal long-range plan for depository library services	1	2	3	1	2	3
8. Knowledge of U.S. Census publications	1	2	3	1	2	3
9. Ability to implement collection development techniques	1	2	3	1	2	3
10. Ability to organize and maintain access to U.S. GPO microfiche	1	2	3	1	2	3

* NOTE: The skills/abilities listed are examples only and are intended to suggest the importance of determining *specific* areas perceived as important for staff training related to the handling and use of government publications. As reworded in the above alternative format, information can be obtained that provides specific *input* for decision making and planning in terms of staff training. This format is suggested as an alternative to question 29, "Does the documents staff need more training in the handling of documents and their use?"

Reliability

Adequate attention cannot be given here to all the instances in the 1983 *Biennial Survey* where the data are likely to be unreliable. The three criteria suggested in Figure 6-2 under the heading "Reliability" neatly summarize the problems inherent with the survey data, and a number of questions on the 1983 *Biennial Survey* fail to meet *any* of these three criteria of freedom from bias, standardized definitions and data collection procedures, and verifiability. For example, returning once again to question 29—"Does the documents staff need more training in the handling of documents and their use?"—none of these criteria are met. Thus, if unreliable data are obtained, the degree to which the data are then understandable, sufficient, or practical is also affected.

Clearly, the question is biased because self-reported data are not likely to produce answers which are indictments of the individual or the institution responding to the question. It is further biased in that the categories for answering the question are limited to "yes" or "no"—nothing in between. Since these factors tend to encourage a positive reply, as a measure of documents staff knowledge and need for training, the information resulting from the question is limited.

The reliability of the same question is further limited because it lacks definition. The terms "handling of documents" and "their use" are vague and open to a broad range of interpretation. One respondent can answer the question thinking of handling of documents as checking them in on a serials Kardex, while another might associate handling of documents with reshelving them. Further, individual interpretation of "Does the documents staff need more training?" is likely to occur. Since there is no definition or example of what type of performance is or is not acceptable, "more training" is a judgement call by the individual respondent—not likely to be consistent and certainly not likely to aid in decision making.

The reliability of the data is closely associated with data collection procedures. An example of problems that can result here is the GPO's attempt in the 1983 *Biennial Survey* to include questions that called for answers based on in-house sampling and computation of statistics. The original instructions and worksheets provided (*Administrative Notes*, no. 7, 1983, p. 2 +) were superficial and inadequate as they

- called for sampling of selected activities during summer months, which are notoriously slow for academic libraries (this was later revised by the GPO)
- failed to explain adequately *how* the sample was to be taken, *how many* items should be included in the sample, or what confidence levels were acceptable
- made huge assumptions about the appropriateness of the times selected for sampling

- relied on written definitions, some of which were vague, simplistic, and not generally accepted by other works in the field, to describe services

Later instructions offered by the GPO (*Administrative Notes*, nos. 8 and 9, 1983) attempted to clarify some of these difficulties, but the credibility of the process was damaged. In addition, inadequate procedures were offered for how the sampling was to be done, no instructions were provided governing the actions that librarians should take when only two instances of an activity could be observed on a sample day, and numerous other methodological problems were ignored. The GPO's efforts to revise the procedures were "too little, too late."

Although the GPO can be commended for its attempt and interest in obtaining more useful and relevant data, its inability to develop clear procedures and guidelines for how the sampling and data reporting would be done was embarrassingly evident. Numerous research methods and statistics books are available which summarize steps for how such sampling and data gathering should be done. And recent publications, such as *Library Data Collection Handbook* (Lynch, 1981), are available to provide definitions of key data elements.

The end result of this data collection effort is more data of questionable reliability. Worse, many users of the survey results may look at the summary information resulting from these questions and not realize that the sampling procedures and data collection techniques were superficial, generalized, and inappropriate. This incident is noted as it demonstrates the lack of sophistication and competency of those in the GPO and JCP responsible for the *Biennial Survey* in not providing adequate instructions and procedures for conducting even a rudimentary data collection procedure such as sampling. As such, the lack of clear and adequate instructions and procedures is an obvious indicator of the lack of reliability with which the data collection process is administered.

Another criterion in the area of reliability has to do with verifiability, i.e., the degree to which additional measures (either from the survey or from other data) show similar results. A number of the responses from the *Biennial Survey* can be verified, in part, by comparing them to similar questions asked during the inspection process. For instance, question 66 from the 1983 *Biennial Survey*—"How many professional staff work with documents [FTE]?"—can be compared to responses from questions on the Inspection Visit Form (IV.C and D), having to do, respectively, with the classification of the person responsible for the depository collection, and the educational background of that person (*U.S. Depository Library Inspection Visit Form*, n.d.). If a comparison between responses to the *Biennial Survey* and Inspection data for selected libraries shows that for the library under consideration similar responses were received, the data have some outside verification. However, users of the data outside the GPO and the JCP have no knowledge of such indicators of reliability.

Where there are opportunities for outside verification of the data, the results are not encouraging. For instance, 36% of the responses to question 29, regarding the perceived need for more training in the handling of documents and their use, indicated the need for more training. However, 64% responded that such training was not needed (*Depository Library Biennial Survey for 1983: U.S. Summary*, 1984). In contrast, on a very specific measure of "correct answer fill rate" (a performance measure which is an indicator of the quality of reference service), another study that sampled academic librarians found that on the average only 37% of the factual and bibliographic questions were answered correctly (McClure and Hernon, 1983). Using such data for outside verification of this response from the *Biennial Survey*, one must question the validity of those respondents who believed that no additional training in the "handling of documents and their use" is needed. But unless an attempt is made to verify such responses, users of the data could significantly misjudge the value of that information.

Space does not permit an item-by-item analysis of the questions in the 1983 *Biennial Survey* in terms of reliability. Further, the purpose of this section is to advocate the formulation of clear objectives and to point out the criteria by which an assessment of reliability can be made. Figure 6-4 provides an overview of reliability problems with *selected* questions from the 1983 *Biennial Survey*. Because numerous questions have reliability problems, the degree to which the data can be used for decision making is severely limited.

In short, freedom from bias, and standardized definitions and data collection are absolutely essential if the survey is to have credibility and value for decision making. Currently, this self-reported data is only as good as the degree to which analysts believe that the responses are, in fact, accurate and measure what they claim to measure. Until many of the survey questions are reworded and carefully defined, obtain data on one activity only, and are free from bias and multiple interpretations, their reliability will be severely limited.

Understandability

The reliability problems limit the degree to which data are understandable; criteria for understandability are suggested in Figure 6-2. Although some of the terms in the survey are consistent with current user and librarian concepts, data should be presented in a quantifiable format and the

Figure 6-4. Selected Questions from the 1983 *Biennial Survey*
with a Reliability Problem

Question	Problems
17. Is the depository material accessible to the public during regular hours? (answered by yes/no)	The terms "accessible" and "regular hours" are vague and the answer forces an either/or response.
18. What percentage of the depository collection is in storage? (answered in 6 percentage categories between 0 and 100)	The term "in storage" is vague, assumes that the librarian has a "count" of total materials, and that the method for determining that count will be the same for all respondents.
23. Is the library equipped with enough map cases to house the volume of maps it will select from GPO during the next two years? (answered by yes/no/doesn't select maps)	The question assumes that the librarian knows how many maps will be selected and how many fit into a map case, and that the selection of items producing maps will deliver the same number of maps over the two-year period.
26. What percentage of the depository documents is checked into a centralized record, such as a shelf list? (answered in 4 percentage categories between 0 and 100)	The term "centralized record" is unclear; there are numerous types of "centralized records," and many such centralized records for documents are simplified, or "partial," records and thus are not likely to be comparable.
30. What level of reference service does the library offer to all potential patrons? (answered by checking all categories that apply: no reference assistance; minimum directional assistance; reference queries answered or referrals made; and user privileges extended to all patrons)	Reference service cannot be provided to "potential" patrons; the definitions for "minimum directional" and "reference queries either answered or referrals made" are vague and unclear; the quality or success in answering questions becomes confused with the doing of the activity; and the response "reference queries answered or referrals made" are two different choices within the same response.
33. Is documents reference service available? (answered by all hours library is open; same as general reference; fewer hours than general reference; or more hours than general reference areas)	The term "reference service" is likely to be widely interpreted, i.e., if someone is at the reference desk, is that providing reference service? It does not allow for the answer, "No reference service is provided."
34. Is there adequate professional and non-professional staff for the operation and maintenance of the depository collection? (answered by yes; only for technical services; only for public services; and no)	No criteria are suggested to determine what is adequate or what is inadequate (the rubber yardstick problems). The question seeks information on *two* areas, i.e., professional and non-professional staff; if the library believes it has adequate professional staff but inadequate non-professional staff, how can it reply accurately?

data analysis should be simple and straightforward. At present, data are presented too simply and straightforward, and are not comparable.

The degree to which the data are comparable is an important consideration. Comparable data are those which

- are defined, collected, and analyzed in the same manner by all those providing and using the data
- provide standardized or indexed measures within similar depository types, e.g., academic depository library total budget *per users in the service area*[6]
- can be examined as trend data over time, i.e., the definitions, administration, and analysis techniques are the same for each *Biennial Survey*

Further, data should be comparable (1) among the various type of depositories; (2) among the various surveys that are administered; and (3) by the individual library over time.

In addition to problems related to widely different interpretations of the questions—which injure comparability—some of the questions in the survey tend to vary over the years, are worded differently, or are eliminated altogether. For instance, question 22 on the 1983 *Biennial Survey* asks

> Is the library equipped with enough microfiche cabinets or boxes to house the volume of microfiche *it will select* [authors' emphasis] from the GPO during the next two years?

However, question 38 on the 1981 *Biennial Survey* asks

> Is the library equipped with enough microfiche cabinets or boxes to house the volume of microfiche *it would like to select* [author's emphasis] from the GPO during the next two years?

Responses from these two questions cannot be compared because one queries about the microfiche that the library *will* select, while the other asks about microfiche it *would like to* select; these are two entirely different questions.

The lack of comparability among the information produced from the *Biennial Survey* severely minimizes the degree to which the survey can be

---

[6] Standardization of performance measures simply means that the measures include factors which produce a scale comparable to other settings. For example, by assessing the linear shelf space available in an academic depository library, in terms of total student enrollment (linear shelving per student), academic depository libraries can better compare their *relative* shelving capacity. See Zweizig and Roger (1982) and Kantor (1984) for additional information on this topic.

used as input for decision making, planning, and evaluation over time. Further, as a basis for either developing data collection instruments or national guidelines, or standards, for depository library services, non-comparable data are misleading at best and disastrous at worst. This non-comparability, then, also limits the relevance of the *Biennial Survey* as well as its sufficiency.

Sufficiency

Indicators of sufficiency include validity, methods of data analysis and presentation, and completeness (see Figure 6-2). The concept of validity has already been introduced in this chapter and descriptions of both internal and external validity were presented. Internal validity is closely associated with the degree to which measures actually represent or describe the activity or things being studied. Thus, measurement can be seen as the process by which numbers are assigned to describe or represent some object or phenomenon in a standardized manner (Kaplan, 1964, pp. 172–178).

The developers of the *Biennial Survey* have provided minimal information about the "measures" which are used and tend simply to report frequency counts for the various questions. Because *measures* apparently have not first been determined, users of the *Biennial Survey* are left to decide for themselves if variables are, in fact, indicators of a measure. Clearly, the users of the surveys require a listing of appropriate measures and definitions for how those measures are to be put into operation in terms of the various questions.

For example, a measure of interest to many documents librarians might be "publicity." Question 51 asks, "In a five-day period, how many hours were spent on tours, bibliographic instruction, presentations, publications, exhibits, or other publicity for documents?" The concern, in terms of validity, is the degree to which this question actually measures the activity described as "publicity." Questions 44–47 ask for the number of directional questions, reference/research questions, database reference questions, and referrals given. Do these questions intend to measure the extent of *reference services?* In short, little thought appears to have been given to the *measures* in the survey; thus, when survey readers assume the measures, their assumptions may not be valid.

Numerous questions on the 1983 *Biennial Survey* do not appear valid as measures for an activity or phenomena. For example, question 51 lacks validity as a measure of "publicity" because

- data are based on a sample of a "five-day period" during August or September (in this case, 1983), a time of year *least* likely for publicity programming for many libraries

- the question did not explain if the publicity was to be initiated only by documents staff or if it involved other library staff
- the question assumes that the number of hours (time) engaged in the listed activities comprise an accurate measure of the extent to which publicity is offered
- the question ignores the cost for these activities, the number of people contacted by such activities, the impact of the publicity on its intended audience, and the *quality* of the publicity activities

Thus, the question makes a number of assumptions about how the activity, "publicity," should be described. Conducting similar analysis on other questions would show that the validity of other "measures" which the *Biennial Survey* seeks to address is limited.

As previously noted, the 1983 *Biennial Survey* marked the first time that depository librarians were asked to provide data based on a sampling process. The poor administrative guidelines and procedures which were developed for this data collection process severely reduced the reliability of the data. In addition, the validity of the data, or the degree to which they can be generalized to the subgroups of the population such as those reported in Chapter 4, is limited.

The problems with the sampling process used by the GPO for questions 43–65 have been previously discussed, and an assessment of the value of the information resulting from them has been termed as "useless" (Morton, 1984, p. 198). While the sampling process severely injured the validity of the data, consumers who read and attempt to make sense out of the printed results are not likely to know that the sampling process (an important criterion of validity) defied generally accepted research procedures.

Another concern about the *Biennial Survey* relates to is its completeness, or the scope or degree to which the information covers necessary topics and phenomena. Since the *Biennial Survey* is incomplete, it is insufficient in two major areas. First, the topics covered are "inputs," or resource related, and, second, the survey fails to provide information on the "quality" or effectiveness of the reporting depositories, e.g., their ability to accomplish specific objectives. Both of these limitations are significant.

In recent years the library community has moved away from relying on descriptive data which only measure inputs.[7] Yet, the majority of questions on the *Biennial Survey* for 1983 describe inputs, or resources: percentage of items selected, titles purchased, microfiche readers available,

---

[7] Examples of this trend are best seen in a number of publications and policy statements issued by the American Library Association, Public Library Association (ALA-PLA). See, for example, "National Standards for Public Libraries: A Discussion Paper" (ALA-PLA, May 1984).

etc. Such information is not sufficient for depository libraries because it represents data already available to many of them.

Further, this emphasis on input- or resource-oriented data does not inspire confidence about the effectiveness of the GPO's internal data collection process. Questions having to do with the percentage of items selected, claims, titles purchased, etc., should be easily obtained from *in-house* GPO records and depository libraries need not be burdened with reporting the same information. Thus, the GPO should be able to eliminate a number of those questions and simply supply the depository libraries with a summary report of the depository's activities during the past year.

The emphasis on inputs removes attention from the collection of more important data related to the quality or effectiveness of the depository program. Thus, not only is the *Biennial Survey* insufficient in describing a depository library and the depository program, it is also misleading by covertly linking quantity of resources (inputs) to quality of services (outputs). Simply because certain resources are obtained or are present in the library *does not* insure that appropriate activites and objectives are being accomplished.

As an example, questions 44–47 ask for the number of directional questions, reference/research questions, database reference searches, and referrals given during the sampling period. Providing ten referrals per day is an indicator of *activity*, not of quality or effectiveness. It is possible that each of those referrals was to incorrect or inappropriate sources. Yet, there is an underlying sense when reading through the various questions that providing more (of whatever—be it referrals, microfiche, or titles) is better.[8]

Depository librarians need less data which describe their library in terms of inputs and require more data on the effectiveness or quality of the results, or outputs, of their collection and services. The national move toward the development and reporting of performance measures is indicative of this new awareness (Zweizig and Rodger, 1982; Kantor, 1984). Further, the effort and time that it takes to report on all the various inputs related to the collection (many of which the GPO should already have available) takes precious time away from efforts that could be made toward collecting data that could be used for the development of performance measures.

Finally, it should be noted that an indicator of sufficiency is the degree to which the data are analyzed and presented to users in an appropriate

---

[8] An underlying assumption of the depository library program is that "public access" can be equated with the number of participating libraries in the program, i.e., the larger the program and the more publications deposited in the libraries, the better the access. Research from a broad range of studies related to public access to government information challenges this simplistic assumption (Hernon and McClure, 1984, pp. 6–10).

format. On this criterion, the Biennial Survey fails dismally. Generally, the format by which the results of the survey are made available is a computer printout or a microfiche copy of the printout. Further, the analysis of the data is rudimentary and only provides frequency counts and percentages.

No attempt is made to provide correlational analysis to determine *relationships* or possible relationships between the variables; sophisticated statistical analyses that include analysis of variance, regression analysis, or tests of significance are not provided; and there is no attempt to interpret the findings or relate the results to other data on the depository library program. Indeed, the manner of data presentation and distribution is woefully inadequate, and only with individual effort can users (1) obtain original copies of the printout summary sheets or (2) use the microfiche version of the data summaries.

This lack of sufficiency for the information resulting from the *Biennial Survey* affects other areas as well. For instance, because the data are resource oriented and do not describe the quality of services, the information is of limited value as input into the planning process (*not relevant*). And because many of the questions on the survey have limited validity, they cannot be compared (*not understandable*). In addition, this insufficiency has created a group of "uncommitted record keepers," i.e., depository librarians, who are beginning to believe that the *Biennial Survey* is simply not practical, given the espoused benefits.

Practicality

The criterion of practicality suggests (1) the degree to which the information is collectable, accessible, timely, necessary, and appropriate, and (2) the degree to which benefits of the collection outweigh the collection costs. It can be argued that much of the data *required* to complete the *Biennial Survey* is accessible. Further, copies of the *Biennial Survey* results are sent to depository librarians and copies can be requested directly from the GPO. However, the *ease* of that accessibility is another question and a number of depository librarians have voiced some concern about the simplicity with which the information based on sampling, for example, was obtained (Morton, 1984).

Accessibility of the data can also be considered in terms of acquiring the original computer tapes of the survey data files. In a letter from the Superintendent of Documents dated April 12, 1984, it was noted that the data files of the 1983 *Biennial Survey* can be made available from the GPO at a cost of $55 per tape. However, the letter also noted that the GPO Data Systems Tape Library maintains a two-year retention schedule for such tapes, and thus "the 1981 file is no longer available," nor, one would assume, are any of the tapes for the previous Biennial Surveys (DiMario, 1984). Disposal of these tapes *eliminates* the possibility of access unless copies were purchased prior to the retention date limit.

The timeliness of the information can be considered from at least two perspectives. The first relates to whether data were collected in a timely fashion, that is, whether the actual data collection took place during the designated time period. On this criteria there is some concern since during the fall of 1983 a note was attached to a depository shipment list indicating that some 250 depository libraries had failed to complete and return their *Biennial Survey* questionnaire. Further, the actual times of the data collection could have varied significantly between August and October 1983, and such differences would have a significant impact on the data that called for sampling. For instance, an academic library which responded to the sampling questions in August is likely to have decidedly different results from one that responded in October simply because it was not practical for the latter to do the data collection in August or September.

At a second level, the timeliness of the information can be considered in terms of when the results are made available. Although computer printouts which summarize the data were available on request and for a fee directly from the GPO in late spring 1984, general distribution and availability of the survey results were not provided as late as one year after the collection of the data. Thus, the timeliness of the information as input for decision making and planning is indeed limited.

Another criterion for practicality is the degree to which the information is perceived as necessary or appropriate by users of that information. Although there is little formal evidence to present in this area, it can be suggested that discussions by the Government Documents Round Table (GODORT) Statistics Task Force, American Library Association, clearly question the necessity and appropriateness of the information collected from the *Biennial Survey* ("Statistics Task Force Minutes," 1984, p. 31). Further, practicing depository librarians have begun to disagree formally with the necessity and appropriateness of the information in terms of its ability to assist in planning and decision making (Morton, 1984).

These considerations, as well as additional ones discussed under the categories of relevance, reliability, understandability, and sufficiency, suggest that the benefits resulting from the *Biennial Survey* do not compensate for the costs (both direct and indirect) of

- depository librarians maintaining appropriate records, obtaining the data (through the sampling process, for instance), organizing the necessary data, and reporting that data on the survey form

- GPO officials developing, administering, and analyzing the data resulting from the survey

An additional cost which should also be considered is that related to time and resources spent preparing and gathering data for the *Biennial Survey*. Depository librarians might use their time more productively to provide services and resolve user information needs, while GPO officials develop improved goals, objectives, policies, and procedures related to the depository library program.

In short, the *Biennial Survey* includes direct as well as indirect costs (costs associated with *not* being able to accomplish other activities). The GPO places all significant labor, service, and materials costs associated with the 1983 *Biennial Survey* at $37,923.50. Figure 6-5 represents a breakdown of costs and shows that they are not insignificant. Given the analysis of the *Biennial Survey* presented here, the "benefits" (if they could be listed) probably would not outweigh the costs.

An Untapped Resource

As currently administered, the *Biennial Survey* has little value as an aid for decision making, planning, and evaluation While GPO officials might argue that the data collected assists them in having a better understanding of the depository library program, depository librarians receive little benefit from the process. Further, there is little formal evidence that the GPO does, in fact, have formal mechanisms for utilizing the data derived from the *Biennial Survey* or rely on it for policy development and assessment.

Judged against its stated purposes, the 1983 *Biennial Survey*, as currently administered does not (1) "determine whether publications are being used [by the depositories] to the best advantage of the American Public," (2) "provide depositories with meaningful statistics which will enable them to draw conclusions about services in their libraries," nor will it (3) "provide the GPO with an accurate picture of conditions in depositories," which would (4) "be helpful in administering the Depository Library Program."

The continued "charade" of data collection and analysis that generally fails to meet recognized criteria for reliability, validity, and utility encourages

- an attitude on the part of GPO and JCP officials that they *really* are collecting useful data
- loss of credibility in the overall process and in the importance of data collection among depository librarians

Figure 6-5. GPO's Costs Associated with the 1983 *Biennial Survey* Project*

Activity	Hours	Materials/ Salary Costs
1. Preparation: reviewing survey literature, writing questions, making changes, responding to librarians' letters and phone calls on sampling techniques	63	$ 756.00
2. *Typing:* original text, by secretary	3	22.50
3. *Proofreading:* galley and page proofs	1	12.00
4. *Printing:* 1500 booklets		524.00
5. *Duplicating:* answer sheets, fact sheets, definitions; 1500 copies = 6000 sheets @ $8 per 1000 Return envelopes @ $10 per 1000	3½	48.00 35.00 15.00
6. *Mailing:* first class mail @ $.69 per envelope in postage; stapling answer sheets, collating, stuffing envelopes Manila envelopes @ $37 per thousand	36	966.00 216.00 55.00
7. Opening return envelopes, verifying, batching for FPI, xeroxing for JCP Committee Print	48	336.00
8. Data Systems support computer costs: Programming, testing program, edit report corrections, producing corrected tape, etc. (DSS charges @ $29.35 per hour)		28,646.00
9. Services of Technical Support Group analyst through project	200	2,900.00
10. Original keystroking of responses plus producing tape for edit report by Federal Prison Industries ($1 per response)		1,300.00
11. Proofreading and correcting edit report printouts	120	1,4000.00
12. Producing microfiche silver masters @ $.75 per sheet (24 masters)		18.00
13. Generating 1475 diazo duplicates for depository libraries		550.00
14. Quality control of diazos	1	7.00
15. Distributing fiche in the line to the libraries	½	5.00
16. Refiling the *Biennial Survey* into depository administration master files	16	112.00
Total:	492	$37,923.50

* The figure includes all significant labor, service, and materials costs (Letter, DiMario, August 1984).

166

- greater difficulty at a later time to institute data collection reforms since depository librarians will have been "conditioned" about the futility of such efforts
- erroneous and misleading decision making, planning, and evaluation for those individuals who rely on data from the *Biennial Survey*
- little likelihood that depository librarians and government officials can justify the importance or benefits of the depository library program since poor empirical evidence is available to support specific arguments or positions

Thus, the *Biennial Survey* as currently administered may be causing greater harm than good.

The roots of the problem lie in the lack of clear guidance for what the *Biennial Survey* is to accomplish, other than simply to collect data. Further, no formal mechanisms take the data and integrate them as input for decision making, planning, or evaluation, at either the federal, state, or local library level. The data collected from the instrument have minimal reliability, validity, or utility, and the GPO fails to report to the users of the data the degree of reliability and validity of those data.

Although "good" survey research (like any type of research) is difficult to conduct and time consuming, there simply is no excuse for the poorly constructed questionnaire that is administered to the depository libraries every two years. Numerous texts explain how questionnaires can be constructed and administered to insure accuracy (e.g., Berdie and Anderson, 1974; Busha and Harter, 1980; and Swisher and McClure, 1984). And numerous texts explain the rudiments of statistical analysis and data presentation techniques (e.g., Jaeger, 1983; and Roscoe, 1975). Until the administration of the *Biennial Survey* is based on standard practices of survey research, it will not have reliability, validity, utility, and thus has little value for decision making, planning, and evaluation.

Interestingly, Title 44, the *U.S. Code*, specifies that the GPO has the legal responsibility to obtain information about the depository library program and that "the designated depository libraries shall report to the Superintendent of Documents at least every two years concerning their condition" (44 *USC* 19:1909). Yet a review of the percentage responses on individual questions from the 1983 *Biennial Survey* suggests that at least 100 to 125 depository libraries either did not return the survey or returned the survey and did not answer the questions. Assuming the lack of responses from 100 of the approximately 1,373 depository libraries, about 7% of the depository libraries failed to fulfill their statutory obligation to "report to the Superintendent of Documents...concerning their condition." One wonders what, if any, remedial actions are taken by the GPO in such instances.

Despite these "failures," the fact remains that the mechanism is in place for the administration of these Biennial Surveys, that the surveys will continue in the future, and that unless drastically improved, they will continue to provide information of limited value. Since the manner in which the data collection process is to be done, as described in Title 44, the *U.S. Code,* is left largely to the imagination of the GPO, there is ample opportunity for improvement, *without having to obtain additional legislative guidelines.* As long as the statutory obligation is present for some form of data collection to take place, every effort should be taken to improve *immediately* the reporting process and increase the usefulness of the resulting information.

Chapter 7

Provision of Information for Improved Depository Library Program Decision Making

The information environment in which the depository library program competes is complex and contains many players. If the program, and thus, the depository libraries are to compete effectively as providers of government information, they must establish appropriate goals and objectives, obtain the necessary resources to accomplish those objectives, implement the most effective programs and activities in light of these objectives, and market the importance, benefits, and services provided by the program. All of these activities require an information base for decision making and planning.

In addition, future success of the depository library program will depend on the degree to which the mission of the program is clarified, distinguished, and politically supported vis-à-vis other federal government information services; on the ability of JCP and GPO officials and depository librarians to work together, constructively, toward the resolution of critical issues and policies related to the collection, organization, distribution, and access of government information; on the degree to which new technologies can be exploited throughout the program to enhance public access to government information; and on the ability of government officials, depository librarians, and other key players related to the depository library program to more effectively utilize existing resources and marshal additional resources for improvement and change in the program.

Throughout these processes, provision of timely, reliable, and valid information as a basis for decision making is essential. Indeed, in the highly politicized arenas of federal information policy even the use of accurate, timely, and understandable information as a basis for decision making may be inadequate because political agendas frequently play an important role in any decision-making process. However, if depository librarians, JCP and GPO officials, and other supporters of the depository library program cannot present their position and *support it* from a strong basis of factual evidence, their position will be weakened.

This conclusion is supported by the continuing efforts of the Reagan administration to limit access to government information, to "privatize" the federal information dissemination programs, and to weaken the structure of the GPO as a primary disseminator of such information (Stokes, 1984; and Abrams, 1983). Despite this *political* philosophy of the Reagan administration, it must be said that, as a group, supporters of the depository library program (regardless how much they might disagree on specific policies of the program) have been poorly equipped to present strong evidence in support of their positions, to justify the need for better resource allocation, or to counteract political diatribe with empirical information.

Depository librarians and other interested information specialists outside the Washington, D.C., area must recognize the highly politicized setting of federal decision making—especially in an area such as information acquisition and distribution (Hoduski, 1982). Equally, JCP and GPO officials must recognize the institutional and organizational constraints typically encountered by depository librarians as they attempt to provide access to government information. Although the perspectives from these two primary groups (GPO and JCP officials and depository librarians) are different, *both* have requirements for information (1) describing the depository library program, (2) assessing the degree of "success" of the program and each library's involvement in that program, and (3) evaluating specific aspects of that program to justify changes in policy and procedures.

In short, the success with which the JCP and GPO can improve the depository library program is linked both to how well they "play the political game" in the federal governmental milieu *and* present evidence to support its various positions and proposals for change. But the success with which the political game is played is often linked to how well a government agency has developed empirical evidence which supports its position. Clearly, the degree to which such evidence exists for the depository library program is limited. Thus, a primary activity that must be enhanced by all is the establishment of a reliable and valid information database which describes and evaluates the depository library program. Such a database is mandatory for documenting the activities of the program, justifying its existence, and determining the degree to which objectives and performance measures are met.

The purpose of this chapter is to suggest specific strategies to improve the information basis for decision making related to the depository library program. Although numerous topics can be used as a vehicle to discuss these strategies, the exploitation of the *Biennial Survey* process will be stressed as a means to accomplish this objective. Despite the political complications of effecting change in the federal government, the authors believe that success in intra-governmental politics between the GPO and other agencies can be significantly improved with empirical evidence which supports proposals for change. Further, the *Biennial Survey* has great potential as a mechanism to provide data necessary for portions of such an information system.

The Context for Establishing a Decision Support System (DSS)

The term decision support system (DSS), which has been introduced relatively recently, has been defined as "a category of information systems used in organizations to assist managers in semi-structured decision processes" as opposed to the more routine and programmed decisions (Akoka, 1981, p. 131). An effective DSS supplies accurate and timely information to decision makers in an individualized format and answers not only basic factual questions but also the "what if. . ." type of question. Typically, it is interactive with the user and provides for immediate exchanges between the user and the system (McClure, 1984a).

If a DSS is to be established for the depository library program, it must be based on a philosophy inherent in notions of information resources management (IRM). IRM recognizes the overall importance of organizational information process and the impact of individuals who utilize information for both strategic planning and decision making. It is based on the assumption that "information is a valued resource in the organization and should be managed in a similar manner as we manage human, fiscal, material, and natural resources" (Marchand, 1982, p. 59). Specific objectives for a program of IRM include (Levitan, 1982, p. 237)

- establishing an environment where only relevant information flows into organizational decision making
- encouraging the practice of comparing costs and creating or collecting information with projected benefits derived from its use
- analyzing organizational requirements *before* acquiring information
- establishing staff training and educational programs regarding information acquisition, evaluation, organization, and dissemination
- making depository librarians responsible for their information production by including them in information systems design and making them accountable for resources needed to produce the needed information
- including information management considerations during the establishment and operation of organizational tasks on a routine basis

Without these philosophical underpinnings, the establishment of a DSS system is not likely to be successful.

Statutory Considerations

Responsibility for federal government IRM and, thus, departmental or agency development of a DSS for the depository library program is confused at best and is outside the scope of this chapter.[1] Suffice to say, that recent factors such as the Paperwork Reduction Act of 1980, the increased role of the Office of Management and Budget (OMB) in federal information policy development, and legal challenges to the authority of the GPO to serve as a central distribution point for depository and other government information (Zagami, 1985), to name a few such factors, have muddled the bureaucratic waters for responsibility in areas of IRM.

Despite interagency political squabbles and turf protection, the statutory basis of the authority for the JCP and the GPO to administer a *Biennial Survey* appears to be clear and straightforward. Title 44, *U.S. Code*, section 1909, states that "the depository libraries shall report to the Superintendent of Documents at least every two years concerning their condition." Since there is no additional information on this point, the method by which the reporting is to be done and the criteria by which the depository's "condition" is to be described, is to be determined by the GPO. Further, as shown in Chapter 1, precedent has established the regular use of the *Biennial Survey* as the primary means by which this reporting has been done.

In addition, the JCP has oversight responsibility for the GPO and its statutory authority as set forth in Title 44, *U.S. Code*, section 103: "the Joint Committee on Printing may use *any measures it considers necessary* [authors' emphasis] to remedy neglect, delay, duplication, or waste in the public printing and binding and the distribution of government publications." Given these two statutes, there is ample opportunity for the GPO (with the encouragement and support of the JCP) to design, extend, and improve decision support services via the *Biennial Survey*.

GPO Information Systems Development

In recent years, the GPO has given some attention to the development of information systems to support activities related to the depository library program (McClure, 1982a, pp. 270–272). In 1984, Dennis R. Chastain, Deputy Director, Data Systems Service, GPO, indicated that "there are fifty-seven separate data systems of varying complexity currently operational in GPO with another twenty-five under development" (*Administrative Notes*, June 1984, p. 9). However, in the context of a DSS, the

---

[1] A useful overview of IRM in the federal government can be found in Levitan (1982, pp. 240–244).

degree to which these various information systems have the potential to support *strategic planning and decision making* directly is unclear.

The system with the greatest potential for decision support appears to be the Federal Documents Data Base (FDDB). The proposed requirements for the system are impressive and will produce more than sixty major output products, many of which have a potential for decision support (*Federal Documents Data Base: Detailed Functional System Requirements*, 1983, vol. 1, section IV). This decision support is planned to have two primary parts, an operational support system (information on daily in-house GPO activities), and a bibliographic database available to all users. Other features of interest for decision support include electronic messaging among depository librarians, provision of depository library profiles, and information about the distribution of materials to depository libraries ("Federal Documents Data Base: A Conceptual Summary," 1983).

But the implementation of the FDDB appears (as this is written, in the fall of 1984) to be questionable at best. Chastain has expressed a "number of concerns" having to do with "availability of personnel resources, accommodating to conflicting priorities within the GPO..., handling the appropriations and procurement process..., and developing a realistic phased implementation" (*Administrative Notes*, June 1984, p. 10). Under "ideal conditions" the FDDB could be in place by late 1987, but it is not likely that "ideal conditions" will prevail until after that date. In the meantime, continued reliance on the less than effective Depository Distribution and Information System (DDIS) is likely.

A formal review of the various GPO information systems is beyond the scope of this chapter, but one critical point needs to be stressed. Most of the information systems currently being developed by the GPO are intended to provide *operational* support as opposed to *decision* support, i.e., control over daily operational procedures rather than information structured to support decision making, evaluation, and policy assessment. Further, creating automated systems is *not* the same as creating systems which produce decision support information (Lancaster, 1983) or which are designed *specifically* as management information systems (Rush, 1984). And despite the breadth and potential of the FDDB, and assuming that it can serve as a basis for a DSS, GPO officials and depository librarians remain with poor quality descriptive information about the depository library program.

Enhancing the Biennial Survey Program

Given the breadth of existing statutory authority, the inadequate development of a GPO information system that provides accurate and timely descriptive information about the depository library system, and the needs of GPO officials and depository librarians for such descriptive information, expansion and redesign of the Biennial Survey process appears to be a viable proposal because

- the administrative mechanism to collect and analyze data from the *Biennial Survey* is already in place
- depository librarians are required by law to report on their condition and, by precedent, this reporting has been accomplished via the *Biennial Survey*
- establishment of a DSS based on *Biennial Survey* data can be integrated into other GPO information systems (such as the FDDB) at a later time
- compared to the establishment of broad-based multipurpose information systems (such as the FDDB) establishment of a DSS based on the *Biennial Survey* data would be significantly less expensive

In short, a significant improvement can be made in the provision of descriptive information about the depository library program immediately, with minimal costs, under existing statutory authority, and with maximum benefits for a broad number of constituencies—including librarians, government officials, and users.

However, the redesign of the Biennial Survey process calls for a number of changes—of which the revision of the actual survey instrument along guidelines suggested in Chapter 6 is only the beginning. Of primary importance is the establishment of a rationale to explain why specific types of information will be collected. Four such functions that should be considered as a basis for collecting information for strategic planning and decision making are (Brown, 1982, p. 190)

- *reducing ambiguity by providing an empirical basis for decision making:* empirical information reduces uncertainty, provides a validity check on intuition and values, and forces assumptions to be stated openly
- *providing intelligence about the environment:* information about the GPO's and depository library's environment is essential to (a) evaluate the current status of member libraries; (b) identify opportunities; (c) isolate objectives consistent with those opportunities; and (d) define activities for the depository library program which fit into the environmental milieu
- *assessing historical, current, and future states:* information about the past, present, and predictable future gives a basis for weighing the strengths and limitations of the depository library program; the difficulties not withstanding, prediction is *essential* to the design of any possible future activities

- *evaluating process and monitor progress:* evaluation data should monitor progress towards measurable objectives; remedial actions can only be taken when as assessment has shown what, specifically, requires attention and has identified the variables associated with the activity under consideration

Based on these functions, information from four critical areas requires attention for effective planning and decision making: the environment; specific target groups, markets, or clientele; resources; and programs, activities, and objectives (Ibid).

The *Biennial Survey,* as currently devised, neither addresses these four functions nor collects information in the four specific areas. Indeed, the philosophical base of the various surveys, specific objectives for what each is intended to accomplish, a rationale for why specific types of data are to be collected, and a statement for how users of the survey are expected to profit from it have not been considered, or at least publicly reported. Nonetheless, the value of the *Biennial Survey* for support of strategic planning and decision making can be enhanced considerably.

Specific Recommendations

The possible structures, formats, administration techniques, and methods for data analysis from the *Biennial Survey* are unlimited, and ultimately, the designers of a DSS based on that survey must decide what is to be included, how it is to be administered, and to what purposes the data will be used. The suggestions offered in this section are intended to provide a first step toward the constructive development and improvement of the process so those data which have reliability, validity, and utility can be used as a basis for planning, evaluation, and decision making. These suggestions are not comprehensive, nor are they given in any specific order of importance. They do, however, suggest that a number of steps can be taken to improve the quality and the usefulness of the data from a *Biennial Survey* process.

Survey Goals, Objectives, and Research Questions

Careful consideration should be given to specifying the overall goals of the survey as well as detailing specific objectives. Why is the survey done? What are the expected results? How are the results to be used and by whom? The purposes of the 1983 *Biennial Survey* (see Chapter 6) are vague and contradictory and until goals and objectives are established and clarified, the survey will continue to produce few tangible results.

Goals and objectives provide a *general guide* for administering a survey, but research questions give *specific instructions* for which variables will be investigated (Swisher and McClure, 1984, pp. 46–47). Administrators should be able to list a set of research questions intended to be answered from the survey *prior* to the administration of the survey. For example:

- has the composition of member libraries changed since the last survey?
- has the percentage of items selected by depository libraries, within specific Sudocs class numbers, changed during the last two years?
- what is the relationship between the staffing of depository libraries and the quality of the services provided?
- what are the demographic characteristics of users of the depository library program and how do they differ among the various types of depository libraries?
- what are the characteristics of those depositories that relinquished status?

None of these research questions can be answered by the existing survey process. The first calls for trend data (presentation of data over time); the second asks to determine the relationship between two variables—one of which calls for the establishment of a *measure* (quality of service); and the third requests information on a topic (users) currently ignored in the survey.

Insuring the Quality of the Data

The need to collect and produce quality data detailed in the previous chapter and specific criteria for insuring the quality of the data were summarized in Figure 6-2. Overriding concerns of reliability, validity, and utility *must* be addressed and specific strategies incorporated in the administration of the survey and its analysis to insure that these and other criteria listed on Figure 6-2 are met.

Further, users of the survey must be given assurances about the degree to which the data are, in fact, reliable and valid. Use of appropriate statistical techniques as well as methods to *verify* the accuracy of the data are absolutely essential with self-reported data such as those collected by the survey. GPO administrators of the survey have a responsibility to the researchers and users of the data as well as to taxpayers, to justify the value, importance, and accuracy of the survey and its findings.

Expanding the Research Design and Methodology

Although it is understood that the *Biennial Survey* is likely to continue as a survey, a number of different research designs can be incorporated within that process. For example, in the 1983 *Biennial Survey*, the GPO experimented with the use of conducting a study of selected activities based on a sample of observations. Although the process as administered was badly flawed, there is great potential to increase the utility of the survey by use of such techniques—assuming they are done correctly.

Additional designs to be considered include, for instance, unobtrusive and obtrusive testing. Recent research has shown that unobtrusive testing is a powerful instrument in studying government publications reference service (McClure and Hernon, 1983). Unobtrusive analysis can also be used to study the use of the collection, equipment, and even technologies such as online searching and microforms. Increasing the reliance of reported data in the survey from designs that do not require self-reporting but are based on actual observations (e.g., obtaining selected data from the inspection process) would significantly improve the quality of the data.

Another area where attention is needed is in the design of survey instruments which are administered to carefully selected *samples*, in much the same manner as census data are collected by the Bureau of the Census. Thus, additional questions could be included and more information could be obtained by stratifying the sample and including "special" questions to a selection of the depositories. Thus, there could be various forms of the survey instrument, some with 100% questions and others with 20% or 10% sample questions.

Finally, it can be suggested that the design techniques for the data collection can include the opportunity for the individual depository libraries to collect and report specific data elements which *they* believe are appropriate for their specific situation. The GPO, then, would simply provide analyses of those data elements *for that particular library* and not compare them to other libraries. Further, the Depository Library Council, professional associations such as the Government Documents Round Table of the American Library Association (ALA-GODORT) might design additional data elements believed to be important and recommend that they be included in the survey. In short, the survey design needs greater flexibility to allow individual participation and specialization—both to improve the quality of the data and to increase individual library commitment to the use of the data.

Reassessing the Topics to be Covered in the Survey

As pointed out in Chapter 6, the current *Biennial Survey* stresses inputs or resources. Careful reconsideration is needed to determine the broad areas that should be covered by the survey as well as the specific variables (and measures) that need to be collected. Earlier in this chapter four broad areas for strategic planning and decision making were noted:

- the environment
- specific target groups, markets, or clientele
- resources
- programs, activities and objectives

Currently, the *Biennial Survey* collects information primarily on resources and, on a limited basis, programs and activities.

Special attention should be given to collecting data elements and providing information on variables and measures needed by depository libraries for *their* departmental and organizational decision making. Data on salaries, linear feet of shelving or cabinet space, and performance-related criteria having to do with the ability of the depository to accomplish predetermined objectives (among others) are necessary. Topics covered in part by the sample questions on the 1983 *Biennial Survey* need to be expanded and the method for their collection/analysis improved. Further, the GPO could obtain direct input from the depositories about what *specific* data elements are needed as part of a pretest for future surveys.

A broad range of information currently is ignored surrounding the depository library program. No composite picture can be produced depicting the nature and characteristics of depository clientele, limited information is available on environmental factors affecting depository library service, and the *Biennial Survey* provides no information that describes GPO activities, resources, or clientele. Indeed, the need for descriptive information about the activities, resources, programs, and clientele of the GPO depository libraries is especially apparent (e.g., see Chapters 3 and 4). The existing data collected from the depository libraries relate to the activities and resources of the GPO, but these activities and resources are not considered when *Biennial Survey* data are analyzed and reported.

For example, data from the depositories about item selections, titles obtained, microfiche selected, etc., *must be* assessed in terms of what the GPO made available during that year; problems related to depository use of GPO cataloging tapes must be considered in the context of the percentage of GPO resources allocated to tape development; or the number of claims submitted by depository librarians may be related to personnel allocations within the GPO. In short, information needed for decision support of the depository library program must have a wider scope than is currently provided; it *must* relate information about depository libraries to a number of other topics—including users, the GPO, and outputs or results of the depository program.

Finally, it should be noted that the printed results from a *Biennial Survey* do not have to be limited *only* to the data requested from the survey instrument. As pointed out in Chapter 6, much internally produced data and data obtained from the GPO would be of interest to users of the survey data. Other GPO information systems could be incorporated into the database from which the *Biennial Survey* results would be prepared. Such a strategy would increase the breadth of the information made available for depository library program decision making, without additional data-reporting responsibilities falling on depository librarians.

Establishing Performance Measures

The use of the descriptive data provided by the Biennial Surveys is limited because they do not indicate the outputs from the depository library program or the program's effectiveness. Although it is nice to know that 75% of the respondents believe that there is adequate professional and paraprofessional staff for their depository (*Depository Library Biennial Survey for 1983*, 1984), such *descriptive* information says nothing about the *quality* of the services, the degree to which depository library program *objectives* are accomplished, or the degree to which user *information needs* are resolved.[2]

To exploit the use of performance measures and insure that data from the survey will be reported so that performance measures can be computed, the following general steps need to be taken:

- clear and measurable objectives have to be established for both the depository library program and the individual depository libraries
- a set of performance measures must be agreed upon, data elements for these measures defined, and methods to collect the data detailed and made available to participating depository libraries
- the data elements needed to compute the performance measures should be reported via the *Biennial Survey* or another appropriate method
- during the computer analysis of the data reported from the survey, the performance measures for both the depository program as a whole, and for the individual depository libraries, are to be computed and reported
- the results from the computation of the performance measures are to be used as a basis to reassess the degree to which objectives are accomplished

---

[2] The lack of performance measures is symptomatic of larger problems having to do with the need for meaningful depository library program goals, restating the points specified in the *Guidelines for the Depository Library System* as objectives, and the apparent limited concern on the part of the GPO about what actually happens to depository publications and how they are used and accessed *after* receipt by the depository libraries.

This process is feasible, and a number of state library agencies are currently in the process of developing data collection procedures as outlined above. Further, a number of performance measures have been developed which can be easily adapted for use in the depository library program or by depository libraries (Zweizig and Rodger, 1982; Kantor, 1984; and McClure, 1984b). In addition, a summary of thirty-one library performance measures (many of which can be adapted for use by depository libraries), with descriptions of their data elements, can be found in McClure and Reifsnyder (1984).

The benefits resulting from the use of performance measures and the inclusion of data elements on the *Biennial Survey* to compute those performance measures include

- indicating the degree to which depository library program objectives and individual depository library objectives are accomplished
- allowing comparison of the performances of depository libraries to each other
- providing a basis for both the depository library program and individual depository collections to *justify* their services and demonstrate the *benefits* resulting from their activities
- assisting the GPO and the depository libraries to determine which services and activities should be supported and which could be eliminated
- encouraging *direct* patron input about the program or a depository library
- providing meaningful data useful to administrators, governing boards, and elected representatives in assessing the depository program outside a purely political context
- encouraging the use of long-range planning since performance measures are used in the planning process

Performance measures have already been developed which can be modified for depository library use, the GPO already has in place a data collection and analysis process, documentation exists on how performance measures can be computed and administered, and there is a clear need for the production of data with the above benefits. The question remaining is, "Why have the GPO and depository community not moved to include the use of performance measures in the *Biennial Survey?*"

Expanding the Data Analysis

Currently, improved use of data analysis techniques and the employment of appropriate statistical procedures will *not* improve the quality of the data since the data have limited reliability and validity. However, once the data collection instruments are improved and acceptable levels of reliability and validity established, the GPO must do a better job of analyzing the reported data in terms of (1) presenting correlations between, and among, variables; (2) computing performance measures; (3) providing trend data on selected variables and statistics; (4) reporting coefficients of the reliability and validity of the data; and (5) providing more detailed breakdowns of data by type of libraries or by other criteria.

An example of the inadequate detail and description provided with the 1983 *Biennial Survey* summary can be seen in the results for questions 43–73 which provide only an "average count," but no frequency information by categories. The average count of 1,212 is given for question 56, "How many titles were purchased from GPO?" But what were the range, median, and standard deviation? What percentage of respondents had 0–500 purchases as opposed to 501–1000 purchases? In terms of additional breakdowns, what was the average number purchased by academic libraries as opposed to public or law school libraries? These and other questions calling for greater detailed analysis of data and cross-tabulation of results among different variables cannot be determined from the current summary data.

Another example of where additional analysis is needed has to do with relationships between variables. An example of such an analysis might be correlating results from question 43—"How many library patrons used the documents department?"—with results from other questions:

- 66: how many professional staff work with documents?
- 67: how many clerical, support staff, and student aides work with documents?
- 71: how many microfiche readers are available for users of documents?
- 26: what percentage of depository documents is checked into a centralized record, such as a shelf list?

If, for instance, there was a significant relationship between patron use (question 43) and percentage of documents checked into a centralized record (question 26) depository librarians would have an indicator for *explaining, understanding,* and possibly *predicting* why things happen the way they do. An example of the format for the resulting correlation table for this analysis is given in Table 7-1.

The type of analysis suggested here is simply a chi square test of association between two categorical variables. Although such a test does not explain cause and effect, it does test for correlation between two variables. Further analyses are needed to assess the correlation between one variable and numerous variables. Statistical procedures, such as analysis of vari-

Table 7-1. Example of a Correlation Table*

Size of Library Holdings, (i.e., title count of non-government publication (question 14)	Length of time person coordinating depository activities has been in that position (question 28)		
	more than two years	between 1 and 2 years	less than one year
Less than 10,000			
10,000–100,000			
100,001–500,000			
500,000 or more			

* NOTE: This table would show a *cross-tabulation,* e.g., the number of depository libraries with holdings of 100,001 to 500,000 where the person coordinating the collection has held that position for less than one year; it could also compute a *correlation coefficient* (such as a chi square statistic) to indicate if there is a relationship between the size of the library holdings and the time a person has been coordinator of the depository collection.

ance, can be used in such instances but require more reliable and valid data than currently exists. Using the above questions as examples, an analysis of variance might indicate that 20% of the variance attributable to depository use comes from the number of professional staff assigned depository responsibility, 16% from size of the general collection, 12% from number of microfiche readers owned, and so on. Knowing this, depository library administrators wishing to change depository performance could then concentrate their attention on variables where the data analysis has shown the greatest variance.

A detailed listing of all the shortcomings of the data analysis techniques is beyond the scope of this chapter. But the lack of reporting the number of missing cases for a specific variable, indicating whether the data are based on the total number of respondents to the survey or the total number of responses to the question, and explaining why some percentages do not total 100% suggests a very naive approach to data analysis. Clearly, the current procedure of providing *only* frequency counts and percentages is inadequate and does not assist decision makers to *explain, understand, interpret,* and *predict* as a result of the data.

Standardized Data Element Definitions

An important and significant movement in library/information science during recent years has been the effort to standardize the definitions of data elements used to describe and report libraries and library activities.

The data elements used on a GPO survey must be (1) clearly defined, (2) used consistently each time administered, (3) appropriate for the unique situations of depository collections, and (4) defined as closely as possible to other national standards.

Success in this area will be difficult because of the general lack of attention government documents-related statistics have received from the two primary players in this area, the National Center for Educational Statistics (NCES), which conducts the Higher Education General Information Survey (HEGIS) and the Library Survey, and the American National Standards Institute (ANSI), which recently published standard ANSI Z39.7-1983, "Library Statistics."[3] Both of these agencies have been criticized for inadequate attention to data elements, statistics, and reporting techniques for government publications (Morton, 1984).

Nonetheless, any national survey or data collection effort by the GPO must take into consideration the issues and problems related to a standardized set of data elements and definitions. While it is certain that there will always be disagreement and controversy regarding any set of standards, the new ANSI standard Z39.7-1983 can provide a basis from which statistics on government publications can be developed and expanded. Indeed, this area of standards development is one in which leadership is critically necessary and the GPO, NCES, ANSI, and professional associations such as ALA-GODORT must work together to design standards which are feasible, appropriate, meaningful, and useful.[4]

Including Multisource Data

While it is essential that the GPO improve and redesign its efforts to establish a national reporting system and decision support system for information about the depository library system, numerous other data collection efforts related to the depository library program should be included in the system. Currently, there is little cooperation between government agencies in the development, coordination, and sharing of information resulting from various surveys about the program. Secondly, data from different agencies are often duplicative, non-comparable, and, apparently, contradictory at times. And finally, access to the individual data tapes from

---

[3] Additional information about ANSI standards can be obtained from the American National Standards Institute, 1430 Broadway, New York, NY 10018. Additional information about NCES data collection activities can be obtained from the National Center for Education Statistics, Statistical Information Office, 400 Maryland Avenue, NW (Brown Building, Rm 606), Washington, DC 20202.

[4] Despite the title "Minimum Standards for Depository Library System" as adopted October 22, 1976, and published with the *Guidelines for the Depository Library System* (1977), these "standards" for the depository library program are seriously flawed and are of little utility.

these surveys is difficult, and in the case of the GPO, the data tapes from previous Biennial Surveys are retained only for two years before destroyed.

As an example, three significant surveys of government documents depository libraries/librarians were done in 1983–1984 by the federal government: the *Depository Librarians' Views on GPO's Administration of the Depository Library Program* (GAO, 1984); the *Provision of Federal Government Publications in Electronic Format to Depository Libraries* (JCP, 1984); and *Depository Library Biennial Survey for 1983: U.S. Summary* (1984) and *Depository Library Biennial Survey for 1983: U.S. Summary by Library Type* (1984). Further, the National Center for Education Statistics has produced summary data about government publications holdings in college and university libraries (NCES, 1984). Four different federal agencies conducted four different surveys, and none of the data from one can be analyzed directly with or against data from the other surveys. This is an incredible waste of money and resources.

These four surveys were *major* efforts on the part of the federal government to obtain survey data about the depository library program; other data collection efforts took place during these two years as well. A host of private surveys, such as the one reported in this book, were done by individual researchers and institutions, and additional survey instruments were sent to depository libraries by the GPO on item selection and other topics related to the depository library program.

Assuming the production of reliable and valid data from these surveys, their usefulness would be greatly enhanced if the data were available in one decision support system related to the depository library program. Further, researchers would have access to an important source of information to assist in the study of the depository library program. Once again, a leadership stance is necessary from within both the federal government and the documents library community to make certain that multisource data about the depository library program are captured, reported, and coordinated for strategic planning and decision making.

Reorganization for Collecting Depository Library Program Statistics

Badly needed is a "Center for Depository Library Program Statistics," to coordinate the administration and data analysis of official surveys. Such a center could significantly reduce the total costs for conducting the various surveys related to the depository library program; it could maintain full-time, specially trained researchers and statisticians to conduct the surveys; and the overall usefulness and quality of the survey data could be greatly improved. A potential home for such a center includes a number of possible federal agencies, libraries, schools of library/information science, private research and development firms, or perhaps even professional associations.

Since establishment of such a center at the federal level might require an additional legal basis, immediate improvement of the *Biennial Survey* could be done simply by creating an office within the GPO headed by personnel trained in research methods and statistics, with specific responsibility to administer, analyze, and report information related to the *Biennial Survey*. The priority currently given to the administration of the *Biennial Survey* is apparent in the poor quality of the product, the apparent lack of resources allocated to its administration, and the apparent limited statistical and research competency of staff who work with the survey.

This issue of having adequate staff at the GPO with research and statistical skills is a critical one. The GPO must move to hire individuals with such skills, train existing staff in this area, or obtain such competencies by bringing in outside consultants. The apparent lack of such skills helps to explain the agency's poor performance in the area of survey research as well as other areas of research and evaluation. There is simply no excuse for the GPO to be administering such surveys without staff specially trained in research skills.

Improving Summary Reports

The summary reports from the Biennial Surveys do not qualify for use of the term "report"; it is ironic that the Government Printing Office (with general responsibility for the production and marketing of federal publications) does not produce a summary report in a format that lends itself to use. In truth, the results from the surveys are simply copies of computer printouts and are best described as a question-by-question frequency count of the responses.

The results are not distributed as a "report" with a title page, introduction, summary, and explanation of the data; indeed, they are not marketed and packaged attractively, nor are they widely distributed. Given the existing format and contents of the *Biennial Survey* results, one can easily understand why they are generally ignored. Numerous strategies can be used to enhance the format and contents of the summary so that the report is readable and usable, and so that it provides an accurate representation of the data contents.

Organization of Material

Logical organization and presentation of the material in the summaries are essential. A typical scheme for presenting summary data reports is presented in Figure 7-1. The manner in which the summary is presented can vary, but as currently made available *there is no organization* of

Figure 7-1. Typical Organization of a Report of Survey Data*

TITLE PAGE

TABLE OF CONTENTS

INTRODUCTION

- purpose of the study and study objectives
- description of the data collection process
- assumptions and limitations of the study
- discussion of the reliability and validity of the data

PRESENTATION OF RESULTS

- introduction to how the presentation is organized
- appropriate tables, graphs, figures, and description

SUMMARY OF FINDINGS

- overview of the findings
- relation of findings to other similar studies or surveys

ANALYSIS OF THE SURVEY

- interpretation of the findings (what do they mean?)
- recommendations for what should be done as a result of these findings

APPENDICES

- copy of the survey instrument used for this study
- other items as appropriate

NOTES

BIBLIOGRAPHY

- sources/references referred to in the body of the report
- sources/references for additional information

INDEX

* NOTE: In the summary "reports" of the Biennial Surveys none of the above sections are included except one labeled "Presentation of Results," which is poorly done and provides only elementary presentations of frequency counts and averages.

material. Badly needed is an introduction to the data to explain the method by which the data were collected, the definitions used for the data categorization, and the assumptions and limitations under which the data were collected.

Without such an explanation, the use of the data is extremely limited. For example, the summary from the 1983 *Biennial Survey* analyzes academic libraries as "small, medium, and large," but there is no explanation by the data about how these terms are defined—rendering any meaningful interpretation of the data virtually impossible. Further, the guidelines and procedures for the sampling process (such as they were) from which data for selected questions were based are not included in the summary. Thus, readers are not aware of (1) the fact that some data are based on sampling; (2) the means by which the data were collected; or (3) limitations of the data.

Other elements of content, such as the inclusion of a copy of the actual survey instrument as an appendix, and of an index to the various information given in the summary; organization and presentation of the data by *topics* rather than by question; and the inclusion of notes and/or bibliographic citations to related sources of statistics on the depository library program, beg for attention in the summary.

Format

The format of the summary data, once again, defies all rules for clear, concise, and understandable data analysis and presentation. Research has shown that the format in which information is presented has an independent effect on decision-making facilitation (Bybee, 1981, p. 364). In other words, an unattractive, hard-to-read, disorganized, and incoherent summary is not likely to assist in decision making. Further, the format of the data presentations should be individualized for specific target audiences, e.g., different data presentations (from the same data) for depository libraries, the JCP, and library administrators. Designing the formats of the presentations to meet the needs of specific audiences will make the summaries much more useful.

For example, the national summary and the analysis by library types as presented in the 1983 *Biennial Survey* are both essential. But of significant benefit for individual depositories would be an analysis and summary report of findings just for each depository. Huge potential benefits could result from customizing the content and format of such reports. Provision of individual scores on performance measures, trend data, and analysis on request of key areas of interest to the depository are only a beginning. Such reports would be of significant assistance to the individual regionals and depositories for strategic planning and decision making.

Tables and Graphics

The question-by-question presentation of data does not lend itself to easy readability and comprehension. The summary report should include data presented in tables, figures, and other graphic presentations that assist in the understanding, comparison, and application of the findings. For example, the printed findings for question 14, "Other than government documents, approximately how many volumes does your library contain?", from the 1983 *Biennial Survey*, were reported as[5]

14	1.1%	(A)	10,000 volumes or less
251	19.6%	(B)	Between 10,001 and 100,000 volumes
703	54.8%	(C)	Between 100,001 and 500,000 volumes
308	24.0%	(D)	500,001 volumes or more

Graphic techniques such as bar graphs and pie charts, such as those shown in Figure 7-2, can be used to provide a visual representation of these same figures. Based on even these "simplistic" data representation techniques, a breakdown by library type could be presented for the last three *Biennial Surveys*. Clearly, graphic techniques can be used to enhance the readability of a document.

Correlation tables which provide information on the *relationship* between two variables and offer a *breakdown* of information about one variable in terms of the second are also needed. For example, the information in the preceding paragraph about the holdings of depository libraries could be correlated against data from question 28, "How long has the person coordinating depository activities been in that position?", in a correlation matrix table (see Table 7-1). The use of such tables allows easy presentation and understanding of the data and significantly improves the methods by which the data were analyzed, by providing (1) tests of significance between the two variables, (2) cross-tabulation of variables, and (3) clues to *explain* why certain activities occur the way they do in the depository library program.

Another data presentation technique which would be of great assistance to readers of the summary is trend data. Trend data allow the reader to see how a specific variable has, or has not, changed over time. Currently, the data summaries do not compare results to previous Biennial Surveys. If reliable data were available that indicated the average number of FTE paraprofessional staff working in academic depository libraries were[6]

1979	3.5
1980	3.2
1981	2.8
1982	2.7
1983	2.7

then the data could be presented as a trend line graph such as that shown in Figure 7-3.

---

[5] Interestingly, the response categories from the 1983 *Biennial Survey* on this question are different from those on the 1981 *Biennial Survey*. Thus, direct comparisons and the production of trend data cannot be made.

[6] These figures are imaginary and used only for purposes of example.

Figure 7-2. Example of Bar Graph and Pie Chart Data Presentation

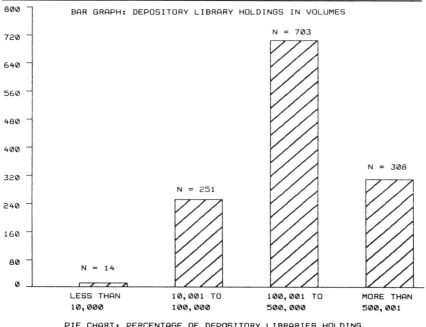

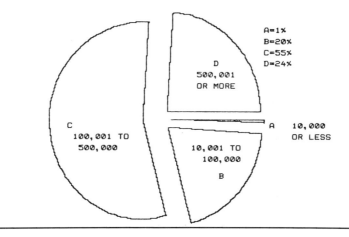

Such presentations can take on increased meaning when the trends for additional variables, such as average number of depository library users per day, are superimposed on the graph. Indeed, by "trending out" variables over specified time periods on the same graph, a much better understanding of the data and their *possible* relationship to other data can be obtained. Unfortunately, none of these data representation techniques

Figure 7-3. Trend Data: Paraprofessional Staffing
1979–1983

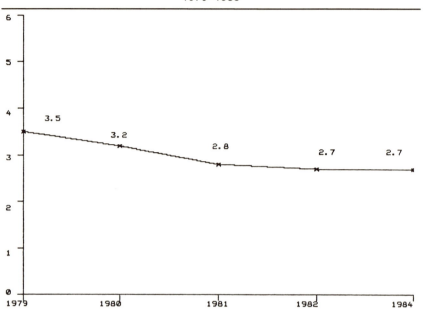

(e.g., data matrices, pie charts, trend graphs, and bar graphs) are used in the summary "reports." The GPO need look no further than such publications from the Bureau of the Census as *Social Indicators* (1980) for examples of how data can be presented graphically for increased readability, understandability, and usefulness.

Since the data are already in machine-readable format and most of the major statistical analysis software programs (e.g., SAS and SPSS)[7] include methods for graphic presentation of data, the reasons for *not* incorporating these data representation techniques are unclear. The complexity of producing such graphics is minimal, to say the least, and usually calls for one or two additional commands in the program or, on interactive software programs, simply hitting a few more keys on the computer terminal. In fact, the graphics presented in Figures 7-2 and 7-3 were produced from a microcomputer software program which cost under $70! Inclusion of graphics to describe and explain the data from a *Biennial Survey* would significantly improve the utility of the data.

[7] SAS information and manuals are available from the SAS Institute, Inc., P.O. Box 10066, Raleigh, NC 27605; and the various manuals for SPSS are published by McGraw-Hill, New York, NY.

Interpretation of the Findings

Noticeably missing from the printouts is a verbal summary of the data which relates the data to similar data, explains the *meaning* of the findings, or attaches an *interpretation* to either the data or the findings. In fact, the primary difference between the term "data" and the term "information" is that "information" typically is organized into some meaningful framework, is placed in a context for the reader, and has been assessed by the issuing body about what meanings and/or interpretations can be attached to the findings.

Interestingly, the three major reports issued by the GAO, the JCP, and the GPO during 1983–1984 regarding the depository library program have minimal explanation, interpretation, or assessment of what the data mean. For example, the report *Depository Librarians' Views Concerning GPO's Depository Library Program* (GAO, 1984), has a brief two-to-three sentence summary of the results from each question, but there is no overview or general assessment of what the survey determined—or to state it another way, there is no discussion of the "so what?" question explained under the criterion of utility in Chapter 6.

Of the three reports, *Provision of Federal Government Publications in Electronic Format to Depository Libraries* (JCP, 1984) makes the best effort to attach meaning to the survey data and does offer specific recommendations for what to do based upon the findings. However, the bulk of this, as well as of the other two survey summaries, is a page-by-page printing of the responses to individual questions with little sophisticated data analysis, explanation of the data, integration of data from one question to another, or relation of the data to other survey instruments.

If time and expense are to be committed to administering a survey describing the depository library program, it is essential that the analysis of the data includes a discussion of what the data mean, how they can be interpreted, and what specific recommendations can result from knowing these findings. Despite the possibility for political interpretations of the data by the various federal agencies responsible for the publication and distribution of the reports, inclusion of an overview, an assessment, an interpretation, and recommendations is essential if the summary is to have utility for strategic planning and decision making.

Online/Interactive Access to the Database

One of the most important aspects of a decision support system is its interactive nature, i.e., the user can communicate directly with the system. Currently, the information from the Biennial Surveys is made available once every two years, and there is no opportunity for users or potential users of the information to access it directly unless they purchase the most recent data tapes from the GPO and load or program the tapes themselves. If the data are to have value for users, they must be accessible *on demand* in much the same manner as information is made available for strategic planning and decision making at Pikes Peak Regional Library District (Dowlin, 1984).

Although the depository library program has been described as a "system" and as a "network," its ability to cooperate and coordinate efforts to accomplish specific objectives, thus far, have been limited (Hernon and McClure, 1984, pp. 299–313). But such a network is in fact possible, and important steps toward that goal have been taken with the development of the FDDB information system by the GPO. Electronic messaging and online access to management information for improved planning and decision making as part of the "network" are technically feasible. The primary difficulties appear to involve the inability of the various stakeholders to agree upon what should be done, how it will be done, who is to be responsible for its development, and from where adequate resources to pay for the system will come.

A Design for Increased Administrative Effectiveness of the Depository Library Program

This book has provided a historical introduction of the depository program and the development and use of the Biennial Surveys; a presentation of summary data about the depository library program that includes a descriptive analysis of specific subgroups of depository libraries (including those relinquishing depository status); an analysis of the quality of the data collected and reported from the *Biennial Survey;* and specific suggestions and recommendations for how survey data describing the depository library program can be enhanced for strategic planning and decision making.

Until a carefully developed plan for better collection, analysis, and presentation of depository library program descriptive data is established and implemented, the decision-making ability of the GPO and other federal government officials, librarians, and others interested in improving the depository library program will be severely reduced. Further, the disjointed, poorly administered, and unreliable descriptive data currently available about the depository program severely limits our ability to improve the program, justify the need for changes, and counteract political policy that may negatively impact the success of the program.

The ongoing administration of private surveys to obtain data about the depository library program (such as the one reported in this book) is evidence that a number of researchers, depository librarians, and others find the descriptive data available from the GPO to be inadequate. Yet the reality is that without adequate fundings, surveys such as the one presented in this book will be infrequently administered and can be seen only as stopgap measures to fill the void left by the GPO in the provision of descriptive data about the depository library program.

The severe weaknesses with the current Biennial Survey process, however, are only part of a larger issue having to do with questions of the effectiveness with which the depository library program is operated. Table 7-2 is a summary of *major* problems analyzed by these and other authors in recent years that require immediate attention. Critical depository library program problems related to inadequate access to government information, no meaningful goals and objectives, an ineffective depository inspection plan, and non-exploitation of information-handling technologies, to name a few, require immediate attention.

Table 7-2. Summary of Selected Major Problems with the Depository Library Program and Sources for Recommendations to Resolve Those Problems

Problem	Sources
1. Inadequate goals and objectives for the depository library program	Hernon and McClure, 1984
2. Need to restructure the depository library program	McClure, 1981; Hernon and McClure, 1984
3. Ineffective collection development	Hernon and Purcell, 1982
4. Inadequate regulations and statutory basis for the depository library program	Hernon and McClure, 1984; McClure, 1984d
5. Poor quality of GPO Cataloging tapes	Myers, 1983; Myers, 1985
6. Ineffective depository library inspection program	Hernon and McClure, 1984
7. Inadequate *Biennial Survey* and need for a decision support system	Hernon, McClure and Purcell, in this book (1985); Morton, 1984
8. Poor quality of reference and referral services from depository libraries	McClure and Hernon, 1983
9. Limited exploitation of technology by the GPO and depository librarians	McClure, 1982a; McClure, 1981
10. Inadequate education and training for government documents librarians	Hernon and McClure, 1984; McClure, 1984c
11. Flawed development of state plans which do not comprise a valid plan or planning process	McClure and Hernon, 1983; Hernon and McClure, 1984

It is important to note that many of the sources listed in Table 7-2 offer *specific* recommendations for how depository librarians, JCP and GPO officials, library administrators, and others interested in the depository library program can take action to improve the program. Although each of these recommendations has been published since 1981, one is hard-pressed to find examples of instances where tangible improvements and changes have been affected for the problems listed in this table.

At the root of many of these problems is the lack of accurate, reliable, and timely information that can be used as a basis for improved strategic planning and decision making. Thus, the need for a decision support system that incorporates access to a broad range of depository library information (in addition to data from the *Biennial Survey*) is interactively linked to decision makers and users of the depository library program. It also provides specific and detailed support for *both* GPO and depository library strategic planning, decision making, and evaluation of services.

In short, during 1981–1984, evidence has been published indicating that the *Guidelines for the Depository Library System*, the inspection process as well as the inspection form, the *Biennial Survey*, the state plans, and the use and production of GPO cataloging tapes (to list a few of the more important topics) are seriously flawed. And although numerous specific recommendations have been offered (such as those in this book related to improving the *Biennial Survey*) corrective action from the GPO has been limited at best.

In recent years, a number of dedicated, concerned, and enthusiastic supporters of the depository library program have spent considerable personal effort and time in providing assessment, suggestions, and recommendations for improvements in the depository library program (see Table 7-2). For whatever reasons, the JCP, the GPO, the Depository Library Council, and ALA-GODORT have been unable to effect significant change to improve the effectiveness of the program. This reality, considered within the current Reagan administrative policy efforts to reduce public access to government information and hobble an already ineffective GPO, does not bode well for the success of the depository library program.

One approach to take is the funding of a retreat where selected representatives from the JCP, the GPO, depository librarians, researchers, and others interested in the success of the depository library program could meet and develop an "agenda" of specific steps to be taken to improve the program. This suggestion has already been articulated (Hernon and McClure, 1984, pp. 419–420), but to date, no action on it or most of the other recommendations offered in Table 7-2 has been taken.

Thus, individuals in support of improving the effectiveness of the depository library program are faced with a dilemma. As with the *Biennial Survey*, much of the structure is in place whereby many of the problems with the depository library program can be significantly improved. But continued identification, analysis, and offering of recommendations to resolve these problems which are then ignored by the GPO force the individuals into a state of apathy or into taking actions that encourage *external* federal controls and assessment to improve the depository library program. A significant problem with the later strategy, especially in these times of Reagan information policies, is that such a position can be interpreted as additional evidence to dismantle and impede the program further, rather than improving it and enabling it to accomplish its statutory purposes.

Clearly, the "ball is in the court" of the Joint Committee on Printing, the Government Printing Office, and members of the depository community. The specific recommendations offered in this book regarding the design and improvement of the Biennial Survey process are important not only to improve the survey itself, but also to provide a decision support system which would significantly assist in providing adequate information to resolve the problems listed in Table 7-2. With the improved quality of descriptive data about the depository library program, increased access to that data by decision makers, the formal design and implementation of a decision support system related to the depository library program, and well-articulated goals and objectives, an informed basis for strategic planning, decision making, and policy development to improve the depository library program can be realized.

Appendix *A*

Biennial Report of Depository Libraries (October 1983)

Depository Library Number _____

UNITED STATES GOVERNMENT PRINTING OFFICE
WASHINGTON, D.C. 20401

OFFICE OF THE
PUBLIC PRINTER

Report Series No. 17

October 1983

BIENNIAL REPORT OF DEPOSITORY LIBRARIES

The Superintendent of Documents under the direction of the Public Printer is charged by Title 44, U.S. Code, with responsibility for administration of the Depository Library Program.

Current statute governing the Depository Library Program requires all designated Depository libraries to report to the Superintendent of Documents every two years. The purpose of this report is to determine whether the publications are being used to the best advantage of the American public. The Superintendent of Documents uses this report as a means of obtaining other information which is helpful in administering the Depository Library Program. The date is valuable in addition, for on-site inspections of Depository Libraries, which are performed as resources permit.

Newly designated Depositories are asked to complete this questionnaire even though they have recently submitted the six month "Check of Condition of Depository Libraries" (Investigation Series No. 4) which is designed especially for newly designated Depository libraries. Libraries inspected in the past two years are also required to complete this questionnaire.

The Biennial Report consists of several sections. Questions are grouped together according to subject. *All* Depository libraries are required to answer questions 1–42, 75–76. Follow instructions printed in *Administrative Notes,* vol. 4, no. 11, August 1983, for statistics collection, questions 43–74. An appendix with definitions is included. Please check all answers that apply to your depository. You may write your answers for your records in the booklet provided but please complete the answer sheet, and return only the answer sheet to the CHIEF, LIBRARY DIVISION (SLL), U.S. Government Printing Office, 5236 Eisenhower Ave., Alexandria, VA 22304 not later than November 15, 1983. A pre-addressed franked envelope is enclosed for your convenience. Please be sure to use it.

Depository Number _____

GENERAL INFORMATION

1. State the depository library number_____

2. State the full name and *mailing address* of the depository library.

   Name_____

   _____

   Address_____

   _____

   City/State_____ Zip Code_____

3. State the address to be listed in the Joint Committee Print *Government Depository Libraries (Street address)*

   Address_____

   _____

   City/State_____ Zip Code_____

4. State the name and title of the person in charge of the library.

   Name_____

   Title_____

5. State the name and title of the person coordinating depository services.

   Name_____

   Title_____

6. Give the area code and telephone number where the coordinator can be reached.

   Area code_____ Telephone number and extension _____

7. Give the area code and telephone number the general public can use for documents reference service.

   Area code_____ Telephone number and extension _____

2

197

8. Is the library's address and telephone number listed correctly in the Joint Committee on Printing's Joint Committee Print (98–1) *Government Depository Libraries*, revised May 1983?

_____(a) YES   _____(b) NO

9. DOES THIS LIBRARY WISH TO CONTINUE AS A DEPOSITORY? (IF THE ANSWER IS "NO", IT IS NOT NECESSARY TO COMPLETE THE REMAINING QUESTIONS ON THIS FORM. RETURN THE SURVEY IMMEDIATELY.)

_____(a) YES   _____(b) NO

10. When was the depository collection last inspected?

_____(a) 1983   _____(f) 1978
_____(b) 1982   _____(g) 1977 or earlier
_____(c) 1981   _____(h) It has never been inspected.
_____(d) 1980
_____(e) 1979

11. Does the library feel it needs to be inspected within the next year?

_____(a) YES   _____(b) NO

12. Is the depository a:

_____(a) Selective depository
_____(b) Regional depository
_____(c) Full depository (the depository receives 100% of the items available but is not a Regional)

13. Is the library primarily:

_____(a) Academic general   _____(f) court
_____(b) Academic law   _____(g) Federal agency/department
_____(c) Academic sci/tech   _____(h) Public
_____(d) Academic medical   _____(i) State library agency
_____(e) Historical society or museum _____(j) Other

14. Other than government documents, approximately how many volumes does your library contain?

_____(a) 10,000 volumes or less
_____(b) between 10,001 and 100,000 volumes
_____(c) between 100,001 and 500,000 volumes
_____(d) 500,001 volumes or more

INSPECTION INFORMATION

15. Who can gain access to the depository documents? (Check all that apply)

_____(a) Anyone can gain access to the material
_____(b) Special procedures are required for those without an appropriate library card
_____(c) This library is for a special clientele therefore patrons are often asked to use other depositories or get a letter of reference
_____(d) Other

3

198

16. Is there a charge for patrons to gain access to the library(ies) in general?
_____(a) There is a fee for a library card, which is required to gain access to the library
_____(b) There is a fee for a library card, but it isn't required for a patron to use the depository documents
_____(c) There is no charge for a library card or to use documents.
_____(d) Other

17. Is the depository material accessible to the public during all regular hours?

_____(a) YES _____(b) NO

18. What percentage of the depository collection is in storage?

_____(a) Between 75–100% _____(d) Between 10–24%
_____(b) Between 50–74% _____(e) Between 1–9%
_____(c) Between 25–49% _____(f) None

19. Does the library keep accurate and accessible records in the documents area which indicate what materials are in storage? (Check only one.)

_____(a) YES _____(b) NO
_____(c) Nothing is in storage

20. How long does it take to retrieve materials in storage?

_____(a) Doesn't apply, nothing is in storage
_____(b) Within a day of the request
_____(c) Within a three-day period after the request
_____(d) Other

21. Does the library have enough shelf space to house the volume of hard copy documents it will select from GPO during the next two years?

_____(a) YES _____(b) NO

22. Is the library equipped with enough microfiche cabinets or boxes to house the volume of microfiche it will select from GPO during the next two years?

_____(a) YES _____(b) NO

23. Is the library equipped with enough map cases to house the volume of maps it will select from GPO during the next two years?

_____(a) YES _____(b) NO _____(c) Doesn't select maps

24. How frequently are item selections reviewed to consider collection development needs?

_____(a) Semiannually
_____(b) Annually
_____(c) Every two years
_____(d) Longer than a two-year interval
_____(e) Doesn't apply (Regional)

4

25. Does the library review its depository collection on an annual basis so that documents retained for five years or longer can be discarded?

_____(a) YES
_____(b) NO, there is no Regional, so the library cannot dispose of documents
_____(c) NO
_____(d) This library chooses to keep most materials for historical or reference purposes
_____(e) Doesn't apply because this library is a Regional or federal government depository

26. What percentage of the depository documents is checked into a centralized record, such as a shelf list?

_____(a) 75–100%   _____(c) 25–49%
_____(b) 50–74%   _____(d) 0–24%

27. What percentage of documents is cataloged by the library?

_____(a) 75–100%   _____(c) 25–49%
_____(b) 50–74%   _____(d) 0–24%

28. How long has the person coordinating depository activities been in that position?

_____(a) More than two years   _____(c) Less than a year
_____(b) Between 1–2 years   _____(d) There is no one in that position

29. Does the documents staff need more training in the handling of documents and their use?

_____(a) YES   _____(b) NO

30. What level of reference service does the library offer to all potential patrons? (Check all that apply.)

_____(a) No reference assistance
_____(b) Minimum directional information
_____(c) Reference queries either answered or referrals made
_____(d) User privileges extended to all patrons

31. Does the library have adequate facilities and equipment to serve handicapped library patrons?

_____(a) YES
_____(b) NO
_____(c) NO, but measures are underway to correct problems

32. How are documents in a series checked in? (Check all that apply)

_____(a) Kardex (visible file)
_____(b) Shelf list
_____(c) Online system
_____(d) Most series are not checked in, except for periodicals
_____(e) Most series are not checked in, item number records are kept
_____(f) Most series are not checked in anywhere
_____(g) Other

33. Is documents reference service available?

_____(a) During all hours the library is open
_____(b) The same as the general reference areas
_____(c) Fewer hours than in the general reference areas
_____(d) More hours than in the general reference areas

5

34. Is there adequate professional and non-professional staff for the operation and maintenance of the depository collection?

       _____(a) YES, there is adequate staff
       _____(b) Only for technical services
       _____(c) Only for public services
       _____(d) NO

EQUIPMENT SURVEY

35. Is there a computer(s) in your library? (Check all that apply)

       _____(a) YES, a mainframe
       _____(b) YES, a minicomputer
       _____(c) YES, a microcomputer
       _____(d) NO, there is no computer in the library

36. Please describe the make and model of the computer(s) in your library.

       _____(a) Mainframe Make and Model_____
       _____(b) Minicomputer Make and Model_____
       _____(c) Microcomputer Make and Model_____
       _____(d) Microcomputer Make and Model_____

37. If your library does not have an on-site computer facility/terminal, is there a local computer facility that could receive electronic messages for your library? (e.g., campus computer center, government computer center, etc.)

       _____(a) YES
       Describe make and model
       _____

       _____(b) NO

38. Does your library have a terminal to access an outside computer?

       _____(a) YES
       Describe make and model of terminal and system accessed
       _____
       _____

       _____(b) NO

39. Are your terminals dedicated (i.e., limited to accessing an internal or local computer system or commercial database) or can they link with multiple networks?

       _____(a) Dedicated local terminal
       _____(b) Dedicated terminal limited to a commercial database (LEXIS, OCLC, etc.)
       _____(c) Multiuse terminal

40. Does your library subscribe to a telecommunications network?

       _____(a) YES, TYMENET
       _____(b) YES, TELENET
       _____(c) YES, UNINET
       _____(d) YES, Other. Specify_____
       _____(e) NO

41. Does your library have a teletype facility?

      _____(a) YES

      Describe make and model_____

      _____(b) NO

42. Does your library have telefacsimile equipment to receive and transmit printed material electronically?

      _____(a) YES

      Describe make and model_____

      _____(b) NO

STATISTICS COLLECTION

The following group of questions refer to the collection of statistics concerning reference and use of the collection. Your library should have kept statistics for a *five day period* to answer these questions. If you haven't collected data to answer these questions, please do so now. Write the total number for all five days in the space provided after the question. A worksheet for data collection was provided in *Administrative Notes,* vol. 4, no. 11, August, 1983.

43. If your library has a separate documents collection, how many library patrons used the documents department in a five day period?

      _____

44. In a five day period, how many directional questions were asked?

      _____

45. In a five day period, how many reference/research questions were asked?

      _____

46. In a five day period, how many database reference searches were done?

      _____

47. In a five day period, how many referrals were given?

48. In a five day period, how many items that the library selects were not available for use for which the library staff searched stacks and other locations?

      _____

49. In a five day period, how many interlibrary loan requests were sent out?

      _____

50. In a five day period, how many interlibrary loan requests were filled?

      _____

51. In a five day period, how many hours were spent on tours, bibliographic instruction, presentations, publications, exhibits, or other publicity for documents?

      _____

The following questions refer to data collected over a *one month* period. Worksheets for data collection were provided in *Administrative Notes,* vol. 4, no. 11, August, 1983.

52. Excluding legislative documents (classes X and Y), how many depository print pieces did your library receive over a one month period?

_____

53. Excluding legislative documents (classes X and Y), how many microfiche titles did your library receive over a one month period?

_____

54. How many paper maps did your library receive over a one month period through the GPO depository library program?

_____

55. How many individual claims did you submit to GPO's Library Programs Service?

_____

56. How many titles were purchased from GPO?

_____

57. How many titles were offered on exchange lists?

_____

58. How many titles previously offered on exchange lists were sent to other libraries?

_____

59. Besides superseded titles, how many documents offered on exchange lists were approved for disposal by the Regional and discarded?

_____

60. How many print pieces (excluding classes X and Y) were cataloged or are a continuation of a previous cataloged entry?

_____

61. How many print pieces (excluding classes X and Y) were included in a shelflist, serial check-in, or other locater file?

_____

62. How many print pieces (excluding classes X and Y) were not included in any record?

_____

8

63. How many microfiche titles were cataloged? (Excluding classes X and Y)

_____

64. How many microfiche titles were included in a shelflist, serial check-in, or other locater file? (Excluding classes X and Y)

_____

65. How many microfiche titles were not included in any record? (Excluding classes X and Y)

_____

These questions require previous gathering of statistics.

66. How many professional staff work with documents? (Add all the hours librarians spend with documents in a week and divide by 40 to arrive at a Full Time Equivalent number, e.g., 1.5.)

_____

67. How many clerical, support staff, and student aides work with documents? (Again, give the number of FTE.)

_____

68. How many volunteers work with documents? (State number in FTE.)

_____

69. How many seats are available for users of documents?

_____

70. How many microche readers are available to documents users?

_____

71. How many microfiche reader/printers are available to documents users?

_____

72. How many computer terminals are available to documents users and/or staff for searching files relating to documents?

_____

73. How many photocopiers, staffed and unstaffed, are provided on library premises for documents users?

_____

74. Does your library have a fiche-to-fiche duplicator that can be used to duplicate depository microfiche?

_____(a) YES _____(b) NO

9

204

USER PREFERENCES

75. Sometimes GPO receives a short supply of an item and distributes some copies in microfiche and some copies in paper. Which option would you prefer?

_____(a) Always receive paper when the item is short
_____(b) Always receive microfiche when the item is short
_____(c) Prefer a random system in which the library sometimes would receive paper and sometimes microfiche

76. Some items GPO distributes are printed in looseleaf format with a basic manual and periodic updates. If your library selects that item after the basic manual was distributed, would you prefer:

_____(a) To receive the updates and expect to purchase the basic manual
_____(b) Not receiving any updates until after the next basic manual was issued

10

DEFINITIONS TO BE USED FOR THE 1983 BIENNIAL SURVEY

The staff at the Library Division appreciates the many helpful comments and suggestions received about the collection of data for the 1983 Biennial Report. Here are some general comments and definitions which should clarify most of the problems.

Sampling schedule

The sampling schedule for use and circulation statistics should reflect one week's use of the collection. As in many libraries collecting circulation statistics, the sampling days are spread out over a 5-week period. If your depository has Saturday and Sunday hours, add the weekend hours into Friday's statistics as we are to collect data for one week's use.

Federal documents

The survey is only to reflect the use of Federal Government documents, not state, local, or international documents.

Number of users in the documents department

Only libraries with separate documents departments need to answer this question. As library users come into the department or call, count them.

Database reference searches

Count searches on databases such as OCLC or Biological Abstracts when the results yield document titles. Do not include OCLC searches when a cataloger is cataloging a document.

Referrals

The term referral pertains to referral to other libraries, state agencies, bookstores, and other institutions outside the library. Having other staff members help answer reference questions doesn't constitute a referral.

Items not available for use for which the staff searches stacks and other locations

Count only items that are included in the library's holdings but are missing, at the bindery, or circulating. Do not include items the library does not own.

Receipts

Exclude the line in which we requested a count of the *Number of Bills and Legislative Documents (Classes X and Y)*. GPO is able to track this information and it was included under the receipts category in error. Receipts are counted excluding legislative documents so that the number of items received can be correlated with items cataloged or shelflisted. (A definition of cataloging is included later in this article.) With regard to the number of microfiche, count titles, not pieces, and do not count legislative microfiche or print titles. You should be able to get your counts from shipping lists.

Acquisitions

Number of claims refers to claims submitted to the Library Programs Service.

With regard to items purchased from GPO Sales, count each subscription as one item and count items ordered, not items ordered and received.

Do not count superseded items as a part of the number of items disposed of. Do count items that were included in discard lists not selected by other libraries and approved for discarding.

11

Record Maintenance

For print pieces and microfiche cataloging statistics, include items for which a cataloged entry is included in a public catalog. A cataloged item will usually have more than one entry. If a series or serial title has previously been included in the public catalog, you may include that issue in the cataloging statistics.

When counting microfiche shelflisted or cataloged, count titles, not individual fiche.

Staffing

Include the number of hours non-documents librarians and support staff work with documents. (Ex., hours spent by catalogers and shelvers)

Include student aide time with clerical and support staff.

Equipment

Equipment refers to equipment accessible to documents staff and users.

If there are several OCLC terminals in the library, count OCLC only once.

Directional Questions

Questions that can be answered without using any reference sources other than schedules of staff, floor plans, handbooks or policy statements. Examples of this type of question include giving directions for locating departments within the library, current periodicals, etc.

12

Appendix *B*

Survey Questionnaire (Reported in Chapters 3 & 4)

Dear Depository Librarian:

We are currently surveying all GPO depository libraries in order to obtain basic descriptive information about the collection, servicing, and organization of depository collections. These data, along with other data collected from published sources, will be compiled into a book, to be published by Ablex Publishing Corp. of Norwood, New Jersey, and will provide the most current statistical profile of the depository library program. This profile will be of value to you, to the administrators of the depository program, and to the library profession in that it will furnish a wealth of comparative data to provide new insights and perspectives into the operation of the depository program.

Note that your depository library number is included on the questionnaire. This will be used to coordinate your response to other data which we have compiled. However, in the book, no library will be identified individually. Our analysis will be limited to a composite profile of depositories and, thus, your response will be held in confidence.

Please take a few moments from your busy schedule to complete the brief questionnaire and return it in the postage free envelope provided. Thank you for your cooperation.

Sincerely,

DEPOSITORY LIBRARY NUMBER_____   STATE_____

1. How does your library classify the depository collection: (CHECK ONE)
   a. SuDocs____
   b. Dewey____
   c. Library of Congress____
   d. Combination of these____
   e. Other (please specify)_____

2. Describe how documents are housed in relation to the rest of the collection: (CHECK **ALL** THAT APPLY)
   a. Most depository materials are in a separate department, or other unit of the library____
   b. Most depository materials are integrated throughout the library____
   c. Most documents are divided in different physical areas of the library____

d. Some documents are housed separately from other depository materials because of their format (e.g., microfiche or maps)____

e. A large percentage (20% or more) of the documents are housed in branches of the library system____

f. A large percentage (20% or more) of the documents are sent to one or more locations outside of the depository library (e.g., to other institutions)____

3. If the majority of documents is a) integrated, b) split among areas of the library, or c) sent to other institutions, what percentage remains in a separate collection: (CHECK ONE)

a. 41-50%____
b. 31-40%____
c. 21-30%____
d. 11-20%____
e. 1-10% ____
f. Doesn't apply because most documents are kept in a separate collection____
g. Doesn't apply because none are kept in a separate collection____

4. Does your library provide online bibliographic data base searching for U.S. government publications (e.g., through DIALOG, SDC, or BRS):

a. Yes____
b. No____

If "yes," is the terminal located in the: (CHECK ONE)

a. Documents Department____
b. General Reference Department____
c. Both____
d. Other (please specify)_____

5. Does the library use any of the following for its depository collection: (CHECK ALL THAT APPLY)

a. OCLC____
b. RLIN____
c. WLN____
d. Other bibliographic utility____
e. Purchase GPO tapes for local use____
f. Use computer for key word indexes to the documents collection____
g. Use computer for documents holdings file____
h. Other (please specify)_____

6. How many depository items do you currently select: (use the actual number from your latest GPO printout)_____

7. Do you select depository items in microfiche:

a. Yes____
b. No____

If yes, (CHECK ONE)

a. They are housed exclusively in the documents area____
b. They are housed exclusively in the central microforms area____
c. They are housed in both places____
d. Other (please specify)_____

8. Indicate the full-time equivalent number of staff members who work with U.S. government publications deposited by the GPO. (INDICATE NUMBERS FOR ALL THAT APPLY)

a. Professional_____
b. Para-professional_____
c. Clerical_____

d. Students_____
e. Other (please specify)_____

9. Is the library a depository for other federal agency publications programs: (CHECK ALL THAT APPLY)

   a. Census Bureau____
   b. Defense Mapping Agency (maps)____
   c. Department of Energy____
   d. Environmental Protection Agency_____
   e. Geological Survey (maps)____
   f. National Aeronautics and Space Administration____
   g. National Ocean Service____
   h. Patent Office____
   i. Other (please specify)_____
   j. None of the above____

Questionnaire for Defunct Depositories (Chapter 5)

Dear Library Director:

We are currently surveying the approximately 1,400 libraries participating in the depository program operated by the U.S. Government Printing Office in an effort to ascertain basic information about their collection, organization, and servicing of United States publications received on deposit.

A part of the study includes an analysis of those libraries which have terminated depository status. As your library was one of these, we would appreciate your taking a few minutes of your time to answer seven, brief questions. The information gathered will be of value to depository libraries and the library profession in that it will furnish a wealth of comparative data to provide new insights and perspectives into the operation of the depository program.

Please return the completed form in the enclosed, stamped, self-addressed envelope.

Sincerely,

FEDERAL DOCUMENTS DEPOSITORY SURVEY

1. Please estimate the percentage of depository categories that you received at the time that your depository status terminated?

    a. 85-100%_____   e. 25-39%_____
    b. 70-84%_____   f. 10-24%_____
    c. 55-69%_____   g. under 10%_____
    d. 40-54%_____

2. Please specify the number of people (both professional and clerical) who serviced documents when status terminated.

    Total:_____

3. Did you employ a full-time documents librarian?

    a. Yes_____   b. No_____

4. If you answered "yes" to question 3, what happened to the position?

5. In what year did your library become a depository?_____

6. Does your library still retain publications received on deposit?

    a. Yes_____   b. No_____

7. Please specify the reason(s) depository status was dropped (check as many options as apply).

   a. Documents can be acquired more easily through other sources (e.g., jobbers or congressional staff)____
   b. Documents were more easily obtained through institutional sources (e.g., interlibrary loan or the main library)____
   c. Library staff did not perceive government publications as comprising an important resource____
   d. Participation in the depository system was a financial burden____
   e. Since our collections are not intended for use by the general public, we could not accept the proviso that depository publications be available for such use____
   f. The government publications duplicated materials already received____
   g. The publications acquired were seldom utilized____
   h. The Superintendent of Documents terminated our depository status; we did not voluntarily relinquish it____
   i. We had severe space limitations____
   j. We lacked the professional staff to maintain the status____
   k. We lacked the support staff necessary to maintain the status____
   l. We thought that another library in the area was a better choice for depository status____
   m. Other (please specify)_____

   _____

Thank you for your participation.

Bibliography

Articles

Abrams, Floyd. "The New Effort to Control Government Information," *The New York Times Magazine* (September 25, 1983), 22–28, 72–73.

Akoka, J. "A Framework for Decision Support Systems Evaluation," *Information and Management* (1981), 131–141.

Armstrong, Ann and Judith C. Russell. "Public Access," *Information World*, 1 (October 1979): 1, 11.

Bower, Cynthia E. "OCLC Records for Federal Depository Documents: A Preliminary Investigation," *Government Information Quarterly*, 1 (1984): 379–400.

Brock, Clifton. "The Federal Depository System: A Proposal for Change," *College and Research Libraries*, 23 (May 1962): 197–206, 247–250.

Bybee, C. R. "Fitting Information Presentation Formats to Decision Making: A Study in Strategies to Facilitate Decision Making," *Communication Research*, 8 (1981): 343–370.

Cook, Kevin L. "Varying Levels of Support Given to Government Documents Departments in Academic Libraries," *College and Research Libraries*, 43 (November 1982): 459–471.

Eastin, R. B. "Let's Use Public Documents," *Library Journal*, 73 (November 1, 1948): 1554–1558.

Faull, Sandra K. "Cost and Benefits of Federal Depository Status for Academic Research Libraries," *Documents to the People*, 8 (January 1980): 33–39.

———. "The Development of State Plans and Their Untapped Potential for Regional Depository Libraries," *Government Information Quarterly*, 2 (1985): 157–168.

Ferriero, David S. and Kathleen A. Powers, "Burnout at the Reference Desk," *RQ*, 21 (Spring 1982): 274–279.

Florance, Valerie. "Presidential Policy and Information Dissemination: An Analysis of the Reagan Moratorium on Government Publishing," *Government Information Quarterly*, 1 (1984): 273–284.

Goehlert, Robert. "Promoting the Use of Federal Documents: An Experimental Current Awareness Service," *Government Publications Review*, 7 (1980): 27–32.

Hernon, Peter. "Academic Library Reference Service for the Publications of Municipal, State, and Federal Government: A Historical Perspective Spanning the Years up to 1962," *Government Publications Review*, 5 (1978): 31–50.

———. "Information Needs and Gathering Patterns of Academic Social Scientists, with Special Emphasis Given to Historians and Their Use of U.S. Government Publications," *Government Information Quarterly*, 1 (1984): 401–429.

————. "Use of Microformatted Government Publications," *Microform Review*, 11 (Fall 1982): 237–252.

———— and Maureen Pastine. "Student Perceptions of Academic Librarians," *College and Research Libraries*, 38 (March 1977): 129–139.

———— and Clayton A. Shepherd. "Government Publications Represented in the *Social Sciences Citation Index:* An Exploratory Study," *Government Publications Review*, 10 (1983): 227–244.

McCaghy, Dawn and Gary R. Purcell. "Faculty Use of Government Publications," *College and Research Libraries*, 33 (January 1972): 7–12.

McClure, Charles R. "An Assessment of the 1983 *Biennial Survey*," *Government Information Quarterly*, 2 (1985): 77–168.

————. "Government Publications Education: Issues and Recommendations," *Administrative Notes*, 5 (May 1984c) 32–50.

————. "Online Government Documents Data Base Searching and the Use of Microfiche Documents Online by Academic and Public Depository Librarians," *Microform Review*, 10 (Fall 1981): 245–259.

————. "Output Measures, Unobtrusive Measures, and Assessing the Quality of Reference Service," *The Reference Librarian*, 4 (1984b): 215–233.

————. "Proposed Regulations from the Joint Committee on Printing: Patchwork Remedies for Complex Problems," *Government Information Quarterly*, 1 (1984d): 309–326.

————. "Technology in Government Document Collections: Current Status, Impacts, and Prospects," *Government Publications Review*, 9 (1982a): 255–276.

———— and Keith Harman. "Government Documents as Bibliographic References and Sources in Dissertations," *Government Publications Review*, 9 (1982): 61–72.

———— and Betsy Reifsnyder. "Performance Measures for Corporate Information Centers," *Special Libraries*, 75 (July 1984): 193–204.

Moody, Marilyn K. and Jean L. Sears. "SDI Service for Government Publications in an Academic Library: A Description and Evaluation," *Government Publications Review*, 9 (1982): 55–60.

Morton, Bruce. "An Items Record Management System: First Step in the Automation of Collection Development in Selective GPO Depository Libraries," *Government Publications Review*, 8A (1981): 185–196.

————. "Random Thoughts on Numbers: The Need for Minimum Uniform Statistical Reporting Standards for U.S. Depository Libraries," *Government Publications Review*, 11 (1984): 195–202.

Myers, Judy E. "The Government Printing Office Cataloging Records: Opportunities and Problems," *Government Information Quarterly*, 2 (1985): 27–57.

National Center for Education Statistics. "Three Years of Change in College and University Libraries," *College & Research Libraries News*, 45 (July/August 1984): 359–361.

Reeves, Edward B., Benia J. Howell, and John Van Willigen. "Before the Looking-Glass: A Method to Obtain Self-Evaluation of Roles in a Library Reference Service," *RQ*, 17 (Fall 1977): 25–32.

Richardson, John V., Jr. "Theses and Dissertations in Documents," *Government Publications Review*, 4 (1977): 363–367.

————, Dennis C. W. Frisch, and Catherine M. Hall, "Bibliographic Organization of U.S. Federal Depository Collections," *Government Publications Review*, 7A (1980): 463–480.

Saunders, W. L. "The Library Schools: Aims and Objectives," in "Theory and Practical Vocational Training: A Forum," *Aslib Proceedings*, 23 (May 1971): 230.

Schwarzkopf, LeRoy C. "The Depository Library Program and Access by the Public to Official Publications of the United States Government," *Government Publications Review*, 5 (1978): 147–156.

————. "The Proposed National Depository Agency and Transfer of the Public Documents Library to the National Archives," *Government Information Quarterly*, 1 (1984): 27–47.

————. "Regional Depository Libraries for U.S. Government Publications," *Government Publications Review*, 2 (1975): 91–102.

Sears, Jean L. and Marilyn K. Moody. "Government Documents Use by Superintendent of Documents Number Areas," *Government Publications Review*, 11 (1984): 101–112.

"Statistics Task Force Minutes," *Documents to the People*, 12 (March 1984): 31–32.

Stokes, Judith E. "Federal Publications Cutbacks: Implications for Libraries," *Government Information Quarterly*, 1 (1984): 49–57.

Vertrees, Robert and Marjorie E. Murfin. "Teaching the Legislative Process: An Evaluation of Classroom and Library Instruction and a Legislative History Exercise," *Government Publications Review*, 7A (1980): 505–515.

Waldo, Michael. "An Historical Look at the Debate over How to Organize Federal Government Documents in Depository Libraries," *Government Publications Review*, 4 (1977): 319–329.

Watts, Carol. "The Depository Library Inspection Program," *Reference Services Review*, 10 (Summer 1982): 55–62.

Whitbeck, George W., Peter Hernon, and John V. Richardson, Jr. "The Federal Depository Library System: A Descriptive Analysis," *Government Publications Review*, 4 (1978): 253–267.

Yannarella, Philip A. and Rao Aluri. "Circulation of Federal Documents in Academic Depository Libraries," *Government Publications Review*, 8 (1976): 43–49.

Zagami, Anthony. "JCP Regulations," *Government Information Quarterly*, 2 (1985): 1–3.

Books

The American Library Directory. New York: Bowker, 1982.

American Universities and Colleges. 12th ed. New York: Walter de Gruyter, 1983.

Barron's Guide to the Two-Year Colleges. 7th ed., vol. 1. Woodbury, NY: Barron's Education Series, Inc., 1981.

Berdie, Douglas R. and John F. Anderson. *Questionnaires: Design and Use*. Metuchen, NJ: Scarecrow Press, 1974.

Boyd, Anne M. and Rae E. Rips. *United States Government Publications.* New York: H. W. Wilson, 1949.

Busha, Charles H. and Stephen P. Harter. *Research Methods in Librarianship: Techniques and Interpretation.* New York: Academic Press, 1980.

Carmines, Edward G. and Richard A. Zeller. *Reliability and Validity Assessment.* Beverly Hills, CA: Sage Publications, 1979.

Chen, Ching-chih and Peter Hernon. *Numeric Databases.* Norwood, NJ: Ablex Publishing Corp., 1984.

Directory of Law Libraries. Published for the American Association of Law Libraries, with the compliments of Commerce Clearing House, 1978.

Directory of Special Libraries and Information Centers. 2 vols. Detroit, MI: Gale, 1983.

Dowlin, Kenneth E. *The Electronic Library.* New York: Neal-Schuman, 1984.

Harrison, E. F. *The Managerial Decision Making Process.* 2nd ed. Boston: Houghton Mifflin, 1981.

Hernon, Peter. *Use of Government Publications by Social Scientists.* Norwood, NJ: Ablex Publishing Corp., 1979.

―――― and Charles R. McClure, *Public Access to Government Information: Issues, Trends, and Strategies.* Norwood, NJ: Ablex Publishing Corp., 1984.

―――― and Gary R. Purcell. *Developing Collections of U.S. Government Publications.* Greenwich, CT: JAI Press Inc., 1982.

Huck, Schuyler W., William H. Cormier, and William G. Bounds, Jr. *Reading Statistics and Research.* New York: Harper and Row, 1974.

Isaac, Stephen and William B. Michael. *Handbook in Research and Evaluation.* San Diego, CA: EDITS Publishers, 1971.

Jaeger, Richard M. *Statistics: A Spectator Sport.* Beverly Hills, CA: Sage Publications, 1983.

Janis, Irving L. and Leon Mann. *Decision Making.* New York: The Free Press, 1977.

Kantor, Paul B. *Objective Performance Measures for Academic and Research Libraries.* Washington, D.C.: Association of Research Libraries, 1984.

Kaplan, Abraham. *The Conduct of Inquiry.* Scranton, PA: Chandler Publishing Co., 1964.

Katzer, Jeffrey, Kenneth H. Cook, and Wayne W. Crouch. *Evaluating Information: A Guide for Users of Social Science Research.* 2nd ed. Reading, MA: Addison-Wesley Publishing Co., 1981.

Kerlinger, Fred N. *Foundations of Behavioral Research.* 2nd ed. New York: Holt, Rinehart and Winston, 1973.

King, William R. *Marketing Management Information Systems.* New York: Petrocelli/Charter, 1977.

Lancaster, F. Wilfred, ed. *Library Automation as a Source of Management Information.* Urbana-Champaign, IL: University of Illinois, Graduate School of Library and Information Science, 1983.

Lynch, Mary Jo, ed. *Library Data Collection Handbook.* Chicago: American Library Association, 1981.

Matthews, Joseph R., Gary S. Lawrence, and Douglas K. Ferguson. *Using Online Catalogs: A Nationwide Survey.* New York: Neal-Schuman, 1983.

McClure, Charles R. and Peter Hernon. *Improving the Quality of Reference Service for Government Publications.* Chicago: American Library Association, 1983.

Nakata, Yuri. *From Press to People.* Chicago: American Library Association, 1979.

Palmour, Vernon E., M. C. Bellassai, and Nancy V. De Wath, *A Planning Process for Public Libraries.* Chicago: American Library Association, 1980.

Roscoe, John T. *Fundamental Research Statistics for Behavioral Sciences.* 2nd ed. New York: Holt, Rinehart and Winston, 1975.

Rush, James E. *Library Systems Evaluation Guide: Management Services.* Powell, OH: James E. Rush Associates, Inc., 1984.

Selltiz, Claire, Lawrence C. Wrightsman, and Stuart W. Cook. *Research Methods in Social Relations.* 3rd ed. New York: Holt, Rinehart and Winston, 1976.

SPSS: Statistical Package for the Social Sciences. 2nd ed. New York: McGraw-Hill, 1975.

Swisher, Robert, and Charles R. McClure. *Research for Decision Making: Methods for Librarians.* Chicago: American Library Association, 1984.

The World Almanac and Book of Facts 1983. New York: Newspaper Enterprise Associates, 1983.

Zweizig, Douglas, and Eleanor Jo Rodger. *Output Measures for Public Libraries.* Chicago: American Library Association, 1982.

Contributions to Books

Brown, Maryann K. "Information for Planning," in *Planning for Library Services,* edited by Charles R. McClure. New York: Haworth Press, 1982, pp. 188–216.

Hoduski, Bernadine E. Abbott. "Political Activism for Documents Librarians," in *Communicating Public Access to Government Information,* edited by Peter Hernon. Westport, CT: Meckler Publishing, 1983, pp. 1–12.

Levitan, Karen B. "Information Resource(s) Management," in *Annual Review of Information Science and Technology,* edited by Martha E. Williams, vol. 17. New York: Knowledge Industry Publications, 1982, pp. 227–266.

McClure, Charles R. "Management Information for Library Decision Making," in *Advances in Librarianship,* edited by Wesley Simonton, vol. 13. New York: Academic Press, 1984a, pp. 1–47.

————. "Structural Analysis of the Depository System: A Preliminary Assessment," in *Collection Development and Public Access of Government Documents,* edited by Peter Hernon. Westport, CT: Meckler Publishing, 1982b, pp. 35–56.

Marchand, Donald A. "Information Management in Public Organizations: Defining a New Resources Management Function," in *Information Management in Public Administration,* edited by Forest W. Horton and Donald A. Marchand. Washington, D.C.: Information Resources Press, 1982, pp. 58–69.

Myers, Judy E. "The Effects of Technology on Access to Federal Government Information," in *New Technology and Documents Librarianship,* edited by Peter Hernon. Westport, CT: Meckler Publishing, 1983, pp. 27–42.

Pope, Nolan F. "Providing Machine-Readable Numeric Information in the University of Florida Libraries: A Case Study," in *Numeric Databases*, edited by Ching-chih Chen and Peter Hernon. Norwood, NJ: Ablex Publishing Corp., 1984, pp. 263–282.

Richardson, John V., Jr. "The Nature of Research in Government Publications: Preliminary Findings," in *Communicating Public Access to Government Information*, edited by Peter Hernon. Westport, CT: Meckler Publishing, 1983, pp. 125–133.

Schwarzkopf, LeRoy C. "Depository Libraries and Public Access of Government Documents," in *Collection Development and Public Access of Government Documents*, edited by Peter Hernon. Westport, CT: Meckler Publishing, 1982, pp. 7–33.

Wilcox, Jerome K. "Proposed Survey of Federal Depository Libraries," in *Public Documents*, Papers Presented at the 1938 Conference of the American Library Association, edited by Jerome K. Wilcox. Chicago: American Library Association, 1938, pp. 26–66.

Government Documents (United States)

Administrative Notes, unnumbered; 4 (nos. 8, 9, and 10); 5 (May 1984 and June 1984). Washington, D.C.: GPO, n.d., 1983, and 1984.

Annual Report of the Public Printer. 1895, 1907, 1923, 1929, 1931, 1932, 1936, 1937, 1938, and 1947. Washington, D.C.: GPO, 1895, 1907, 1924, 1929, 1931, 1932, 1936, 1938, 1939, and 1947.

Annual Report of the U.S. Government Printing Office, Fiscal Year 1981. Washington, D.C.: GPO, 1982.

Biennial Report of Depository Libraries. Washington, D.C.: GPO, 1975, 1977, 1979, and 1981.

Biennial Report of Depository Libraries. Report Series No. 17. Washington, D.C.: GPO, October 1983.

Biennial Survey. Washington, D.C.: GPO, n.d.

Bregent, Ann. "Cost of Regional Library Services in the State of Washington." Washington, D.C.: GPO, 1979.

Bureau of the Census. *1980 Census of Population: General Population Characteristics*. Washington, D.C.: GPO, 1982–1983.

Depository Library Biennial Survey for 1983: U.S. Summary. Washington, D.C.: GPO, 1984 (computer printout).

Depository Library Biennial Survey for 1983: U.S. Summary by Library Type. Washington, D.C.: GPO, 1984 (computer printout).

Estimate of the Population of States: July 1, 1981 to 1983 (Advance Report). Washington, D.C.: Bureau of the Census, 1984. (Bureau of the Census, Series P-25, No. 944).

"Federal Documents Data Base: A Conceptual Summary," Handout by the GPO distributed at the Fall 1983 Depository Library Council Meeting. Seattle, WA, September 15–17, 1983.

Federal Documents Data Base: Detailed Functional Systems Requirements. 2 vols. Washington, D.C.: GPO, Library Programs Services, 1983.

Federal Government Printing and Publishing: Policy Issues. Prepared for the Ad Hoc Advisory Committee on Review of *Title 44*, Joint Committee on Printing. Washington, D.C.: GPO, 1979.

General Accounting Office. *Depository Librarians' Views on GPO's Administration of the Depository Library Program.* Report to the Chairman, Joint Committee on Printing, April 9, 1984.

Government Depository Libraries. Joint Committee Print. Washington, D.C.: GPO, 1982 and 1983.

Guidelines for the Depository Library System. Washington, D.C.: GPO, 1977.

Instructions to Depository Libraries. Washington, D.C.: GPO, 1977.

Joint Committee on Printing. *Provision of Federal Government Publications in Electronic Format to Depository Libraries.* Report of the Ad Hoc Committee on Depository Library Access to Federal Automated Data Bases. Washington, D.C.: GPO, 1984.

"Minimum Standards for the Depository Library System," as adopted by Depository Library Council, October 22, 1976. Washington, D.C.: GPO, 1976.

National Center for Education Statistics. *Education Directory: Colleges and Universities, 1980-1981.* Washington, D.C.: GOP, 1981a.

———. *Library Statistics of Colleges and Universities.* Washington, D.C.: GPO, 1981b.

———. *Statistics of Public Libraries, 1977-78.* Washington, D.C.: GPO, n.d.

———. *100 GPO Years, 1861-1961.* Washington, D.C.: GPO, 1961.

Powell, Benjamin E., and William R. Pullen. "The Depository Library System— An Examination with Recommendations for Increasing Its Effectiveness," In *Revision of Depository Library Laws*, hearings.... Washington, D.C.: GPO, 1958, Appendix H, pp. 172-181.

Public Documents Highlights. Washington, D.C.: GPO, 1983.

Social Indicators. Washington, D.C.: Department of Commerce, Bureau of the Census, 1980.

Statistical Abstract of the United States, 1982-1983. Washington, D.C.: GPO, 1982.

11 *Statutes at Large* 379.

44 *United States Code*, Section 1909.

U.S. Congress. Senate. Judiciary Committee. Subcommittee on Library. *Depository Libraries*, Hearings.... 87th Cong., 2nd sess., 1962.

U.S. Depository Library Inspection Visit Form. Washington, D.C.: GPO, n.d.

"Use of GPO/MARC Tapes," *Administrative Notes*, 5, no. 7 (May 1984): 30-31.

Theses and Dissertations

Miller, Sara J. "The Depository Library System: A History of the Distribution of Federal Government Publications to Libraries of the United States from the Early Years of the Nation to 1895," D.L.S. dissertation, Columbia University, 1980.

Mimeographed Materials

American Library Association. Public Library Association. New Standards Task Force. "National Standards for Public Libraries: A Discussion Paper." Chicago: ALA-PLA, 1984.

Paisley, William J. *Behavioral Studies on Scientific Information Flow: An Appendix on Method.* New London, NH: Gordon Research Conference on Scientific Method, July 14–18, 1969.

Unpublished Materials

Letter from Raymond Mason Taylor, then Superintendent of Documents, to Peter Hernon, August 5, 1982.

Letter from Michael F. DiMario, then Superintendent of Documents, to Peter Hernon, May 11, 1983.

Letter from Michael F. DiMario, then Superintendent of Documents, to Peter Hernon, April 12, 1984.

Letter from Michael F. DiMario, then Superintendent of Documents, to Charles R. McClure, August 29, 1984.

Biographical Notes
on Authors

PETER HERNON is Associate Professor at the Graduate Library School, University of Arizona, Tucson. From 1978 until the fall of 1983, he was at the Graduate School of Library and Information Science, Simmons College, Boston. His teaching interests relate to government publications/information, research methods, and planning and evaluation of library services. He received his M.A. (L.S.) from the University of Denver and his Ph.D. from Indiana University, Bloomington, Indiana. Formerly Associate Editor of *Government Publications Review*, he is now Editor of *Government Information Quarterly* (Greenwich, CT: JAI Press Inc., 1984–). He has written in the documents field since 1972 and has authored thirteen books and over forty other publications. Examples of his writings include *Use of Government Publications by Social Scientists* (Norwood, NJ: Ablex Publishing Corp., 1979), and "Use of Microformatted Government Publications," *Microform Review*, 11 (Fall 1982): 237–252. He is also co-author of *Developing Collections of U.S. Government Publications* (Greenwich, CT: JAI Press Inc., 1982) and *Improving the Quality of Reference Service for Government Publications* (Chicago: American Library Association, 1983).

CHARLES R. McCLURE is Associate Professor at the School of Library Science, University of Oklahoma, where he teaches courses in government publications/information, administration, and planning and evaluation of information services. He completed his M.L.S. at the University of Oklahoma and his M.A. in history at Oklahoma State University. He served as head of the Government Documents Department at the University of Texas at El Paso Library, completed his Ph.D. degree in Library and Information Services at Rutgers University, and is currently president of Information Management Consulting Services, Inc.

McClure has written widely in areas of library administration and government publications, including *Information for Academic Library Decision Making* (Westport, CT: Greenwood Press, 1980); *Strategies for Library Administration* (Littleton, CO: Libraries Unlimited, 1982); and *Improving the Quality of Reference Service for Government Publications* (Chicago: American Library Association, 1983), which he co-authored with Peter Hernon. Together they also wrote *Public Access to Government Information: Issues, Trends, and Strategies* (Norwood, NJ: Ablex Publishing Corp., 1984), a textbook covering critical issues facing documents librarianship across levels of government. He currently serves as Associate Editor of *Government Information Quarterly* (Greenwich, CT: JAI Press Inc., 1984–).

GARY R. PURCELL is Professor at the Graduate School of Library and Information Science, University of Tennessee, Knoxville. He received his M.L.S. degree from the University of Washington and both his M.A. and Ph.D. degrees from Case Western Reserve University; his doctorate is in Library and Information Science. He teaches in the areas of government publications/information, reference service, and information science. Purcell is co-author, with Peter Hernon, of *Developing Collections of U.S. Government Publications* (Greenwich, CT: JAI Press, 1982) and co-author, with Gail Schlachter, of *Reference Sources in Library and Information Services: A Guide to the Literature* (Santa Barbara, CA: ABC-Clio, 1984). He is also the author of several articles concerned with technical report literature, state publications, and the use of government publications. Together with Mary Sue Stephenson, he is writing a series of four articles on the use of new technology and systems analysis for the management of depository collections. These articles began appearing in the third issue of volume 1 (1984) of the *Government Information Quarterly* (Greenwich, CT: JAI Press Inc.).

Name Index

Subject/Title Index